Neurolinguistic Programming in Clinical Settings

Neurolinguistic Programming in Clinical Settings provides a theoretical framework for the clinical applications of Neurolinguistic Programming (NLP) protocols in mental health. It offers evidence-based models for a range of conditions; including PTSD, anxiety and depression, grief, phobias, and binge-eating.

Providing a follow up to the 2014 book *The Clinical Effectiveness of Neurolinguistic Programming*, this book updates the existing research evidence for NLP interventions with mental health clinical conditions. It includes further evidence for its use with somatoform disorders, anxiety and depression, and as a general psychotherapy modality. The book outlines up-to-date evidence from clinical trials that demonstrate the success rate of NLP with PTSD populations and discusses how ongoing randomised clinical trials at Kings College London are demonstrating the clinical effectiveness of NLP protocols and are becoming more widely accepted by mainstream mental health care.

Written by a team of internationally academically informed clinicians and researchers, the book will be key reading for academics, researchers, and post-graduate students in the field of mental health research, psychotherapy, and counselling. It will also be of interest to clinicians and mental health professionals interested in NLP as a therapeutic modality.

Lisa de Rijk is the owner of Awaken School of Outcome Oriented Psychotherapies Ltd, training director of the Research and Recognition Project, and visiting research fellow at Kings College, London.

Richard Gray is the research director for the Research & Recognition Project. He is on the faculty of the Touro School of Osteopathic Medicine, Middletown, New York. He was previously a tenured faculty member at Fairleigh Dickinson University, Teaneck, NJ.

Frank Bourke is the CEO and founder of the Research and Recognition Project. He has lectured at Cornell University and has more than 33 years of professional experience in Executive, Clinical and Research roles.

Advances in Mental Health Research series

Books in this series:

Video and Filmmaking as Psychotherapy
Research and Practice
Edited by Joshua L. Cohen and J. Lauren Johnson with Penelope P. Orr

Group Therapy for Adults with Severe Mental Illness
Adapting the Tavistock Method
Diana Semmelhack, Larry Ende, and Clive Hazell

Narratives of Art Practice and Mental Wellbeing
Reparation and Connection
Olivia Sagan

The Prevention of Suicide in Prison
Cognitive Behavioural Approaches
Edited by Daniel Pratt

Schizotypy
New Dimensions
Edited by Oliver Mason and Gordon Claridge

Supervision and Treatment Experiences of Probationers with Mental Illness
Analyses of Contemporary Issues in Community Corrections
Babatunde Oluwaseun Adekson

Mental Wellbeing and Psychology
The Role of Art and History in Self Discovery and Creation
Sue Barker with Louise Jensen and Hamed Al Battashi

Neurolinguistic Programming in Clinical Settings
Theory and Evidence-Based Practice
Edited by Lisa de Rijk, Richard Gray, and Frank Bourke

Neurolinguistic Programming in Clinical Settings

Theory and Evidence-Based Practice

Edited by Lisa de Rijk, Richard Gray, and Frank Bourke

Routledge
Taylor & Francis Group
LONDON AND NEW YORK

First published 2022
by Routledge
2 Park Square, Milton Park, Abingdon, Oxon OX14 4RN

and by Routledge
605 Third Avenue, New York, NY 10158

Routledge is an imprint of the Taylor & Francis Group, an informa business

British Library Cataloguing-in-Publication Data
A catalogue record for this book is available from the British Library

Library of Congress Cataloging-in-Publication Data
A catalog record has been requested for this book

ISBN: 978-1-032-05720-0 (hbk)
ISBN: 978-1-032-05719-4 (pbk)
ISBN: 978-1-003-19886-4 (ebk)

DOI: 10.4324/9781003198864

Typeset in Times New Roman
by MPS Limited, Dehradun

Contents

Illustrations

Figures

Tables

Contributors

Frank Bourke PhD, Research and Recognition Project; 50+ years of professional experience in business (clinical administration), academia (lecturer, Cornell University) and direct clinical service (psychotherapy in numerous settings including one year in NYC post 9/11. Currently, CEO of the Research and Recognition nonprofit founded to research the effective components of NLP.

Lisa de Rijk PhD, is a Psychotherapist, visiting research fellow Kings College, London, registered nurse and master trainer of NLP. She is director of Awaken Consulting & Training Services Ltd, and Awaken School of Outcome Oriented Psychotherapies Ltd, a UKCP Member Organisation. Lisa is also clinical training director for the NLP Research & Recognition Project.

Lucas Derks, PhD, Netherlands, 1950, is a social psychologist who encountered the first book by Bandler and Grinder (later NLP) in 1977 within his psychology study. The links to psychological research and NLP has been his focus since. The integration of NLP and social psychology he made in the mid 1990s in The Social Panorama Model. He currently is an independent researcher with The Society for Mental Space Psychology.

Richard Gray, PhD, research director, the NLP Research and Recognition Project; adjunct instructor of Behavioral Medicine, Touro College of Osteopathic Medicine, Middletown, NY. Recipient of the 2004 Neuro-Linguistic Programming World Community Award in Education. He is the author of Archetypal Explorations (Routledge, 1996); co-author with Lisa Wake and Frank Bourke of The Clinical Effectiveness of NLP (Routledge, 2012).

Jacqueline Heemskerk (the Netherlands) works with NLP, Social Panorama and Mental Space Therapy in her practice for coaching and therapy since 1994. In 2017, Jacqueline started her research into the representation of food and obesity in the mental space in women with binge eating and its treatment with NLP techniques.

Rob Kamps is the founder of BPD training Holland and is director and head coach.

Will Murray was the training director for the Research and Recognition Project's Reconsolidation of Traumatic Memories Protocol (RTM), was a member of the RTM research team and is a certified RTM administrator and is a certified triathlon coach licensed by USA Triathlon.

Phil Parker PhD, is principal of the Phil Parker Training Institute and a researcher and lecturer in Coaching and Drugs Counselling at London Metropolitan University. He designed the Lightning Process and has authored papers and books on NLP, coaching and health, which have been translated into a range of languages.

Przemysław Turkowski is a psychologist and psychotherapist, IANLP fellow member trainer, member of Section of Science and Research in Polish Society for Neurolinguistic Psychotherapy. He studied biology and psychology at the Interdisciplinary College of Math and Science at Warsaw University.

Acknowledgements

We recognise that we stand on the shoulders of the originators and early developers of NLP, Andreas, Bandler, Cameron, DeLozier, Grinder, Lewis, McLendon, Pucelik, and Dilts. We acknowledge their work and the desire at the time of its creation, to not have NLP be a testifiable and researchable methodology. We bow to those of you who have gone before us.

We also acknowledge the shoulders that they stood on: Bateson, Erickson, Galanter, James, Korzybski, Miller, Pavlov, Perls, Pribram, Rogers, Satir, Watzlawick.

Without all of the above contributors and all those who came after them, too numerous to mention, we would not be in the position today of presenting a second edition of clinical research evidence for NLP.

Each of the researchers mentioned in both of these editions has driven their research often voluntarily without the big funding that comes with RCT's, with a head wind of anti-research rhetoric from a significant majority within the field of NLP.

The three editors of this series offer our thanks, acknowledgement and honour to each and every one of you who have made this happen. You have firmly placed NLP on the map of significant contributor to mental and physical wellness.

Lisa de Rijk, Rick Gray, and Frank Bourke

Part I

Introduction and theoretical framework for the clinical application of NLP

1 Introduction and summary of the first edition

Dr Frank Bourke and Dr Lisa de Rijk

The first edition

The first edition of the *Clinical Effectiveness of Neurolinguistic Programming* set the agenda for establishing the clinical evidence base for NLP as an emerging and growing field of therapy. The book brought together contributions from 14 authors and leaders in the field of NLP therapy from eight different countries. Authors were psychologists, psychiatrists, psychotherapists, and coaches from within the field, many of whom had already made significant academic and scientifically informed contributions in their own countries. The first edition focused on three primary areas: existing clinical and practitioner evidence, contemporary research in NLP, and the future of NLP and research.

The Introduction to that edition included a reflection on the quality of evidence that NLP must provide if it is to be taken seriously. Since that date there has been an increased number of published A-level research including positive responses from outside reviewers that are discussed in Part 2 of this volume.

Part 1, included clinical research studies of phobias, PTSD, the application of NLP, and Neurolinguistic Psychotherapy (NLPt) to a broad array of issues and diagnoses, reviews of the evidence for NLP in the treatment of anxiety disorders, addictions, and depression symptom clusters.

In Part 2, Contemporary Research in NLP, the authors focused on two areas, indirect research supporting the principles, tools, and techniques of NLP, and the methodological flaws inherent in the prior criticisms of NLP research. Indirect research included neuroscientific and behavioural studies that support, albeit without intending to, a significant number of NLP's basic premises and practices. The authors addressed the controversial nature of NLP and the historic avoidance by the early developers of creating an evidence base for the approach.

Part 3, concluded with discussions surrounding the need for standardization in certification and training, and future directions for the field, with a call for greater scientific rigour as the research progresses.

DOI: 10.4324/9781003198864-1

Acknowledgements

Here, we would like to mention the support of a number of NLP experts who believed in, helped begin and are helping to continue the development of research studies. This level of academic research has been a requirement of the academic and professional communities that NLP has largely neglected and is necessary for the validation of NLP's claims of clinical effectiveness. While this list is by no means exhaustive, we hope it will help to inspire other members of the community to engage in the long-needed dialogue between open-minded academic and professional health experts and experts from the NLP field. Prominent among these supporters, including a number who helped develop the RTM Protocol are, Connirae and Steve Andreas, Tim and Kris Hallbom, Richard Bolstad, Richard Gray, Shelle Rose Charvet, Richard Churches, Lucas Derks, Charles Faulkner, Michael Hall, Jaap Hollander, Rachel Hott, Steven Leeds, Bill McDowell, Peter Schutz, Paul Tosey, and the authors of these two Volumes.

We would like to thank and pay tribute to Steve Andreas, who has been, from NLP's beginning – with his wife Connirae – one of the most prodigious mentors and clinical developers of NLP in the United States. Steve died in 2018. He gave his more than significant clinical knowledge and energy to the development of the RTM protocol, helping to guide the rigorous development of this effective clinical tool. Given the breath of the clinical skills they taught, the level of professional and personal integrity with which they did it together (and that she continues to do), the value of their contributions is hard to convey.

Outline of this edition

This volume offers a follow on to *The Clinical Effectiveness of Neurolinguistic Programming* (2013) published through Routledge's Advancing Mental Health Series. Since the first edition, a number of research developments have added to the evidence base demonstrating the clinical effectiveness of NLP and NLP-based interventions. One of the most exciting is a series of clinical trials with PTSD populations using a protocol derived from the classic NLP intervention, the visual kinesthetic dissociation (VK-D). The pattern, Reconsolidation of Traumatic Memories (RTM-patent pending), has established a growing evidence base that is gaining strong scientific attention in trauma treatment both in the US and the UK.

As a result of the quality of its published evidence and additional clinical evidence supporting RTM, Kings College, London has commenced a Randomised Clinical Trial in Belfast. The lead editor for this book, Dr Lisa de Rijk, is also the clinical lead for the RTM arm of this Randomised Clinical Trial. This series of clinical trials is expected to demonstrate the clinical effectiveness of an NLP-derived protocol that is becoming more widely accepted and used by mainstream mental health care. These trials, along with a number of additional advances, will be discussed extensively in this edition.

This follow on edition also updates the existing research evidence for NLP interventions with clinical mental health conditions. It includes further evidence for its use with somatoform disorders, anxiety and depression, and as a general psychotherapy modality. Along with additional publications, conferences, and supporting NLP organizations, the authors call for the recognition of a genuine Research Movement within the field of NLP.

With this increasing evidence base researched by psychologists, psychotherapists, and psychiatrists, the book includes a considered argument for the use of NLP with clinical populations as a licensed activity.

The book is divided into three parts.

Part 1 provides an introduction and a theoretical framework for the clinical applications of NLP protocols in mental health. It includes a rational for a clinical evidence base and an update on direct research on NLP since the last volume. This is followed by an extensive report on the clinical evidence for, and the neuroscientific hypothesis supporting RTM. The section ends with a discussion of an NLP-based approach to clinical diagnosis.

Part 2 offers in-depth discussions of five evidence-based protocols and models with analysis of scientific research for each condition and approach. They discuss complex mental health conditions, phobias and depression, grief and bereavement, neurophysiological conditions, and binge eating and obesity.

Part 3 begins with an update of the indirect evidence-base since 2013, focusing on the formal elements of NLPs strategy analysis. It is followed by a discussion of the design and implementation of training standards with special attention given to the training and implementation of new protocols. We conclude with suggestions for future research.

Reference

Wake, L., Gray, R. M., & Bourke, F. S. (Eds.) (2013). *The clinical effectiveness of neurolinguistic programming: A critical appraisal.* Routledge.

2 The rationale for a clinical evidence base

Dr Lisa de Rijk, Dr Richard Gray, and Dr Phil Parker

Introduction

The clinical evidence base for NLP as a therapeutic modality and clinical intervention has now gained impetus with a number of randomised clinical trials published and further RCTs in progress.

This chapter provides an update to the clinical evidence base presented in the first edition in this series and has added a further subsequent 17 clinical studies that have been published in peer-reviewed journals. Studies include a continuation of research in PTSD and the RTM protocol; anxiety and general psychotherapy treatment; post-surgical pain management; medical birth interventions; occupational stress; strokes; and a new protocol called the Lightning Process that has been developed specifically for those with neurobiological conditions such as Chronic Fatigue Syndrome, ME and MS, (Crawley, Mills, Hollingworth, et al., 2013; Crawley et al., 2018), physical function, pain, anxiety, and depression (Parker, Aston & de Rijk, 2020), or addictive patterns with alcohol dependency.

A more recent systematic review and meta-analysis has been conducted by Kitchiner, Lewis, Roberts, & Bisson (2019) and for the first time proposes the NLP RTM (reconsolidation of traumatic memories) protocol as emerging evidentiary medicine using ISTSS (International Society for Trauma Stress Studies) criteria. The implications of this are discussed in the concluding part of this chapter.

Development of the evidence base

The changes observed by the addition of NLP approaches to existing psychotherapy models in the 1970s resulted in an initial flourishing of research interest. Unfortunately, a number of factors appear to have negatively affected the development of that early research. First, the NLP pioneers were influenced by the counter cultural movement prevalent in the USA at this time, that questioned and rejected existing structures (Grinder & Pucelik, 2013) and this included a wariness of 'old school' research institutions. Second, the early research (Sharpley, 1984) with its limited understanding of

DOI: 10.4324/9781003198864-2

NLP and poor methodology resulted in confused conclusions and misunderstandings. These included mis-casting the concept of the potential link between eye movements and what information the brain was processing as being central to NLP which was then used as the basis for the development of further studies (Wake, Gray & Bourke, 2013). Because of their incorrect assumptions about what constitutes NLP and how to test it these early studies discouraged further investigation of NLP. Unfortunately, these same studies continue to affect attitudes to NLP into the present (Gray, Liotta, Wake, & Cheal, 2013).

However, this situation has changed over the last decade as a new generation of researchers with a good working knowledge of the field has begun to address the previous issues in the evidence base.

Current evidence base

A PubMed search for the term 'Neuro Linguistic Programming' undertaken in 2021 returned 150 papers of which 58 had the term in the title of the paper and a further 34 included the term as a keyword, in the abstract or in the paper's text. No date limits were set for the search and the papers' publication dates ranged from 1980 to 2021. A wide range of areas of interest was identified in the papers. These included a trial evaluating NLP for assisting the turning of babies from the breech position to aid delivery compared to treatment as usual (NLP was significantly (p = .009) better than treatment as usual (Reinhard et al., 2013); a qualitative study on the development of self-esteem, using NLP, for women who had suffered rape attacks (Vianna, Bomfim, & Chicone, 2006); a randomised control trial (RCT) on the Lightning Process (an approach derived from NLP) for those with Chronic Fatigue Syndrome/Myalgic Encephalitis (the combination of the Lightning Process and specialist medical care (SMC) provided significant improvements in a range of outcomes compared than SMC alone (Crawley et al., 2018)); evaluating the effects of neuro-linguistic programming, and guided imagery on the pain and comfort after open-heart surgery (both approaches produced significantly better outcomes than treatment as usual (p < .005) (Doğan & Saritaş, 2021)).

This search also identified the range of quality and type of studies undertaken. The lowest quality studies are represented by opinion pieces and case histories, but there is an increasing number of RCTs (Arroll et al., 2017; Crawley, Mills, Hollingworth, et al., 2013; Gray, Budden-Potts, & Bourke, 2019; Gray, Budden-Potts, Schwall, & Bourke, 2020; Parker, Banbury, & Chandler, 2020), systematic reviews (Kotera, Sheffield, & Van Gordon, 2018; Parker, Aston, & de Rijk, 2020); and meta-analyses (Adams & Allan, 2019; Sturt et al., 2012; Zaharia, Reiner, & Schütz 2015) which greatly increase the strength of the evidence base.

The few A level studies identified in the Systematic Review have been reviewed in detail in other chapters and are included in the table within this chapter. The limited albeit developing evidence base makes it necessary for NLP to continue producing the kind of research that will be critical to its acceptance in the world of main line psychologies. There is a need for more good quality studies of the types mentioned above. An important step towards this is the need to foster an even deeper recognition of the importance of supporting and working with those involved in research within the world of NLP as a whole. For researchers, the lack of standardisation in the delivery of NLP processes raises methodological concerns that they are correctly evaluating one 'uniform intervention' within studies. Others reasonably argue that interactive interventions such as psychotherapy, coaching and NLP require new models for research that value the differences present in each consultation that are tailored to meet the needs of that particular client practitioner interaction (The European Association of Psychotherapy, 2021). Finally, the unscientific bias and stigma against NLP that has been noted by others need to be resolved. This double standard has resulted in: on one hand poor quality papers such as Wiseman's eye movements study, which debunks a you-tube video that claims 'NLP can identify if you are lying', being accepted for publication (Wiseman et al., 2012). This confused study repeats the failings found in early research whilst acknowledging this 'claim' was made by the NLP originators. By contrast authors such as Arroll were informed by a reviewer that the phrase 'NLP' would need to be removed from a paper reporting on a well-designed RCT on phobias (Arroll et al., 2017) before it could be accepted for publication (Arroll & Henwood, 2017).

Hopefully the growing weight of evidence reported above, supported by the chapters in this book, will move these conversations to a more scientifically grounded basis where transparent criteria can be applied to help clients make informed choices about appropriate interventions.

Existing evidence

In 2013, Wake and colleagues cited The Agency of Health Care Policy and Research and their research grades as a guide for the quality of research that NLP must produce. This agency defined four levels of research:

- Level A evidence, based on randomized well-controlled clinical trials for individuals, including Meta-Analyses and Systematic Reviews.
- Level B evidence, based upon well-designed clinical studies, without randomization or placebo comparison for individuals.
- Level C evidence, based on service and naturalistic clinical studies combined with clinical observations that are sufficiently compelling to warrant the use of the treatment technique or follow the specific recommendations.
- Level D evidence, based on long-standing and widespread clinical practice that has not been subjected to empirical tests.

Table 2.1 provides a summary of A, B, C, and D level studies included in the first edition. New studies conducted since then are included and are shaded for ease of referencing.

Evidentiary medicine status and NLP

Evidence-based medicine is hotly contested despite the common-sense nature of its position that clinical decisions should be made based upon the most up to date, solid, and scientific evidence (Greenhalgh, Howick, & Maskrey, 2014; Ioannidis, 2016). If this is then considered with regard to the practice of psychotherapy, the debate becomes more about the effectiveness of the therapist, rather than the therapy (Stiles, Barkham, Twigg, Mellor-Clark, & Cooper, 2006).

Yet funding for and access to psychological therapies remains the privilege of those therapies that can demonstrate clinical and cost effectiveness through RCTs. CBT is the most prolific beneficiary of that privilege (Axelsson, Andersson, Ljótsson, & Hedman-Lagerlöf 2018; Fineberg et al., 2018; Jonsson et al., 2016; Lunkenheimer et al., 2020; Matsumoto et al., 2020; Morrell et al., 2016; Morriss, Xydopoulos, Craven, Price, & Fordham, 2019; Osborne et al., 2019; Rasing et al., 2019; Richards et al., 2018; Richards et al., 2016; Ross, Vijan, Miller, Valenstein, & Zivin, 2019; Skapinakis et al., 2016; Tie et al., 2019).

Sturt et al. (2012) conducted a systematic review of neurolinguistic programming and the effect on health outcomes within the NHS (National Health Service). At that time, she concluded that'*... there is little evidence that NLP interventions improve health-related outcomes. This conclusion reflects the limited quantity and quality of NLP research, rather than the robust evidence of no effect. There is currently insufficient evidence to support the allocation of NHS resources to NLP activities outside of research purposes'.* (p757). Sturt is now Principal Investigator for the PETT Study (https://doi.org/10.1186/ISRCTN10314773) comparing trauma focussed CBT (CBT-TF) and the RTM protocol, an NLP based method, for the treatment of PTSD in UK military veterans.

Kitchiner et al. (2019) has more recently conducted a systematic review and meta-analysis of all studies investigating the use of all psychotherapies in the treatment of active duty and ex-serving military personnel with PTSD. The aim of the review was to determine which studies were effective in treating active serving and veteran military personnel diagnosed with PTSD. At the same time Kitchiner included this review alongside others to update the International Society for Traumatic Stress Studies (ISTSS) treatment guidelines.

Working within the Cochrane Collaboration guidelines, the review team identified 5554 records, of which 5351 were excluded. 203 articles were screened for eligibility and 177 of these were excluded. Of the remaining studies, 24 were included in the final meta-analysis of 2386 study participants. The evidence demonstrated that CBT-TF (n = 10 studies) was

Table 2.1 Clinical Studies in NLP

Authors	*Publication*	*Study Title*	*Study Level*	*Measurement tools*	*Comments*
Crawley, E., Mills, N., Hollingworth, W., Deans, Z., Sterne, J., Donovan, J., Beasant, L., & Montgomery, A.	Archives of Disease in Childhood, 103,155–164, 2018	Clinical and cost-effectiveness of the Lightning Process in addition to specialist medical care for paediatric chronic fatigue syndrome: randomised controlled trial	A	SF-36-PFS school attendance (days per week), the Chalder Fatigue Scale, pain (visual analogue scale), Hospital Anxiety and Depression Scale (HADS), Spence Children's Anxiety Scale (SCAS) and quality-adjusted life-yearsWork Productivity and Activity Impairment: General Health questionnaire (V2.0)	Of the 100 participants, 51 were randomised to SMC+LP. Data from 81 participants were analysed at 6 months. Physical function (SF-36-PFS) was better in those allocated SMC+LP (adjusted difference in means 12.5 [95% CI 4.5 to 20.5], p=0.003) and this improved further at 12 months (15.1 [95% CI 5.8 to 24.4], p=0.002). At 6 months, fatigue and anxiety were reduced and at 12 months, fatigue, anxiety, depression and school attendance had improved in the SMC+LP arm. Results were similar following multiple imputation. SMC+LP was more cost-effective in the multiple imputation data set (difference in means in net monetary benefit at 12 months £1474 [95% CI £111 to £2836], p=0.03) but not for complete cases.The LP is effective and is probably cost-effective when provided in addition to SMC for

					mild/moderately affected adolescents with CFS/ME
Gray, R., & Bourke, F.	Journal of Military, Veteran and Family Health, 2015:1 (2) 13–20	Remediation of intrusive symptoms of PTSD in fewer than five sessions: a 30-person pre-pilot study of the RTM protocol	A	PCL-M	Of 26 subjects meeting standard PCL-M criteria for PTSD (PCL-M >45) at intake, only 77% (2/26) met PCL-M criteria for PTSD at the 2-week follow up and 3.8% (1/26) met the criteria at the 6-week follow up.
Gray, R., Budden-Potts, D, Bourke, F.	Journal of the Society for Psychotherapy Research. 2019: 29 (5) 621–639.	Reconsolidation of Traumatic Memories for PTSD: A randomized controlled trial of 74 male veterans.	A	PSS-I, PCL-M	46 (71%) lost DSM diagnosis for PTSD; 42 (65%) were in complete remission (PSS-I <20) and DSM criteria not met; 4 (6%) others lost the DMS diagnosis and had absence of nightmares and flashbacks.Within-group RTM effect sizes (Hedges' *g)* for PSS-I score changes ranged from 1.45-2.3. The between-group comparison between the treatment group and the untreated controls was significant (*p<0.001)* with an effect size equivalent to two standard deviations (*g*=2.13; 95% CI [1.56,2.0].
Gray, R. M., Budden-Potts, D., Schwall, R. J., Bourke, F.	Psychological Trauma:theory, research, practice and policy. 2020.	An open-label, randomized controlled trial of the reconsolidation of traumatic	A	PSS-I; PCL-M; PCL-S;	RTM eliminated intrusive symptoms and significantly decreased symptom scale ratings in 90% (n=27) of participants, versus 0% of controls (*p<.001)*.

(*Continued*)

Table 2.1 (Continued)

Authors	*Publication*	*Study Title*	*Study Level*	*Measurement tools*	*Comments*
		memories (RTM) in military women.			
Tylee, D. S., Gray, R., Glatt, S. J., Bourke, F.	Journal of Military, Veteran and Family Health. 2017:3 (1), 21–33	Evaluation of the reconsolidation of traumatic memories protocol for the treatment of PTSD: a randomized wait-list controlled trial.	A	PSS-I, PCL-M.	At 6 months post, within group RTM effect sizes (Hedges *g*) ranged from 2.79-5.33. 88% of those treated had lost the DSM diagnosis for PTSD, 15% had lost DSM diagnosis (PCL-M <50 and DSM criteria not met) and 73% were in complete remission from all symptoms (PCL-M <30).
Bigley, J., Griffiths, P. D., Prydderch, A., Romanowski, C. A. J., Miles, L., Lidiard, H., Hoggard. N.,	The British Journal of Radiology, 83 (2010), 113–117	Neurolinguistic programming used to reduce the need for anaesthesia in claustrophobic patients undergoing MRI	B	Spielberger's State Anxiety Inventory.	38 of the original 50 patients were able to complete the MRI scan. 12 patients who did not complete the scan had statistically higher anxiety scores before NLP than the remaining patients. There was a statistically significant reduction in the median anxiety score, and a predicted 65% cost saving if NLP were used compared to an MRI scan under general anaesthetic.
Bowers, L. A.	Thesis (Ph. D.) – Graduate School of the Union Institute, Cincinnati, OH. (1996).	An exploration of holistic and non-traditional healing methods including researching the use	B	Visual Analogue Scale	Average reduction of 6.2 over 2.1 NLP sessions compared to the non-treatment group experiencing a reduction of 1.7 over the same period of time.

		of neuro-linguistic programming in the adjunctive treatment of acute pain.			
Genser-Medlitsch, M., Schütz, P.,	Self-Published, Austria, 1997. Nowiny Psychologiczne (Psychological News) issue 1 2004.	Does Neuro-Linguistic psychotherapy have effect? New Results shown in the extramural section.	B	Individual Discomfort List, IPC questionnaire on locus of control,Self-Report Symptom Inventory,Stress Management Questionnaire, Sociodemographic data	76% of clients experienced positive changes in 25 of 33 dimensions.6 months post treatment 88% (22 scales) were stable
Hossack, A., & Bentall, R. P.	Journal of Traumatic Stress, 9(1), 99–110. (1996)	Elimination of posttraumatic symptomatology by relaxation and visual-kinesthetic dissociation	B	GHQ- 30, SCl-90-R, IES, HAD, Diaries and personal reviews post treatment	Wait condition control. Two patients showed complete cessation of symptoms. One showed decreased IES scores but continued intrusive thoughts.
Parker, P., Aston, J., & de Rijk, L.	EXPLORE, 1–30. (2020)	A Systematic Review of the Evidence Base for the Lightning Process.	B	Systematic review	Identified an emerging body of evidence supporting the efficacy of the LP for many participants with fatigue, physical function, pain, anxiety and depression
Parker, P., Banbury, S., & Chandler, C.	EJAPP, 4(13). (2020)	Efficacy of The Rediscovery Process on Alcohol Use, Impulsivity	B	Alcohol use (TOPS form), Flourishing Scale, Impulsivity	The Rediscovery Process, compared to Treatment As Usual, significantly improves a range of important alcohol misuse

(*Continued*)

Table 2.1 (Continued)

Authors	*Publication*	*Study Title*	*Study Level*	*Measurement tools*	*Comments*
		and Flourishing: A Preliminary Randomised Controlled Study and Preliminary Cohort Study.		(Low self control scale)	outcomes that are maintained over the 3-month period.
Stipancic M, Renner W, Schütz P, Dond R:	Counselling and Psychotherapy Research 10(1) – Routledge: 39–49, 2010.	Effects of Neuro-Linguistic Psychotherapy on psychological difficulties and perceived quality of life.	B	Structured Clinical Interview for DSM-IV Personality Disorders (SCID II) for clinical symptoms.Croatian Scale of Quality of Life (KVZ) for quality of life measures.	Significant decrease in clinical symptoms and increase in quality of life for the study group, with effect sizes (n=54) of 0.65 SCID II, 0.65 KVZ Predictor variable, 0.51 KVZ Criterion variable when measured T1-T2, and, 1.09 SCID II, 0.69 KVZ Predictor variable and 0.73 KVZ Criterion variable at T1-T3 five month follow up.
Witt (2003),	Psychosomatics 4: 33–37	Psychological Treatment Can Modulate the Skin Reaction to Histamine in Pollen Allergic Humans.	B	Skin prick test of saline solution and a histamine provocation as a positive control.	Control group were noted to have a highly significant increased difference in histamine wheal area.
Witt (2008)	International Journal of Psychotherapy 12(1): 50-60	Neuro-Linguistic-Psychotherapy (NLPt) treatment can modulate the reaction in pollen	B	Psychological tests - Krampen-AT-Symptomscale and Rehabilitations-Psychologische-	Psychological test results demonstrated that well-being increased significantly in the study group between t0 and t1 and

		allergic humans and their state of health.	Diagnosesystem. Interval-scale data was normally distributed using the Kolmogorov-Smirnov-Test	remained stable between t1 and t2.
	No significant increase in control group.			
	Variance homogeneity using the Bartlett-Test allowed variance analysis.	Analysis of variance over time showed a highly significant effect in the NLPt group. Mood of well-being showed a highly significant increase in the NLPt group t0-t1 and remained stable t1-t2.		
	Pre-testing using Oneway Anova and Multiple t-Test.	The state of illness decreased significantly in the NLPt group between t0-t1 and stable t1-t2.		
	Medicine consumption and ailments recorded in daily diary entries.	T		
	Ailments were counted using Kruskal-Wallis 1-way	Unexplained decrease in the placebo		

(Continued)

Table 2.1 (Continued)

Authors	*Publication*	*Study Title*	*Study Level*	*Measurement tools*	*Comments*
	Anova to determine if groups ranking was normally populated and effects were measured using Mann-Whitney U and Wilcoxon Rank sum tests. Medication consumption was counted as binary data using Chi-square.	group t1-t2. Study group showed significantly fewer symptoms. Medication use was significantly less in the study group Psychological NLPt intervention has an effect on allergy sensitivity			
Zaharia C, Reiner M, Schütz P.	Psychiatr Danub. 2015 Dec;27(4):355–363. PMID: 26609647.	Evidence-based Neuro Linguistic Psychotherapy: a meta-analysis.	B	Meta-analysis	The overall meta-analysis found that the NLP therapy may add an overall standardized mean difference of 0.54 with a confidence interval of CI= [0.20; 0.88]
Allen, K. L.,	Dissertation Abstracts International 43(3), 861-B University of Missouri at Kansas City. (1982)	An investigation of the effectiveness of Neurolinguistic Programming procedures in treating snake phobics	C	Wait group control.BSS-II, BAT, FT	No difference in treatment groups, both superior to control. NLP group more convinced of success
Brandis, A. D.,	Dissertation Abstracts International 47(11),	A neurolinguistic treatment for	C	Parental Provocation Inventory.Parents'	ANOVA and Eta coefficients showed no significance.Post-hoc

	4642-B California School of Professional Psychology. (Order = DA8626141): 161, 1986.	reducing parental anger responses and creating more resourceful behavioural options.		Report used for comparison	analysis demonstrated strong experimental effect in half of the experimental group, when investigated attributed result to utilisation of resource anchor.
Duncan, R. C., Konefal, J., Spechler, M. M.	Psychological Reports. 1990 Jun;66(3 Pt 2):1323–1330	Effect of neurolinguistic programming training on self-actualization as measured by the Personal Orientation Inventory.	C	Personal Orientation Inventory	Significant positive changes were observed in nine of twelve scales for 18 trainees, and ten of twelve scales for 36 trainees at the end of the training.
Einspruch, E. L., & Forman, B. D.	Psychotherapy in Private Practice. 6:1, 91–100 (1988)	Neurolinguistic Programming in the Treatment of Phobias.	C	BDI, MPQ	Marked improvement.
Field ES.	American Journal of Clinical Hypnosis. 1990 Jan; 32(3):174–182.	Neurolinguistic programming as an adjunct to other psychotherapeutic/ hypnotherapeutic interventions.	C		Both techniques effective in ending hyperactive episodes in the first client and integrating feelings and knowledge into personal consciousness with the second client.
Gray, R. M., Budden-Potts, D., Bourke, F.	Journal of Experiential Psychotherapy. 2017:20 47–61	The Reconsolidation of Traumatic Memories (RTM) Protocol for PTSD:a case study.	C	PCL-MPSS-IBSISUDS	No scores for pre and post reported.

(*Continued*)

Table 2.1 (Continued)

Authors	*Publication*	*Study Title*	*Study Level*	*Measurement tools*	*Comments*
Gray, R., & Teall, B.	Journal of Experiential Psychotherapy. Vol 19, no 4 (76), 59–69, December 2016	Reconsolidation of Traumatic Memories (RTM) for PTSD: a case series	C	PCL-MCase study series	Part of a 26 cohort study group. The four reported cases had an intake mean of 63.5 (± 11.7). Post treatment mean PCL-M dropped 37.75 points (57%) to 24.75 (± 2.98) at the six-week follow-up
HemmatiMasla-kpak, M., Farhadi, M., & Fereidoni, J.	Iranian journal of nursing and midwifery research, (2016). 21(1), 38–44. https://doi.org/10.4103/1735-9066.174754	The effect of neuro-linguistic programming on occupational stress in critical care nurses.	C	Expanding Nursing Stress Scale (ENSS)	Quasi-experimental pre-post test study. Control and experimental groups. N=60.The baseline score average of job stress was 120.88 and 121.36 for the intervention and control groups, respectively (P = 0.65). After intervention, the score average of job stress decreased to 64.53 in the experimental group while that of control group remained relatively unchanged (120.96). Mann–Whitney test results showed that stress scores between the two groups was statistically significant (P = 0.0001).
Koziey, P. W., McLeod, G.,	Professional Psychology: Research and Practice. American Psychological Association. (1987)	Visual-Kinesthetic Dissociation in Treatment of Victims of Rape	C	SCl-90-R, MFS-II, POMS STAI	Clinical report. No control.Unspecified but significant improvement in multiple measures.

		(Research and Practice)			
Liberman, M.B.	Dissertation Abstracts International 45(6), St. Louis University. (1984)	The treatment of simple phobias with Neurolinguistic Programming techniques.	C	Pre-post design.FSS-II SCL,-9DR, FT, SHSS	Reduction in personal distress symptoms; improved approach behaviour, reduced fear, discomfort and overall intensity of symptoms.
Parker, P., Banbury, S. & de Rijk, L.	International Journal of Mental Health Addiction (2021).	A Thematic Analysis of Experiences of Alcohol Users of the Rediscovery Process. Self-control or Flourishing?.	C	Qualitative Study	The major themes of control and flourishing and the range of participants' responses, highlight how the intervention appears to work on many levels, from changing behaviours to shifting ones' sense of self.
Peng, Y., Lu, Y., Wei, W., Yu, J., Wang, D., Xiao, Y., Xu, J., Wang, Z.	J Stroke Cerebrovasc Dis. (2015) Aug;24(8):1793–1802. doi: 10.1016/ j.jstrokecerebro-vasdis.2015.04.009. PMID: 26117212	The Effect of a Brief Intervention for Patients with Ischemic Stroke: A Randomized Controlled Trial.	C	Pre Post questionnaire	RCT of 4 sessions of NLP vs TUA (n=180).Intervention group achieved remission of depressive (OR, 2.81; 95% CI, 1.41-5.59); anxious symptoms (OR, 2.19; 95% CI, 1.15-4.18) after intervention. At the 6-month follow-up, no differences between groups. After intervention, the intervention group had better awareness rates on stroke knowledge (P < .05). Better quality of life and physical function both after intervention and at the follow-up (P < .05).
			C	Prospective Trial	

(*Continued*)

Table 2.1 (Continued)

Authors	*Publication*	*Study Title*	*Study Level*	*Measurement tools*	*Comments*
Reinhard, J., Sänger, N., Hanker, L., Reichenbach, L., Yuan, J., Herrmann, E., & Louwen, F.	Archives of Gynecology and Obstetrics, 287(4), 663–668. (2013)	Delivery mode and neonatal outcome after a trial of external cephalic version (ECV): A prospective trial of vaginal breech versus cephalic delivery.			Reinhard, J., Sänger, N., Hanker, L., Reichenbach, L., Yuan, J., Herrmann, E., & Louwen, F.
Sumin, A. N., Khairedinova, O. P., Sumina, L., Variushkina, E. V., Doronin, D. V., Galimzianov, D.	Klin Med (Mosk) 78(6): 16–20, 2000.	Psychotherapy impact on effectiveness of in-hospital physical rehabilitation in patients with acute coronary syndrome.	C	Exercise tolerance testsCentral haemodynamic measures	NLP, progressive muscular relaxation, Ericksonian hypnosis and metaphors.The test group had higher exercise tolerance and lower reactivity of central haemodynamics in all exercise tests.
Utuza, A. J., Joseph, S., & Muss, D. C.	Traumatology. (2011)	Treating Traumatic Memories in Rwanda with the Rewind Technique: Two-Week Follow-Up after a Single Group Session.	C	IES	Clinical report, no control.21 subjects pre and post test. Pre-test IES 38.5 mean, Post test 15.14 $(n=21)$ $p < .001$

Wake, L.	Current Research in NLP. ANLP. pp.43–53. (2011)	Waking Up and Moving On – A Programme Evaluation of an Intervention with Adolescents Identified as at Risk of Offending Behaviour.	C	Independent Service Evaluation Report. (Tope, Thomas and Jones 2010).	The authors report on number of benefits from workshop: improved behaviour; thinking of the future; positive outlook; changes in social activities. Reported outcomes are validated.
Wake, L., Leighton, M.,	Mental Health Review Journal, Vol. 19 Iss: 4, pp. 251–264 (2014)	Pilot study using Neurolinguistic Programming (NLP) in post-combat PTSD	C	Depression and Anxiety Stress Scale (DASS)	Post cohort study.Pre and post DASS scores were highly significant (T-test).Significant study limitations – study group, incomplete data, therapist effect, therapist training, treatment methodology
Weaver, M.	Current Research in NLP: Proceedings of 2008 NLP Conference. Vol 1. pp. 67–83 (2009)	An Exploration of a Research-Based Approach to the Evaluation of Clients' Experience of Neuro-Linguistic Psychotherapy within a Private Practice Making use of the CORE Model.	C	CORE Systems Research Tool	33 clients.Clients experience a reduction in problems after an average of 7 weekly sessions of psychotherapy.
Baddeley M.	Australian Journal of Clinical Hypnotherapy	The use of hypnosis in marriage and	D	3 case reports.	Combination of Ericksonian hypnosis, analytical hypnotherapy and NLPThese

(Continued)

Table 2.1 (Continued)

Authors	*Publication*	*Study Title*	*Study Level*	*Measurement tools*	*Comments*
	and Hypnosis 13(2): 87–92, 1992	relationship counselling.			processes are more potent than traditional counselling
Bertoli, J. M.	C. R. Figley. Westport, CT US, Greenwood Press/ Greenwood Publishing Group: 207-225. (2002).	The use of neuro-linguistic programming and emotionally focused therapy with divorcing couples in crisis. Brief treatments for the traumatized: A project of the Green Cross Foundation.	D	Project report	Combination of NLP and Emotionally Focussed Therapy with the aim of replacing attachment to the ex-spouse and to reengage with the aim of developing new interactional patterns as co-parents.
Davis, S. L., Davis, D. I.	Journal of Marital and Family Therapy, Vol 9(3), Jul, 1983. pp. 283–291.	Neuro-Linguistic Programming and family therapy.	D	Case report	Overview of techniques used which include dissociated state rehearsal for future oriented behaviours.
Doğan, A., & Saritaş, S.	Journal of Cardiac Surgery. (2021). https://doi.org/10.1111/jocs.15505	The effects of neuro-linguistic programming and guided imagery on the pain and comfort after open-heart surgery.	D	Pain levels, pre and post surgery	Randomized, single-blind clinical study, the participants received NLP with a new behavior formation technique or the guided imagery relaxation technique using an audio compact disc for a duration of 30 min.

Juhnke, G. A., Coll, K. M., Sunich, M. F., Kent, R. R.	*The Family Journal* 2008 16: 391 originally published online 11 August 2008	Using a Modified Neurolinguistic Programming Swish Pattern With Couple Parasuicide and Suicide Survivors	D	Clinical case example	Adapted form of the NLP swish pattern to support couple survivors of suicide and parasuicide. Authors conclude that pattern provides clients with an opportunity to reconnect with memories of their loved one in a more positive way.
Muss, D.	British Journal of Clinical Psychology, 30(1), 91–92. (1991)	A new technique for treating post-traumatic stress disorder.	D	Client report at 2 years	No control. 15 (n=19) return to work and report elimination of intrusive images and thoughts
Parker, P., Aston, J., & Finch, F.	Journal of Experiential Psychotherapy, *21*(2), 8. (2018)	Understanding the Lightning Process approach to CFS/ME; a review of the disease process and the approach	D	Review	This paper resolves the identified gaps in the research and clarifies the hypotheses behind this approach, which has been identified by the evidence base as providing successful outcomes for some. It is hoped this clearer understanding of the approach will assist researchers, clinicians and those with this disabling disease to identify some additional options for potential recovery.
Savardelavar, M., & Kuan, G. (2020).	International Journal of Public Health & Clinical Sciences (2020), 7(2), 14–15. https://doi.org/10.32827/ijphcs.7.2.14	Reducing Performance Anxiety of a Female Dancer Using Neuro-	D	Single case study design	Utilised NLP and Neurosemantics over 40 sessions twice per week. Case study presentation. Less anxiety, increased participation in training sessions, fewer

(*Continued*)

Table 2.1 (Continued)

Authors	*Publication*	*Study Title*	*Study Level*	*Measurement tools*	*Comments*
		Linguistic Programming and Neuro- Semantics: A Case Study.			performance errors, greater communication with other dancers.
Scott, E. K.,	Dissertation Abstracts International 48(7), 1713-A 1714-A Northern Arizona University (Order = DA8715297): 191, 1987	The effects of the Neurolinguistic Programming model of reframing as therapy for bulimia.	D	Group case study	NLP technique of reframing to facilitate change
Shelden, V. E., Shelden, R. G.,	Family Therapy, Vol 16(3), 1989, 249–258.	Sexual abuse of males by females: The problem, treatment modality, and case example.	D	Single Case Study	Utilisation of NLP and biofeedback to alter identified unuseful patterns of behaviour and to focus on a future desired state.
Vianna, L. A. C., Bomfim, G. F. T., Chicone, G.,	Revista Latino-Americana de Enfermagem, Vol 14(5), Sep–Oct, 2006. pp. 695–701.	Self-esteem of raped women.	D	Phenomenological study with 5 groups of women	Combination of psychodrama and NLP techniques Thematic analysis demonstrated that attendees were able to reflect on and develop a change in attitude and perceive new roads ahead.
Wake, L.	Current Research in NLP. Volume 1. p. 50–66. (2009)	A study of the relationship between the core belief structures of neurolinguistic psychotherapy and	D	Grounded theory qualitative study	Relationship between some NLPt processes and their similarity to object relations theory

		object relations theory.			
Zika, B.	Australian Journal of Clinical Hypnotherapy and Hypnosis. Vol 6(2) Sep 1985, 57–66	Transformational hypnotherapy: Historical antecedents and a case example.	D	1 case report	Combination of NLP and analytic therapy models. A positive therapeutic model for maladaptive behaviour.

associated with the largest evidence of effect compared to wait list or treatment as usual. Group CBT-TF was less effective (n = 1 study). All CBT-TF studies demonstrated a greater drop-out rate compared to wait list or person-centred therapy. EMDR (Eye Movement Desensitisation and Reprocessing therapy) was not effective when compared to wait list or treatment as usual (n = 4 studies).

Two NLP studies were included in the RTM protocol (Gray, Budden-Potts, & Bourke, 2017; Tylee, Gray, Glatt, & Bourke, 2017).

When compared against the ISTSS recommend algorithm, no therapies were given a Strong recommendation. CBT-TF was recommended at Standard level. PE (prolonged exposure [a modified CBT]) and CPT were given a Low Effect. CBT-TF, RTM and VRE (virtual reality exposure) were recommended as interventions with Emerging Evidence of effect.

In summarising the findings of this review for the NLP RTM Trauma Protocol:

- RTM is recommended as an intervention with Emerging Evidence of effect
- RTM meets the predetermined threshold for clinical importance
- More work is encouraged to determine if RTM should be seen as a valid alternative to established paradigms

Chapter summary

This chapter has provided a transparent representation of clinical studies and evidence to date. The focus has been on the studies with the highest quality methodology with lower quality studies omitted and we have endeavoured to be critical in our critique of where these selected studies are placed against the research evidence criteria. Much of the research work conducted to date has been done through self-funding, on a voluntary basis or through small grant awards. Yet despite the lack of funding for robust clinical trials, the team of professionals researching three main areas are to be congratulated.

There is a steady stream of evidence in three main areas: The RTM protocol for treating PTSD; the Lightening Process for treating neurobiological disorders and alcohol dependency; and the use of NLP methodology for treating those seeking psychotherapy.

As other chapters will demonstrate, there is more work to be done to gain further clinical recognition and further exciting research studies already in progress.

References

Adams, S., & Allan, S. (2019). Muss' Rewind treatment for trauma: description and multi-site pilot study. *Journal for Mental Health*, 27(5), 468–474. doi:10.1080/09638237.2018.1487539

Allen, K. L. (1982). An investigation of the effectiveness of Neurolinguistic Programming procedures in treating snake phobics. *Dissertation Abstracts International*, 43(3), 861-B. University of Missouri at Kansas City.

Arroll, B., & Henwood, S. M. (2017). NLP research, equipoise and reviewer prejudice. *Rapport*, 54, 24–26.

Arroll, B., Henwood, S. M., Sundram, F. I., Kingsford, D. W., Mount, V., Humm, S. P., Wallace, H. B., & Pillai, A. (2017). A brief treatment for fear of heights: A randomized controlled trial of a novel imaginal intervention. *The International Journal of Psychiatry in Medicine*, 52(1), 21–33. doi:10.1177/0091217417703285

Axelsson, E., Andersson, E., Ljótsson, B., & Hedman-Lagerlöf, E. (2018). Cost-effectiveness and long-term follow-up of three forms of minimal-contact cognitive behaviour therapy for severe health anxiety: Results from a randomised controlled trial. *Behaviour Research and Therapy*, Aug, 107, 95–105. doi:10.1016/j.brat.2018.06.002. Epub Jun 15. PMID: 29936239.

Baddeley, M. (1992). The use of hypnosis in marriage and relationship counselling. *Australian Journal of Clinical Hypnotherapy and Hypnosis*, 13(2), 87–92.

Bertoli, J. M. (2002). The use of neuro-linguistic programming and emotionally focused therapy with divorcing couples in crisis. Brief treatments for the traumatized: A project of the Green Cross Foundation. C. R. Figley (pp. 207–225). Westport, CT US: Greenwood Press/Greenwood Publishing Group.

Bigley, J., Griffiths, D., Prydderch, A., Romanowski, A. J., Miles, L., & Lidiard. H. (2010). Neurolinguistic programming used to reduce the need for anaesthesia in claustrophobic patients undergoing MRI. *The British Journal of Radiology*, 83, 113–117.

Bowers, L. A. (1996). An exploration of holistic and ontratraditional healing methods including research in the use of neuro-linguistic programming in the adjunctive treatment of acute pain. *Dissertation Abstracts International*, 56(11), 6379.

Brandis, A. D. (1986). A neurolinguistic treatment for reducing parental anger responses and creating more resourceful behavioural options. *Dissertation Abstracts International*, 47(11), 4642-B. California School of Professional Psychology. (Order = DA8626141): 161.

Crawley, E., Gaunt, D., Garfield, K., Hollingworth, W., Sterne, J., Beasant, L., Collin, S. M., Mills, N., & Montgomery, A. A. (2018). Clinical and cost-effectiveness of the Lightning Process in addition to specialist medical care for paediatric chronic fatigue syndrome: Randomised controlled trial. *Archives of Disease in Childhood*, 103, 155–164. doi:10.1136/archdischild-2017-31337

Crawley, E., Mills, N., Beasant, L., Johnson, D., Collin, S., Deans, Z., White, K., & Montgomery, A. (2013). The feasibility and acceptability of conducting a trial of specialist medical care and the Lightning Process in children with chronic fatigue syndrome: Feasibility randomized controlled trial (SMILE study). *Trials*, 14(1), 415. doi:10.1186/1745-6215-14-415

Crawley, E., Mills, N., Hollingworth, W., Deans, Z., Sterne, J., Donovan, J., Beasant, L., & Montgomery, A. (2013). Comparing specialist medical care with specialist medical care plus the Lightning Process® for chronic fatigue syndrome or myalgic encephalomyelitis (CFS/ME): Study protocol for a randomised controlled trial (SMILE Trial). *Trials*, 14, 444. doi:10.1186/1745-6215-14-444

Davis, S. L., & Davis, D. I. (1983). Neuro-Linguistic Programming and family therapy. *Journal of Marital and Family Therapy*, 9(3), Jul, 283–291.

Doğan, A., & Saritaş, S. (2021). The effects of neuro-linguistic programming and guided imagery on the pain and comfort after open-heart surgery. *Journal of Cardiac Surgery*. doi:10.1111/jocs.15505

Duncan, R. C., Konefal, J., & Spechler, M. M. (1990). Effect of neurolinguistic programming training on self-actualization as measured by the Personal Orientation Inventory Psychological Reports. Jun, 66(3 Pt 2), 1323–1330.

Einspruch, E. L., & Forman, B. D. (1988). Neurolinguistic programming in the treatment of phobias. *Psychotherapy in Private Practice*, 6(1), 91–100.

Field, E. S. (1990). Neurolinguistic programming as an adjunct to other psychotherapeutic/hypnotherapeutic interventions. *The American Journal of Clinical Hypnosis*, 32(3), 174–182.

Fineberg, N. A., Baldwin, D. S., Drummond, L. M., Wyatt, S., Hanson, J., Gopi, S., Kaur, S., Reid, J., Marwah, V., Sachdev, R. A., Pampaloni, I., Shahper, S., Varlakova, Y., Mpavaenda, D., Manson, C., O'Leary, C., Irvine, K., Monji-Patel, D., Shodunke, A., Dyer, T., Dymond, A., Barton, G., & Wellsted, D. (2018). Optimal treatment for obsessive compulsive disorder: A randomized controlled feasibility study of the clinical-effectiveness and cost-effectiveness of cognitive-behavioural therapy, selective serotonin reuptake inhibitors and their combination in the management of obsessive compulsive disorder. *International Clinical Psychopharmacology*, Nov, 33(6), 334–348. doi:10.1097/YIC.0000000000000237. PMID: 30113928; PMCID: PMC6166704.

Genser-Medlitsch, M., & Schütz, P. (1997, 2004). Does Neuro-Linguistic psychotherapy have effect? New Results shown in the extramural section. Martina Genser-Medlitsch; Peter Schütz, ÖTZ-NLP, Wiederhofergasse 4, A-1090, Wien, Austria/Nowiny Psychologiczne Psychological News. issue 1.

Gray, R., & Bourke, F. (2015) Remediation of intrusive symptoms of PTSD in fewer than five sessions: a 30-person pre-pilot study of the RTM protocol. *Journal of Military, Veteran and Family Health*, 1(2), 13–20.

Gray, R. M., Budden-Potts, D., & Bourke, F. (2017). The Reconsolidation of Traumatic Memories (RTM) Protocol for PTSD: A case study. *Journal of Experiential Psychotherapy*, 20, 47–61.

Gray, R., Budden-Potts, D., & Bourke, F. (2019). Reconsolidation of traumatic memories for PTSD: A randomized controlled trial of 74 male veterans. *Journal of the Society for Psychotherapy Research*, 29(5), 621–639.

Gray, R. M., Budden-Potts, D., Schwall, R. J., & Bourke, F. (2020). An open-label, randomized controlled trial of the reconsolidation of traumatic memories (RTM) in military women Psychological Trauma: Theory, research, practice and policy.

Gray, R., Liotta, R., Wake, L., & Cheal, J. (2013). Research and the History of Methodological Flaws. In Lisa Wake, Richard Gray, & Frank Bourke (Eds.), *The clinical efficacy of NLP: A critical appraisal* (pp. 194–216). London: Routledge.

Gray, R., & Teall, B. (2016). Reconsolidation of Traumatic Memories (RTM) for PTSD: A case series. *Journal of Experiential Psychotherapy*, 19, no 4 (76), 59–69, December.

Greenhalgh, T., Howick, J., & Maskrey, N. (2014). Evidence based medicine: A movement in crisis? *BMJ*, 348, g3725.

Grinder, J., & Pucelik, F. (2013). *Origins of neuro linguistic programming*. Bancyfelin: Crown House Publishing.

HemmatiMaslakpak, M., Farhadi, M., & Fereidoni, J. (2016). The effect of neuro-linguistic programming on occupational stress in critical care nurses. *Iranian*

Journal of Nursing and Midwifery Research, 21(1), 38–44. doi:10.4103/1735-9066.174754

Hossack, A., & Bentall, R. P. (1996). Elimination of posttraumatic symptomatology by relaxation and visual-kinesthetic dissociation. *Journal of Traumatic Stress*, 9(1), 99–110.

Ioannidis, J. P. (2016). The mass production of redundant, misleading, and conflicted systematic reviews and meta-analyses. *Milbank Q*, Sep, 94(3), 485–514. doi:10.1111/1468-0009.12210.

Jonsson, U., Bertilsson, G., Allard, P., Gyllensvärd, H., Söderlund, A., Tham, A., & Andersson, G. (2016). Psychological treatment of depression in people aged 65 years and over: A systematic review of efficacy, safety, and cost-effectiveness. *PLoS One*, Aug 18, 11(8), e0160859. doi:10.1371/journal.pone.0160859. PMID: 27537217; PMCID: PMC4990289.

Juhnke, G. A., Coll, K. M., Sunich, M. F., Kent, R. R. (2008). Using a Modified Neurolinguistic Programming Swish Pattern With Couple Parasuicide and Suicide Survivors. *The Family Journal*, 16, 391.

Kitchiner, N. J., Lewis, C., Roberts, N. P., & Bisson, J. I. (2019). Active duty and ex-serving military personnel with post-traumatic stress disorder treated with psychological therapies: systematic review and meta-analysis. *European Journal of Psychotraumatology*, 10(1). doi:10.1080/20008198.2019.1684226

Kotera, Y., Sheffield, D., & Van Gordon, W. (2018). The applications of neuro-linguistic programming in organizational settings: A systematic review of psychological outcomes. *Human Resource Development Quarterly*. doi:10.1002/hrdq.21334

Koziey, P. W., & McLeod, G. (1987). *Visual-Kinesthetic dissociation in treatment of victims of rape (research and practice) professional psychology: Research and practice*. American Psychological Association.

Liberman, M. B. (1984). The treatment of simple phobias with Neurolinguistic Programming techniques. *Dissertation Abstracts International*, 45(6). St. Louis University.

Lunkenheimer, F., Domhardt, M., Geirhos, A., Kilian, R., Mueller-Stierlin, A. S., Holl, R. W., Meissner, T., Minden, K., Moshagen, M., Ranz, R., Sachser, C., Staab, D., Warschburger, P., & Baumeister, H. (2020). COACH consortium. Effectiveness and cost-effectiveness of guided Internet- and mobile-based CBT for adolescents and young adults with chronic somatic conditions and comorbid depression and anxiety symptoms (youthCOACHCD): study protocol for a multicentre randomized controlled trial. *Trials*, Mar 12, 21(1), 253. doi:10.1186/s13063-019-4041-9. PMID: 32164723; PMCID: PMC7069009.

Matsumoto, K., Hamatani, S., Nagai, K., Sutoh, C., Nakagawa, A., & Shimizu, E. (2020). Long-term effectiveness and cost-effectiveness of videoconference-delivered cognitive behavioral therapy for obsessive-compulsive disorder, panic disorder, and social anxiety disorder in Japan: One-Year Follow-Up of a Single-Arm Trial. *JMIR Mental Health*, Apr 23, 7(4), e17157. doi:10.2196/17157. PMID: 32324150; PMCID: PMC7206520.

Morrell, C. J., Sutcliffe, P., Booth, A., Stevens, J., Scope, A., Stevenson, M., Harvey, R., Bessey, A., Cantrell, A., Dennis, C. L., Ren, S., Ragonesi, M., Barkham, M., Churchill, D., Henshaw, C., Newstead, J., Slade, P., Spiby, H., & Stewart-Brown, S. (2016). A systematic review, evidence synthesis and meta-analysis of quantitative and qualitative studies evaluating the clinical effectiveness, the cost-effectiveness, safety and acceptability of interventions to prevent postnatal depression. *Health Technology Assessment*, 20(37), 1–414. doi:10.3310/hta20370. PMID: 27184772; PMCID: PMC4885009.

Morriss, R., Xydopoulos, G., Craven, M., Price, L., & Fordham, R. (2019). Clinical effectiveness and cost minimisation model of Alpha-Stim cranial electrotherapy stimulation in treatment seeking patients with moderate to severe generalised anxiety disorder. *Journal of Affective Disorders*, Jun 15, 253, 426–437. doi:10.1016/j.jad.2019.04.020. Epub Apr 15. PMID: 31103808.

Muss, D. (1991). A new technique for treating post-traumatic stress disorder. *British Journal of Clinical Psychology*, 30(1), 91–92.

Osborne, D., Meyer, D., Moulding, R., Kyrios, M., Bailey, E., & Nedeljkovic, M. (2019). Cost-effectiveness of internet-based cognitive-behavioural therapy for obsessive-compulsive disorder. *Internet Interventions*, Sep 3, 18, 100277. doi:10.1016/j.invent.2019.100277. PMID: 31890626; PMCID: PMC6926329.

Parker, P., Aston, J., & de Rijk, L. (2020). A systematic review of the evidence base for the lightning process. *EXPLORE*, 1–30. https://doi.org/10.1016/j.explore.2020.07.014.

Parker, P., Aston, J., & Finch, F. (2018). Understanding the Lightning Process approach to CFS/ME; a review of the disease process and the approach. *Journal of Experiential Psychotherapy*, 21(2), 8. https://jep.ro/images/pdf/cuprins_reviste/82_art_2.pdf

Parker, P., Banbury, S., & Chandler, C. (2020). Efficacy of the rediscovery process on alcohol use, impulsivity and flourishing: A preliminary randomised controlled study and preliminary cohort study. *EJAPP*, 4(13). https://www.nationalwellbeingservice.org/volumes/volume-4-2020/volume-4-article-13/

Parker, P., Banbury, S., & de Rijk, L. (2021). Self-control or flourishing? A thematic analysis of experiences of alcohol users of The Rediscovery Process. *International Journal of Mental Health and Addiction*. https://doi.org/10.1007/s11469-021-00520-3.

Peng, Y., Lu, Y., Wei, W., Yu, J., Wang, D., Xiao, Y., Xu, J., & Wang, Z. (2015). The effect of a brief intervention for patients with ischemic stroke: A randomized controlled trial. *Journal of Stroke Cerebrovascular Disease*, Aug, 24(8), 1793–1802. doi:10.1016/j.jstrokecerebrovasdis.2015.04.009. PMID: 26117212.

Rasing, S. P. A., Stikkelbroek, Y. A. J., Riper, H., Dekovic, M., Nauta, M. H., Dirksen, C. D., Creemers, D. H. M., & Bodden, D. H. M. (2019). Effectiveness and cost-effectiveness of blended cognitive behavioral therapy in clinically depressed adolescents: Protocol for a Pragmatic quasi-experimental controlled trial. *JMIR Research Protocols*, Oct 7, 8(10), e13434. doi:10.2196/13434. PMID: 31593538; PMCID: PMC6803889.

Reinhard, J., Sänger, N., Hanker, L., Reichenbach, L., Yuan, J., Herrmann, E., & Louwen, F. (2013). Delivery mode and neonatal outcome after a trial of external cephalic version (ECV): A prospective trial of vaginal breech versus cephalic delivery. *Archives of Gynecology and Obstetrics*, 287(4), 663–668. doi:10.1007/s00404-012-2639-1

Richards, D., Duffy, D., Blackburn, B., Earley, C., Enrique, A., Palacios, J., Franklin, M., Clarke, G., Sollesse, S., Connell, S., & Timulak, L. (2018). Digital IAPT: The effectiveness & cost-effectiveness of internet-delivered interventions for depression and anxiety disorders in the Improving Access to Psychological Therapies programme: Study protocol for a randomised control trial. *BMC Psychiatry*, Mar 2, 18(1), 59. doi:10.1186/s12888-018-1639-5. PMID: 29499675; PMCID: PMC5833053.

Richards, D. A., Ekers, D., McMillan, D., Taylor, R. S., Byford, S., Warren, F. C., Barrett, B., Farrand, P. A., Gilbody, S., Kuyken, W., O'Mahen, H., Watkins, E. R., Wright, K. A., Hollon, S. D., Reed, N., Rhodes, S., Fletcher, E., & Finning, K. (2016). Cost and outcome of behavioural activation versus cognitive behavioural therapy for depression (COBRA): A randomised, controlled, non-inferiority trial. *Lancet*, Aug 27, 388(10047), 871–880. doi:10.1016/S0140-6736(16)31140-0. Epub 2016 Jul 23. PMID: 27461440; PMCID: PMC5007415.

Ross, E. L., Vijan, S., Miller, E. M., Valenstein, M., & Zivin, K. (2019). The cost-effectiveness of cognitive behavioral therapy versus second-generation anti-depressants for initial treatment of major depressive disorder in the United States: A decision analytic model. *Annals of Internal Medicine*, Dec 3, 171(11), 785–795. doi:10.7326/M18-1480. Epub 2019 Oct 29. PMID: 31658472; PMCID: PMC7188559.

Sharpley, C. (1984). Predicate matching in NLP: A review of research on the preferred representational system. *Journal of Counseling Psychology*, 31(2), 238–248.

Savardelavar, M., & Kuan, G. (2020). Reducing performance anxiety of a female dancer using neuro-linguistic programming and neuro-semantics: A case study. *International Journal of Public Health & Clinical Sciences* (IJPHCS), 7(2), 14–15. doi:10.32827/ijphcs.7.2.14

Scott, E. K. (1987). The effects of the Neurolinguistic Programming model of reframing as therapy for bulimia. *Dissertation Abstracts International*, 48(7), 1713-A 1714-A Northern Arizona University (Order = DA8715297): 191.

Shelden, V. E., & Shelden, R. G. (1989). Sexual abuse of males by females: The problem, treatment modality, and case example. *Family Therapy*, 16(3), 249–258.

Skapinakis, P., Caldwell, D., Hollingworth, W., Bryden, P., Fineberg, N., Salkovskis, P., Welton, N., Baxter, H., Kessler, D., Churchill, R., & Lewis, G. (2016). A systematic review of the clinical effectiveness and cost-effectiveness of pharmacological and psychological interventions for the management of obsessive-compulsive disorder in children/adolescents and adults. *Health Technology Assessment*. Jun, 20(43), 1–392. doi:10.3310/hta20430. PMID: 27306503; PMCID: PMC4921795.

Stiles, W. B., Barkham, M., Twigg, E., Mellor-Clark, J., & Cooper, M. (2006) Effectiveness of cognitive-behavioural, person-centred and psychodynamic therapies as practiced in UK National Health Service settings. *Psychological Medicine*, 26, 555–556.

Stipancic, M., Reiner, W., Schütz, P., & Dond R. (2010). Effects of Neuro-Linguistic Psychotherapy on psychological difficulties and perceived quality of life. *Counselling and Psychotherapy Research*, 10(1) – Routledge: 39–49.

Sturt, J., Ali, S., Robertson, W., Metcalfe, D., Grove, A., Bourne, C., & Bridle, C. (2012). Neurolinguistic programming: a systematic review of the effects on health outcomes. *British Journal of General Practice*, Nov, 62(604), e757–e764. doi:10.3399/bjgp12X658287. PMID: 23211179; PMCID: PMC3481516.

Sumin, A. N., Khairedinova, O. P., Sumina, L., Variushkina, E. V., Doronin, D. V., & Galimzianov, D. (2000). Psychotherapy impact on effectiveness of in-hospital physical rehabilitation in patients with acute coronary syndrome. *Klin Med* (Mosk), 78(6), 16–20.

The European Association of Psychotherapy. (2021). *Position Paper on the Proper Nature and Policy Applications of Psychotherapy Research*. https://www.europsyche.org/app/uploads/2021/04/EAP-Research-Statement-March-13-2021-adopted.pdf

Tie, H., Krebs, G., Lang, K., Shearer, J., Turner, C., Mataix-Cols, D., Lovell, K., Heyman, I., & Byford, S. (2019). Cost-effectiveness analysis of telephone cognitive-behaviour therapy for adolescents with obsessive-compulsive disorder. *BJPsych Open*. 2019 Jan, 5(1), e7. doi:10.1192/bjo.2018.73. PMID: 30762502; PMCID: PMC6343121.

Tylee, D. S., Gray, R., Glatt, S. J., & Bourke, F. (2017). Evaluation of the reconsolidation of traumatic memories protocol for the treatment of PTSD: A randomized wait-list-controlled trial. *Journal of Military, Veteran and Family Health*, 3(1), 21–33.

Utuza, A. J., Joseph, S., & Muss, D. C. (2011). Treating traumatic memories in Rwanda with the Rewind Technique: Two-Week Follow-Up after a Single Group Session. *Traumatology*.

VA National Center for PTSD. (2014). *Using the PTSD Checklist for DSM-IV (PCL)* [Internet]. 2014 Jan. Washington, DC: US. Department of Veterans Affairs. http://www.ptsd.va.gov/professional/pages/assessments/assessment-pdf/PCL-handout.pdf. Published January. 2014. Updated March 2016. Accessed July 4, 2016.

Vianna, L. A. C., Bomfim, G. F. T., & Chicone, G. (2006). *Self-esteem of raped women*. Revista Latino-Americana de Enfermagem, 14(5), Sep-Oct, 695–701.

Wake, L. (2009). A study of the relationship between the core belief structures of neurolinguistic psychotherapy and object relations theory. *Current Research in NLP*, 1, 50–66.

Wake, L. (2011). Waking Up and Moving On – A Programme Evaluation of an Intervention with Adolescents Identified as at Risk of Offending Behaviour. *Current Research in NLP. ANLP*, 43–53.

Wake, L., Gray, R. M., & Bourke, F. S. (2013). The clinical effectiveness of neurolinguistic programming: A critical appraisal. Routledge.

Wake, L., Leighton, M. (2014). Pilot study using Neurolinguistic Programming (NLP) in post-combat PTSD. *Mental Health Review Journal*, 19(4), 251–264.

Weaver, M. (2009). An Exploration of a Research-Based Approach to the Evaluation of Clients' Experience of Neuro-Linguistic Psychotherapy within a Private Practice Making use of the CORE Model. *Current Research in NLP: Proceedings of 2008 NLP Conference*, 1, 67–83.

Wiseman, R., Watt, C., ten Brinke, L., Porter, S., Couper, S.-L., & Rankin, C. (2012). The eyes don't have it: Lie detection and neuro-linguistic programming. *PLoS ONE*, 7(7), e40259. 10.1371/journal.pone.0040259

Witt, K. (2003). Psychological treatment can modulate the skin reaction to histamine in pollen allergic humans. *Psychosomatics*, 4, 33–37.

Witt, K. (2008). Neuro-Linguistic-Psychotherapy (NLPt) treatment can modulate the reaction in pollen allergic humans and their state of health. *International Journal of Psychotherapy*, 12(1), 50–60.

Zaharia, C., Reiner, M., & Schütz, P. (2015), Evidence-based Neuro Linguistic Psychotherapy: a meta-analysis. *Psychiatria Danubina*. Dec, 27(4), 355–363. PMID: 26609647.

Zika, B. (1985). Transformational hypnotherapy: Historical antecedents and a case example. *Australian Journal of Clinical Hypnotherapy and Hypnosis*, 6(2), 57–66.

Part II

Evidence-based protocols and models

3 The Reconsolidation of Traumatic Memories protocol (RTM) for PTSD – An emerging evidentiary treatment

Dr Richard Gray

Introduction

This chapter will

- review the published studies (Gray & Bourke, 2015; Gray, Budden-Potts, & Bourke, 2019; Tylee, Gray, Glatt, & Bourke, 2017), including those in process, and the implications of the two systematic reviews/meta-analyses (The International Society for Traumatic Stress Studies ISTSS, 2019; Kitchiner, Lewis, Roberts, & Bisson, 2019),
- describe the ongoing research at Walter Reed and Kings College,
- review RTM's association with the reconsolidation mechanism,
- offer suggestions for future research.

PTSD is a disorder of memory in which certain traumatic memories may intrude into and interfere with everyday life as flashbacks during which the client perceives themselves back in previous traumatizing events, and through its impact on mood and perspective as depression, guilt, or fear that the trauma will be discussed or otherwise confronted. It often disrupts sleep with nightmares that impact the patient's ability to function for hours or days following (American Psychiatric Association [APA], 2013).

Front line treatments for PTSD include Prolonged Exposure (PE), Cognitive Processing Therapy (CPT), Eye Movement Desensitization and Reprocessing (EMDR), and pharmaco-therapy. All four interventions report equivalent efficacy in reducing symptom severity scores (Bisson, Roberts, Andrew, Cooper, & Lewis, 2013; Goetter, Bui, & Ojserkis, 2015; Resick, Williams, Suvak, Monson, & Gradus, 2012; Steenkamp & Litz, 2014; Steenkamp, Litz, Hoge, & Marmar, 2015). None of these treatments, however, has been fully effective in the treatment of PTSD (Kitchiner et al., 2019; Steenkamp et al., 2015). A review of those interventions finds that 60% to 72% of military patients receiving those treatments retain the PTSD diagnosis post-treatment (Steenkamp, Litz, Hoge, & Marmar, 2015).

DOI: 10.4324/9781003198864-3

The Reconsolidation of Traumatic Memories (RTM) Intervention

RTM is a brief, trauma-focused therapy derived from Neuro-Linguistic Programming (NLP) techniques. It is closely related to the Visual Kinetic Dissociation protocol (Gray & Liotta, 2012) from which it is derived and the Rewind Technique (Adams & Allan, 2018; Muss, 1991, 2002). It differs from them in that it relies explicitly upon the syntax of reconsolidation to enhance outcomes; it has been standardized and expanded for scientific evaluation (Gray & Bourke, 2015; Gray & Liotta, 2012; Tylee, Gray, Glatt, & Bourke 2017; Gray, Budden-Potts, & Bourke, 2017).

As a technique derived from NLP, a test of RTM is not a test of the validity of NLP, but only of predicted relationships based upon NLP's structural elements (see Chapter 10). Here, the intervention focuses upon introducing structural changes into the traumatic memory through the purposeful restructuring of the submodality dimensions (see below) of the memory to create a felt dissociation from the events. This felt dissociation, then, allows the newly dissociated memories to be spontaneously reappraised as a normal part of a personal world-map, thus providing workable answers for the client.

RTM has been focused primarily upon PTSD symptoms expressed as immediate, phobic-like responses to triggering stimuli (flashbacks), repeated nightmares or night terrors, and fast arising autonomic reactivity. Nightmares and flashbacks associated with the diagnosis are expected to be related to one or a few identifiable traumatic incidents either by content or feeling tone. The intervention has been tested almost exclusively with combat trauma and victims of Military Sexual Trauma (MST) (Gray & Bourke, 2015; Tylee et al., 2017; Gray et al., 2019; Gray, Budden-Potts, Schwall, & Bourke, 2020), however, recent trainees have extended its applicability to non-military contexts and traumas with equivalent results (Gray, Davis, & Bourke, 2021).

Each treatment session begins with a brief, controlled retelling of the target trauma. That narrative is interrupted as soon as signs of emotional arousal are observed (e.g., changes in posture, breathing, muscular tone, lacrimation, flushing, voice tone, etc.). The evocation is interrupted with the expectation that a very brief exposure to the trauma will initiate labilization of the memory with reconsolidation blockade of the structure of the original memory (Agren, 2014; Gray & Liotta, 2012; Forcato et al., 2007; Kindt, Soeter, & Vervliet, 2009; Lee, 2009; Schiller & Phelps, 2011; Schiller et al., 2010; Schiller, Kanen, LeDoux, Monfils, & Phelps, 2013). Previous research with humans and animals has shown that just such a brief, incomplete, or unreinforced reminder will render the traumatic memory subject to change for a period of from one to six-hours (Nader, Schafe, & Le Doux, 2000; Schiller et al., 2010). After termination of the narrative, calming and reorienting the patient to the present, patients are then guided through a series of dissociative experiences that are designed to perceptually recode the trauma memory as a past, non-threatening event. Insofar as these changes represent new information that is relevant to the target memory and its current level of threat, it is believed that, in accordance with reconsolidation theory (Agren, 2014; Gray & Liotta, 2012; Fernández, Bavassi, Forcato, & Pedreira, 2016; Forcato et al., 2007; Kindt et al., 2009; Lee, 2009; Schiller, & Phelps, 2011; Schiller et al., 2013), those changes will be incorporated into the structure of the target memory. With RTM, the content of the target memory remains unchanged, only its perceptual structure is altered. After treatment, the details of the event may be recalled, narrated, or discussed without the strong arousal that is characteristic of PTSD. Once the intensity of the memory has been attenuated, as verified by SUDs reports and symptom inventories, the meaning of the event is reappraised spontaneously. Partial memories are often restored to more complete narratives and the perspective within the memory typically shifts to a more distant, third-person position (Gray & Bourke, 2015; Gray et al., 2017; Gray et al., 2020; Gray & Liotta, 2012; Tylee et al., 2017).

RTM is designed to introduce perceptual distortions that code the memory as a past event, not threatening in the present. The specific elements involved in this recoding include multiple levels of dissociation that imply that the patient is not "in" the memory. They include the movie theater scenario (as the context for fantasy), the flattening of the event onto a distant movie screen, the loss of color, temporal distortions, the instruction to watch another dissociated self as they watch the movie, and others (see Table 3.1. for an outline of the intervention). These all distance the patient from the trauma content. While each, separately and in combination, decreases the complexity of the visual image, and creates a sense of distance and dissociation, they also reduce its salience, defined as its emotional intensity. At last, the memory is coded as a distant, non-threatening, distributed memory of the target event.

The RTM protocol is distinct from trauma focused Cognitive behavioral therapies (TFCBTs) in that exposure to the trauma memory is not the central effector of treatment change. Here, the brief exposure narrative is believed to initiate a period in which the trauma memory is destabilized and during which information can be incorporated into the structure of the target memory (Agren, 2014; Gray & Bourke, 2015; Gray & Liotta, 2012; Fernández et al., 2016; Forcato et al., 2007; Kindt et al., 2009; Lee, 2009; Schiller, & Phelps, 2011; Schiller et al., 2013). RTM is not an exposure or an extinction-based intervention, it is believed to employ reconsolidations as a memory-updating mechanism.

The cognitive elements of the intervention are well established in the annals of cognitive behavioral research (NLPWIKI, 2014). In RTM they are systematically used throughout the protocol to change the apparent present-time, emergent nature of the trauma material and the patient's response to it, to a more distant perspective consistent with non-pathological memories.

Table 3.1 Treatment outline: reconsolidation of traumatic memories

1	The client is asked to recount the target trauma briefly.
2	As soon as they show signs of autonomic arousal, the clinician stops the narrative and reorients them to the present.
3	Elicit SUDS (Subjective Units of Distress) rating.
4	The clinician aids the client in choosing a recognizable but neutral name for the event.
5	The clinician assists the client in choosing "bookends," times before and after the event: a time before they knew the event would occur, and another when they knew that the event was over and that they had survived.
6	The client is guided to imagine being in a movie theater in which the pre-trauma bookend is displayed in black and white on the screen.
7	They are instructed how to remain dissociated from the material on the screen.
8	As if from behind and above, the client watches their own responses as a black and white movie of the target trauma plays from bookend to bookend. The movie is repeated with structural alterations as needed until the client is comfortable.
9	The client steps into the last frame of the movie, turns on the sound, color, and dimensionality, and experiences the event backwards, as a fast rewind lasting 2 seconds or less. It begins with the post-trauma bookend and ends with the pre-trauma bookend. This is repeated as needed until they are comfortable and show little or no autonomic arousal.
10	The clinician elicits the trauma narrative and probes for responses to stimuli that previously elicited a fast arising, autonomic response. If the response is significant, earlier steps of the process are repeated.
11	SUDS ratings are elicited.
12	When the client is free from emotions in recounting the event, or sufficiently comfortable (SUDS = 1 or 2), they are invited to proceed to the next phase of treatment. If SUDs $\geq$ 3, trending upward, the client is directed to repeat elements of the protocol beginning either with the rewind or the black and white movies.
13	The client is invited to design and experience several alternate, non-traumatizing versions of the event, and rehearses these several times.
14	The client is again asked to relate the trauma, and their previous triggers are probed.
15	SUDS ratings are elicited.
16	When the trauma cannot be evoked, and the client can recount the event without significant autonomic arousal, the procedure is over.

Note: Other versions of the RTM outline can be found in Gray et al., 2019; and Tylee et al., 2017. Full details of the intervention are available from the corresponding author.

Crucially, and perhaps the defining element of the protocol, is the use of the cognitive elements of the intervention during the period of labilization that follows the termination of the trauma narrative. During this period, thought to last from one to six hours (Nader, 2003; Nader et al., 2000; Schiller et al., 2010), relevant information about the target memory that is new, or novel, that provides safety information, or information that changes the status of the threat, may be introduced into the structure of the memory (Agren, 2014; Fernández et al., 2016; Forcato et al., 2007; Kindt et al., 2009; Lee, 2009; Schiller, & Phelps, 2011; Schiller et al., 2013). While the cognitive elements of the protocol may have some value on their own, we hypothesize that it is their presentation in the context of reconsolidation that leads to the fast, largely permanent changes in the index memories that characterize RTM.

Initially, RTM was targeted only at clients expressing the intrusive symptoms of PTSD, especially when experienced as sudden, uncontrollable responses either to the trauma narrative, elements of the narrative, or stimuli known to elicit flashbacks and nightmares. This style of responding has been identified as being particularly susceptible to 'reconsolidative modification' (Kredlow, Unger, & Otto 2016). Since the beginning of training for licensed clinicians, its application has been extended to subsyndromal PTSD, and non-military traumas (Gray et al., 2021).

Studies of RTM efficacy

There have been four randomized waitlist-controlled studies (RCTs) of RTM. The reported scores were based upon the PCL-M for DSM IV (Foa, Riggs, Dancu, & Rothbaum, 1993). The two later RCTs evaluated the protocol using both the PSS-I and PCL-M for DSM IV at intake and at two-weeks post-treatment. At six weeks post and later follow-ups the PCL-M was used either alone or with the PSS-I (Gray et al., 2020; Gray et al., 2017; Tylee et al., 2017; Gray & Bourke, 2015). Three of the studies investigated RTM with samples of male veterans. The fourth study (Gray et al., 2020), examined a mixed group of thirty service-related women, 21 of whom suffered from some degree of Military Sexual Trauma (MST). All studies obtained high effect sizes and significant loss of diagnosis. Those who no longer met diagnostic criteria, as well as those who were merely subclinical but with significant symptom score reductions, reported a complete absence of flashbacks and nightmares after the last treatment.

In their pilot study, Gray and Bourke (2015) evaluated RTM in a population of veterans with current PTSD diagnoses. They reported a mean (PCL-M) intake score of 61.7. After treatment, they reported a mean reduction in trauma severity of 33 points, with a final mean PCL-M score of 28.8 ± 7.5 at 6 weeks or the last measure reported. Hedges' g at 6-weeks post showed a 2.9 SMD difference from intake to follow-up (CI 99% [26.05, 33.71]; p. < 0.001). Informal follow-ups reaching approximately 75% of treatment completers indicated that treatment gains were maintained for up to 4 years (R. Gray, personal communication, August 5, 2019).

Tylee et al. (2017) reported a mean (PCL-M) reduction of 39.8 points (cumulative intake mean = 66.5 ± 8.27), with a final mean PCL-M score of 26.8 ± 13.08 at 6 months. Hedges' g for all treatment completers at 6-months post indicated a 3.59 SMD difference in effect from intake to follow-up (CI 99% [22.06, 33.54]; $p < 0.001$). Data from a one-year follow-up indicated that these improvements were maintained for a full year after treatment. Twelve-month mean PCL-M scores for treatment completers, with 81.5% reporting, were 20.9 (±4.2), a reduction of 46.5 points. These results were significant at the .001 level.

Gray, Budden-Potts, and Bourke (2019) reported a 74-person study following the same randomized waitlist design. In this study, the main measure at all time points was the PSS-I. Mean intake score on the PSS-I was 38.5 ± 6.783 with mean reductions at 6 weeks of 23 points and final mean scores of PSS-I 15.38 ± 15.23. Within-group RTM effect sizes (Hedges' g) for PSS-I score changes ranged from 1.45 to 2.3. The between group comparison, between the treatment group and untreated controls was significant ($p < 0.001$) with an effect size equivalent to two standard deviations ($g = 2.13$; 95% CI 1.56, 2.70]; p. < 0. 001).

In their study of thirty female subjects, Gray and associates (2020) reported that treatment group PSS-I scores decreased from a mean of 43.6 ± 2.5 to 9.7 ± 6.3 at 2-weeks post (decrease, 33.9; $g = 3.7$; 95% CI [2.5, 4.8]), and remained stable to 1-year post. PSS-I scores for treated controls dropped from a mean of 38.6 ± 3.5 to 7.1 ± 5.9 at 2-weeks post (decrease, 31.5; $g = 3.4$; 95% CI [2.3, 4.5]) and remained stable to 1-year. Treatment group PCL-M means decreased from 73.5 ± 3.1 to 28.3 ± 7.2 at 2-weeks post (decrease, 45.2, $p < 0.001$ | $g = 4.2$; 95% CI [3.0, 5.4]). Scores for treated controls dropped from a mean of 67.1 ± 4.5 to 25.6 ± 7.4 at 2-weeks post (decrease, 41.5, $p < 0.001$| $g = 3.5$; 95% CI [2.4, 4.6]), and remained stable to 1 year.

In these studies, we used PTSD symptom inventories based upon DSM-IV-TR (APA, 2000). We did this to ensure comparability with previous studies of the intervention and in light of the large body of research already accomplished using that standard (Hoge et al., 2016).

For all studies, clinical improvement in PTSD symptoms was determined using standard levels of change in PCL-M scores (Schnurr et al., 2007; VA National Center for PTSD, 2014). Response to treatment was regarded as clinically significant for improvements in PCL-M scores of greater than 20 points (Monson et al., 2008).

For all four RCT investigations, loss of diagnosis was determined based upon a combination of standard DSM criteria (scoring below threshold on symptom inventories while failing to endorse all three symptom clusters at the required levels). This accounted for 65% or more of the results in all three studies. A second criterion included scoring below the dichotomous clinical threshold for PTSD as defined for the primary measure (PSS-I ≤ 20,

PCL-M ≤ 45) while showing no autonomic reactivity to relevant stimuli and reporting a total loss of nightmares and flashbacks. Using these combined measures, loss of diagnosis was above 90% for all four studies. A forest plot (Figure 3.1) reveals an overall standardized mean difference of 2.7 SMDs.

PTSD symptom scores

After the pilot study, we inspected the symptom cluster scores for all participants for Intent to Treat (ITT) analysis. In the following table and accompanying figures, we present the changes for each cluster across study arm (Treatment and Control) and symptom inventory (PCL and PSS-I; Gray et al., 2019; Gray et al., 2020; Tylee et al., 2017; see Table 3.2).

These results reflect significant reductions in symptom scores across all of the studies. A visual presentation of the data for PSS-I symptom Clusters appears in Figure 3.1, Figure 3.2 and for PCL in Figure 3.3. For PSS-I, items are scored on a scale ranging from 0 (not at all) to 3 (very much). A PTSD diagnosis was made when at least one reexperiencing, three avoidance, and two arousal symptoms were endorsed with a score of at least 1 (Foa, Riggs, Dancu, & Rothbaum, 1993).

For PCL responses, only scores between 3 and 5 (*Moderately* or above) are regarded as symptomatic and are applied to the following DSM criteria for diagnosis. At least 1 "B" item (Questions 1–5), 3 "C" items (Questions 6–12), and 2 "D" items (Questions 13–17) (Figure 3.3).

Studies pending publication

Lewine et al. (2017) evaluated how quantitative EEG (qEEG) and clinical measures (PCL and PSS-I) from subjects with PTSD were affected by treatment with the Reconsolidation of Traumatic Memories (RTM) protocol as compared to waitlisted controls and a matched set of qEEG results from a database of neuro-normal adults. Twelve PTSD subjects underwent qEEG and clinical assessments at baseline and 1 month after three 90-minute RTM treatment sessions (administered over the course of 1 week). Ten additional PTSD subjects were evaluated at baseline and 1-month following a no-treatment waiting period. Baseline EEG data were also evaluated from twenty-two age and gender-matched neurotypical control subjects. In each case, the individual participants' qEEG data were evaluated with respect to a large normative database. At baseline, only about 14% of control subjects showed some elevation in qEEG, high-beta responses. In contrast, nearly 70% of PTSD subjects showed excessive power in the high-beta range. Waitlist PTSD subjects showed minimal clinical or EEG changes between baseline and follow-up evaluations, while RTM subjects showed highly significant ($p < 0.001$) reductions in PCL and PSS-I scores, along with normalization of the excessive high-beta activity that had previously been associated with their PTSD symptom scores.

Study or Subgroup	RTM Mean [PSS-I seve]	RTM SD [PSS-I seve]	RTM Total	Waitlist Control Mean [PSS-I seve]	Waitlist Control SD [PSS-I seve]	Waitlist Control Total	Weight	Mean Difference IV, Fixed, 95% CI [PSS-I seve]
Gray & Bourke 2015	31.96	11.58	26	67.4	10.04	5	7.1%	-35.44 [-45.30, -25.58]
Gray et al. 2020	9.7	6.3	15	38.6	3.5	14	50.7%	-28.90 [-32.58, -25.22]
Gray et al., 2019	12.9	12.9	36	37.11	9.39	33	24.5%	-24.21 [-29.50, -18.92]
Tylee et al., 2017	9.7	8.3	15	38.93	8.09	12	17.8%	-24.23 [-35.44, -23.02]
Total (95% CI)			**92**			**64**	**100.0%**	**-28.27 [-30.89, -25.65]**

Heterogeneity: $Chi^2 = 4.49$, $df = 3$ ($P = 0.21$); $I^2 = 33\%$

Test for overall effect: $Z = 21.16$ ($P < 0.00001$)

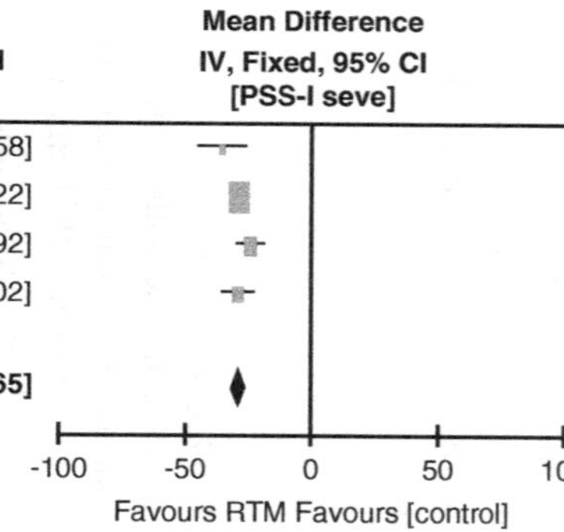

Figure 3.1 Forest plot: Four RCTs of the RTM Protocol.

Figure Note: Forest plot generated using Review Manager (RevMan), 2014.

Table 3.2 PSS-I-5 Results from trainee treatments by initially reported target trauma type-PSS-I-5 results only

Trauma type	*N*	*Mean Baseline PSS-I-5*	*SD*	*Mean Post PSS-I-5*	*SD*	*Δ*	*Δ %*	*ES d*	*ES g*	*95% CI*	
										Lower	*Upper*
Sexual Trauma	21	45.8	12.9	10.2	9.3	35.6	78	3.17	3.11	2.21	4.06
Family Violence	20	49.8	13.7	13.7	12.9	36.1	72	3.58	3.5	2.49	4.57
Other	18	46.9	12.5	11.2	10.1	35.7	76	3.14	3.07	2.11	4.04
Accident	6	41.8	15.76	5.5	4.2	36.3	86	3.14	2.9	1.28	4.52
Combat	4	39.3	11.26	7.5	5.7	31.8	81	3.56	3.1	1.04	5.14
First Responder	2	42	0	2	0	40	95	–	–	–	–
Health Trauma	2	48.5	33.2	4.5	3.5	44	91	1.86	1.05	−1.04	3.14
School Violence	1	42	0	5	0	37	88	–	–	–	–
Means	74	44.5	12.4	7.45	5.7	37.06	83.38	3.075	2.788	1.348	4.245

Table note: Some categories were too small for the computation of effect sizes. n= number of clients; Δ = (Baseline PSS-I-5) – (Post TreatmentPSS-I-5); Δ% = % change; ES d = Cohen's D; ES g = Hedge's g; CI =Confidence Interval. The table is derived from Gray, Davis, and Bourke (2021) and is used with the permission of the authors.

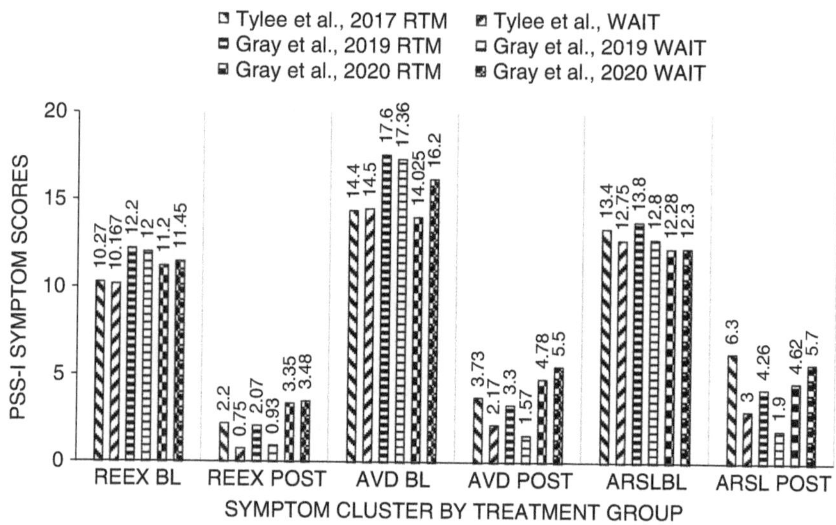

Figure 3.2 DSM IV PSS-I Symptom clusters for all time points.

Figure note: The figure legend lists keys for the RTM and control groups in parallel columns to be read left to right. They are listed consecutively in the figure columns; REEX= reexperiencing; BL = baseline; POST = post treatment; AVD = avoidance; ARSL = arousal.

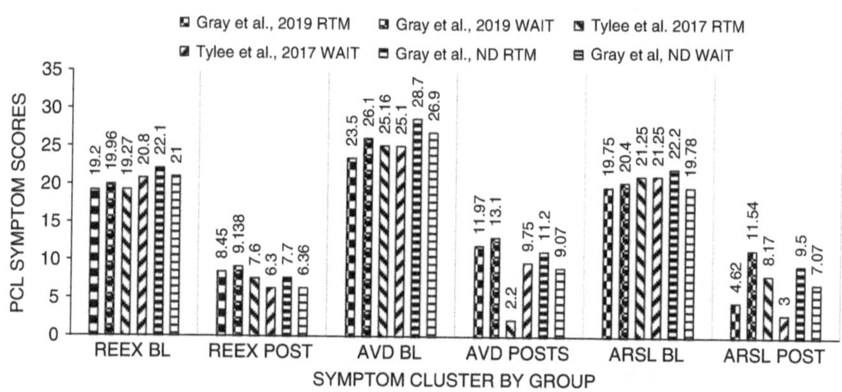

Figure 3.3 DSM IV PCL Symptom clusters for all time points.

Figure note: The figure legend lists keys for the RTM and control groups in parallel columns to be read left to right. They are listed consecutively in the figure columns; REEX= reexperiencing; BL = baseline; POST =post treatment; AVD = avoidance; ARSL = arousal.

The researchers applied a source modeling protocol (the LORETA algorithm) to determine the brain regions most likely to correspond to the observed qEEG results. It showed that the baseline abnormalities in high-beta were mostly generated in medial temporal lobe (hippocampus and amygdalar), insular, frontal, and parietal regions. Post-treatment normalization mostly reflected changes in the medial temporal areas, consistent with changes in the hippocampal and amygdalar regions. Those authors concluded that high-beta activity may be a useful biomarker for PTSD that can be used to objectively track the neurobiological impact of behavioral therapies. That research produced some dramatic visual evidence that may be viewed in Figure 3.4.

Between 2018 and 2020, 18 licensed mental health professionals participated in certification trainings for the use of the reconsolidation of RTM protocol. After completion of the course and subsequent certification, participants collected and reported back anonymized data on 85 clients they had completed treating for PTSD using RTM. Among the reported cases, 74 used the PSSI-5 and 11 others used PCL-5. We had originally hypothesized that trainee results would match or exceed those reported in the above-cited RTM studies, that the protocol's utility would be extended by these practitioners to more trauma types than previously reported, and that their results would validate the efficacy of the training (Table 3.2).

Between 2018 and 2020, 99 patients diagnosed with PTSD were referred for treatment to a professional counseling and therapy organization in Albuquerque NM. Ninety of those patients were deemed eligible and were treated by the 18 certified RTM trainees. Patients averaged slightly more

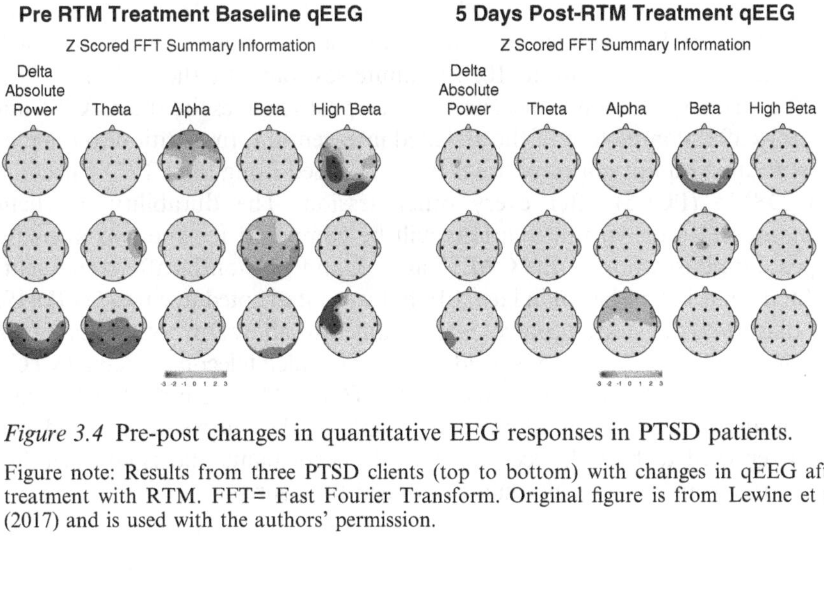

Figure 3.4 Pre-post changes in quantitative EEG responses in PTSD patients.

Figure note: Results from three PTSD clients (top to bottom) with changes in qEEG after treatment with RTM. FFT= Fast Fourier Transform. Original figure is from Lewine et al. (2017) and is used with the authors' permission.

than one trauma each and averaged about 3 sessions per trauma. Data collection beyond symptom severity scores were limited by the exigencies of the COVID-19 epidemic. Of the 90 RTM-eligible clients, 5 dropped out, and 85 completed RTM treatment for at least one trauma. Pre- post- PSS-I-5 or PCL-5 results found that 80 (95%) scored below minimal diagnostic criteria for PTSD, exceeding previously reported success rates. Trainees extended the range of treated traumas beyond military contexts to include family violence, first responder trauma exposure, sexual abuse, school-related traumas, and traffic accidents.

The authors concluded that RTM training appears to be an effective means for developing a cadre of licensed professionals who are able to replicate the results of RTM as previously reported. Moreover, its extension to non-military traumatic events recommends the treatment for a wide range of traumatic memories. The results and effect sizes for those clients reporting PSS-I-5 scores (n = 74) is reported in Table 3.3, ordered by the trauma frequency.

Ongoing research

Several independent university studies of RTM are currently ongoing. The first is a head-to-head comparison with a brief (ten session) version of prolonged exposure sponsored by the Center for Rehabilitative and Neurological Medicine at the Uniformed Services University, Walter Reed Military Medical Center, Bethesda, MD, USA.

This is a randomized, single-blind, two-arm, controlled clinical trial. The study will enroll 108 active duty, reservist, National Guard, or retired military service members who are eligible for care in the DoD healthcare system, and who meet criteria for PTSD, as confirmed by administration of the Clinician-Administered PTSD Scale for DSM5 (CAPS5) by an independent study administrator, blind to the study arm. The study will compare the results of up to 10, 90-minute sessions of either RTM or PE.

The primary outcome measure is pre- post-changes in the CAPS5 inventory after completion of the assigned intervention. In addition to the pre-post results, rapidity of response is being assessed using the PTSD Checklist for DSM5 (PCL5) after every other session. The durability of client responses to the two interventions will be compared for the two arms by repeat administration of the CAPS5 at 2, 6, and 12 months after treatment.

Study enrollment began in late 2019 but was interrupted due to COVID-19. At that time, the study protocol was modified to allow for both assessments and intervention sessions to be held entirely via video teleconferencing (VTC). As of March 2021, 33 participants (28 by VTC) had been enrolled (67% male, Mean age = 42.9), 16 of whom had completed the intervention. RTM has been reported to be well-received by study participants and is considerably easier for them to complete than Prolonged Exposure.

Table 3.3 DSM IV PTSD Symptom clusters for all time points

			REEXPERIENCING						*AVOIDANCE*						*AROUSAL*					
			PCLM			*PSS-I*			*PCLM*			*PSS-I*			*PCLM*			*PSS-I*		
			INTAKE	*INTAKE 2*	*2 WKS*	*INTAKE*	*INTAKE 2*	*2WKS*	*INTAKE*	*INTAKE 2*	*2 WKS*	*INTAKE*	*INTAKE 2*	*2WKS*	*INTAKE*	*INTAKE 2*	*2 WKS*	*INTAKE*	*INTAKE 2*	*2WKS*
Gray, Budden-	TREATMENT	Mean	19.2		8.45	11.2		3.35	23.5		11.975	14.025		4.775	19.75		10.5	12.275		4.625
Potts, &		SD	3.702		4.624	2.574		4.222	6.641		6.375	4.148		5.211	3.564		4.777	1.894		4.081
Bourke, 2020	CONTROL	Mean	19.966	18.655	9.138	11.448	12.0345	3.483	26.103	25.621	13.103	16.172	15.552	5.552	20.414	20.448	11.536	12.276	12.621	5.690
		SD	4.022	4.270	5.330	3.112	4.686	4.197	5.434	5.294	6.241	3.616	3.408	5.415	3.290	3.376	6.191	2.576	2.321	4.936
Tylee, Gray, Glatt,	TREATMENT	Mean	19.267		7.6	10.267		2.2	25		11.067	14.4		3.733	20.2		11.467	13.4		6.333
& Bourke, 2017		SD	2.492		2.874	3.059		3.530	5.305		4.978	3.112		4.949	2.651		5.041	1.183		4.030
	CONTROL	Mean	20.833	20.25	6.333	10.167	11.417	0.75	25.166	25.333	9.75	14.5	14.333	2.167	21.25	21.583	8.167	12.75	12.333	3
		SD	2.552	−3.049	1.497	3.589	2.999	1.357	5.982	5.466	5.011	4.777	5.499	3.786	3.441	3.825	4.064	2.379	2.774	2.860
Gray, Budden-	TREATMENT	Mean	22.133		7.733	12.2		2.067	28.733		11.2	17.6		3.333	22.2		9.533	13.8		4.2667
Potts, Schwall		SD	2.10		3.615	2.484		3.494	3.240		6.0734	2.501		4.952	2.569		4.612	1.265		3.955
& Bourke, ND	CONTROL	Mean	21	20.5	6.357	12	11.214	0.929	26.929	24.57	9.071	17.357	14.786	1.571	19.786	21.071	7.071	12.786	12.429	1.929
		SD	2.320	2.066	1.598	2.038	2.007	1.730	4.160	4.669	2.615	2.530	3.683	2.533	3.355	2.615	1.90	1.578	2.209	1.940

A second study is being completed by Kings College, Belfast, UK. This study is an external randomised pilot trial to compare the RTM protocol with Trauma Focussed CBT delivered by charities for the treatment of PTSD in ex-military veterans. The study was initially offered to only residents of the island of Ireland, however, due to Covid restrictions and limited uptake the trial was opened up to all UK ex-military veterans.

The aims of the trial are:

- to determine the rate of trial recruitment, retention in treatment and research, to understand the reasons for drop out and determine completeness of outcome data.
- to undertake exploratory analyses of the outcome data to support a power calculation for a fully powered non-inferiority trial.
- understand the safety risks.
- to establish an expanded mental healthcare capacity across Northern Ireland (the original site for the trial) to enable both interventions to be delivered closer to the veteran's home.

Cochrane Systematic reviews including RTM

Cochrane Systematic reviews are among the most highly respected analyses of treatment efficacy. Previously, program certification from the U. S. Government (the now-defunct National Registry of Evidence-Based Programs and Practices, NREPP) required multiple publications in peer-reviewed journals and the program's presence in reputable systematic reviews or meta-analyses. RTM has now appeared in multiple Cochrane-based reviews. Two of those studies stand out.

In its 2019, *PTSD Prevention and Treatment Guidelines–Methodology and Recommendations*, The International Society for Traumatic Stress Studies (The International Society for Traumatic Stress Studies [ISTSS], 2019) reviewed more than 5500 RCTs of new studies related to PTSD. Of those, 327 met Cochrane Collaboration inclusion criteria for RCTs of interventions targeted specifically at PTSD. As part of their acceptance criteria, ISTSS adopted the UK NICE standards for the assessment of effect size thresholds. These included effect sizes >.8 for waiting list controls, >.6 for attentional controls, and >.2 for active controls. Two RTM waitlisted RCTs were included. RTM was recognized as a psychological treatment for PTSD with "Emerging Evidence."

In a more recent Cochrane systematic review and meta-analysis, RTM was found to be one of only two psychological treatments to adequately address the needs of active-duty service members and veterans (Kitchiner et al., 2019).

The nature of RTM

RTM relies on two important elements. The first is its hypothesized use of the reconsolidation mechanism and the window of labilization that it creates in order to incorporate structural changes into an updated version of the original trauma memory. The second is its use of cognitive interventions that directly impact the original memory. When introduced within the window of labilization, their relevance to the index memory ensures that those changes are incorporated into the memory. The literature is clear that new content, introduced during the period of labilization, must be relevant to the original memory context or it may not be incorporated into the structure of the original (Agren, 2014; Fernández et al., 2016; Forcato et al., 2007; Kindt et al., 2009; Lee, 2009; Schiller, & Phelps, 2011; Schiller et al., 2013).

Reconsolidation

For most of the 20th century, classical memory research held that long-term memory was largely permanent, not subject to change (Nader & Einarsson, 2010; Schwabe, Nader, & Pruessner 2014). Until the early 21st century, memory change research was dominated by the extinction paradigm dating back to Pavlov's (1927) work in the early 20th century (Clem & Schiller, 2016). Extinction, as we now know, creates a blocking memory in the frontal cortex that renders the target memory somewhat inaccessible but does not modify the memory itself (Bouton, 2004; Bouton & Moody, 2004; Clem & Schiller, 2016; Kindt & van Emmerik, 2016; Kredlow et al., 2016; Monfils, Cowansage, Klann, & LeDoux, 2009; Rescorla, 1988).

Reconsolidation is a neural mechanism for the updating of long-term memory (Agren, 2014; Lee, 2009; Nader, 2003; Nader et al., 2000; Sandrini, Cohen, & Censor, 2015; Schiller et al., 2010). It was first identified in 1968 as retroactive amnesia (Misanin, Miller, & Lewis 1968) but did not become a central focus of memory research until 2000 when Nader, Schafe, and LeDoux brought it into the research spotlight (Nader et al., 2000). Since that time, reconsolidation has become the center of a whirlwind of research (Bonin & De Koninck, 2015; Clem & Schiller, 2016; Schiller & Phelps, 2011).

When a long-term memory is confronted with information that contradicts some essential element of that memory (but not the entire memory), or provides novel information about that event (Pedreira et al., 2004), that memory may briefly become subject to change. During this labilization period, lasting for one or more hours (Nader, 2003; Nader et al., 2000; Monfils et al., 2009), the memory can be strengthened, weakened, or its emotional tone and salience changed. Various researchers have shown that consolidation and reconsolidation are distinct phenomena. Reconsolidation is not consolidation (Johnson & Casey, 2015; Kredlow et al., 2016; Monfils et al., 2009; Nader & Einarsson, 2010; Pedreira et al., 2004).

The process of reconsolidation is related to the observation that prediction error results in memory updating throughout the brain (Kaplan & Oudeyer, 2007; Kroes & Fernández, 2012; Daw, Gershman, Seymour, Dayan, & Dolan, 2011). Prediction errors have been explicitly related to reconsolidation by several authors (Kindt & van Emmerik, 2016; Kroes & Fernández, 2012; Lee, 2009; Agustina López et al., 2016; Pedreira et al., 2004).

Reconsolidation is different from extinction in temporal constraints (Pedreira et al., 2004), neural pathways (Clem & Schiller, 2016; Monfils et al., 2009), and involves the synthesis of different proteins (Merlo, Milton & Everitt, 2015; Nader et al., 2000; Suzuki et al., 2004; Tronson & Taylor, 2007). Reconsolidation modifies the original trace, whereas extinction creates a new blocking memory (Kindt & van Emmerik, 2016; Kredlow et al., 2016; Monfils et al., 2009). The neural locus of extinction for fear memories is generally found in the vmPFC. The rewritten fear memory in reconsolidation is most frequently identified with a locus in the baso-lateral amygdala (Björkstrand et al., 2015; Monfils et al., 2009; Schiller et al., 2013).

In order to effectively induce labilization, several specific constraints must be observed. They are:

1. There must be a stimulus, internal or external, that triggers a specific long term memory schema that serves as a prediction or sets an expectation of what will happen next;
2. That stimulus presentation must be sufficiently brief so as to not set conditions for the creation of an extinction memory;
3. There must be a prediction error, such that the actions or perceptions predicted by the triggered memory are not met.

This might include: the non-presentation of an expected UCS after presentation of a CS (an extinction trial); a change in safety information regarding the expected action or event; a change in the setting of the event; the worsening of the expected circumstance; an interruption of an expected physiological response; the presentation of an unconditioned stimulus of lessened intensity than expected; or other changes.

Once the window of labilization has opened, the original memory may be changed. Most often, reconsolidation means that the memory is renewed without change, that is, reconsolidated in its original form. In reconsolidation blockade, as in the propranolol studies with phobias and PTSD (Dunbar & Taylor, 2017), something, inhibition of protein synthesis, new information, interferes with reconsolidative reinforcement of the memory and the memory is weakened. In trauma memories, new information may be added to the memory so that the original memory is changed. New information may take the form, inter alia, of a worsening of the expected outcome, changes in the context to which the memory applies, new safety information about the memory, or structural changes to the content of the memory. The changes must also be relevant to the original memory context. That is, they should in some manner evoke the original context so that some part of it and not the whole is changed.

Early attempts at behavioral initiation of memory reconsolidation often used an extinction protocol within the window of labilization. This technique often failed to produce the expected reconsolidative effects (Kindt, Soeter, & Vervliet 2009; Kredlow et al., 2016). In RTM, however, the reminder stimulus takes the form of a limited exposure to the trauma memory. Lee, Nader, and Schiller (2017) have presented research regarding this approach in which it was considered that an intervention for PTSD might require a stimulus of broader applicability than a simple Conditioned Stimulus (CS) – Conditioned Response (CR) response system. The successful use of modified Unconditioned Stimulus (UCS) presentations to evoke the reconsolidation mechanism has been used as follows (as cited by Lee et al., 2017): Liu and colleagues treated conditioned fear in rats using a shock of lesser intensity than the original UCS to trigger labilization (Liu et al., 2014); Luo and colleagues (Luo et al., 2015) illustrated the same capacity of a priming (limited) dose of cocaine to block reconsolidation in addicted rats thereby reducing cocaine seeking; and Xue et al. (Xue et al., 2017), in a smoking reduction study using limited exposure to nicotine to evoke cravings in their test of a reconsolidation disruption model using propranolol. In all cases, the limited presentation of the UCS successfully evoked labilization.

Identification of RTM with reconsolidation

RTM has identified reconsolidation as the hypothesized neurological context that confers its observed levels of efficacy. The identity is based upon the following observations as originally noted in Tylee, Gray, Glatt, and Bourke (2017) and as detailed below.

1. The syntax of RTM (Gray & Bourke, 2015; Gray & Liotta, 2012) matches the syntax of reconsolidation (Agren, 2014; Forcato et al., 2007; Kindt, Soeter & Vervliet, 2009; Lee, 2009; Schiller & Phelps, 2011; Schiller et al., 2013); 2. RTM uses an abbreviated reminder stimulus that is too short and lacking in intensity to support extinction (Almeida-Correa & Amaral, 2014; Gray & Liotta, 2012; Lee, 2009; Merlo et al., 2014; Nader, 2003; Perez-Cuesta & Maldonado, 2009; Suzuki et al., 2004); 3. The duration of the exposure is incompatible with the creation of extinction memories (Gray & Liotta, 2012; Kredlow et al., 2016; Nader, 2003); 4. The initiation of labilization requires a novel presentation of the fear stimulus rather than a repeated or extended exposure (Almeida-Correa & Amaral, 2014; Fernández et al., 2016; Kindt & van Emmerik, 2016; Kindt, Soeter, & Vervliet, 2009; Lee, 2009; Pedreira et al., 2004). That novelty may include non-reinforcement (Agren, 2014; Perez-Cuesta & Maldonado, 2009; Schwabe et al., 2014), changes in duration of re-exposure (Almeida-Correa & Amaral, 2014), the presentation of safety information (Clem & Schiller,

2016), retelling the trauma narrative in a clinical setting (Agren, 2014), or the presentation of the UCS in a modified form or with decreased intensity (Lee et al., 2017). RTM introduces multiple levels of novelty (Gray & Liotta, 2012); 5. The results of the intervention tend to be long lasting or permanent (Agren, 2014; Björkstrand et al., 2015; Clem & Schiller, 2016; Kindt & van Emmerik, 2016; Fernández et al., 2016; Gray & Bourke, 2015; Schiller et al., 2013; Schiller et al., 2010; Tylee et al., 2017), and at this point, are not known to be characterized by clinical relapse as reflected in extinction memories (spontaneous recovery, contextual renewal, reinstatement, and rapid reacquisition (Björkstrand et al., 2015; Bouton, 2004; Kindt, Soeter, & Vervliet 2009; Kredlow et al., 2016).

The syntax of RTM and reconsolidation

Donald Lewis, as reported by Schiller and Phelps (2011), was the first to identify the syntax of reconsolidation. Although later researchers (Agren, 2014; Forcato et al., 2007; Kindt et al. 2009; Lee, 2009; Schiller & Phelps, 2011; Schiller et al., 2013) have expanded upon the paradigm, the basic steps are these:

1. Reactivate a consolidated memory by means of a reminder cue;
2. Administer the treatment aimed at altering reconsolidation post reactivation;
3. Test for retention after the effects of the treatment have dissipated and the window of reconsolidation has closed—typically, at least 24 hours after treatment (Schiller & Phelps, 2011, p. 1).

RTM operationalizes these steps as follows.

1. It begins by asking the client to tell the story of their trauma. It is expected that accessing the index trauma imaginally or via narrative exposure, begins to elicit the traumatic response. As soon as autonomic reactivity is observed, the retelling is stopped. and the client is reoriented to the present before the narrative becomes overwhelming.
2. After the client has been reoriented to the present context, RTM leads patients through a series of cognitive operations designed to change the perceived immediacy, reality, and emergent nature of the trauma memory. This is the treatment.
3. In follow-up sessions, the client is asked to recount the narrative with SUDs evaluations following each retelling. This is the testing.

The abbreviated reminder

RTM depends upon the insight that observable sympathetic responsivity is sufficient evidence of the trauma memory's reactivation to make the memory accessible to change. We believe that the narrative, and its component elements, is the trigger for the expected emotional responses that generally follow. This also requires that the client relate a specific instance of the trauma.

We note that LeDoux identified at least two paths for the registration of fear memories. One path was observed to operate quickly and imprecisely. Briefly, this path receives sensory signals that pass from the sense organ to the sensory nuclei in the thalamus and from there directly to the baso-lateral amygdala (BLA) (LeDoux, 2000; Silverstein & Ingvar, 2015). A second, slower path includes the sensory cortices, the hypothalamus and from there takes various paths to the amygdala (LeDoux, 2000; Silverstein & Ingvar, 2015). Silverstein and Ingvar (2015) have identified at least five paths for visual fear traces alone.

There is a broad consensus indicating that fear memories (or the convergence zones by which they are represented; Damasio, 1989) are located in the Baso-Lateral Amygdala (BLA; Clem & Huganir, 2010; Erlich, Bush, & Ledoux 2012; LeDoux, 2000; Nicholson et al., 2016; Schiller et al., 2013). The amygdala has direct projections from the central nucleus to the hypothalamus (Balleine & Killcross, 2006; Hermans, Battaglia, Atsak, de Voogd, Fernandez, & Roozendaal, 2014; Clem & Huganir, 2010; Erlich et al., 2012; Liberzon & Abelson, 2016; Schiller et al., 2013), and can immediately activate the HPA axis via LeDoux's quick and imprecise, reactive pathway (LeDoux, 2000; Hermans et al., 2014; Silverstein & Ingvar, 2015), resulting in a flood of fast-acting neuro-peptides and hormones that prepare the body for fight or flight. It also innervates areas of the brainstem that regulate other fear-related responses (Hermans et al., 2014; LeDoux, 2000; Liberzon & Abelson, 2016).

With regard to the faster thalamo-amygdalo-hypothalamic pathway, there is an immediate and observable set of physiological changes in the client that signal arousal. These may include freezing, shaking, changes in breath rate, heart rate, facial tonus, posture, verbal fluency, etc. (Gray & Bourke, 2015; Gray & Liotta, 2012; Gray et al., 2017; Gray et al., 2020; Tylee et al., 2017). At this point, when enhanced autonomic responses are observed, the patient's narrative is terminated, and they are reoriented to the present context. This is done using an assortment of techniques known collectively as break-state interventions. They include having the client stand, having them change their focus to a different sensory system, returning the topic of discussion to an earlier topic, or an innocuous topic like what they had for breakfast (Gray & Bourke, 2015; Gray & Liotta, 2012; Tylee et al., 2017). This calming is essential to the process (Baldi & Bucharelli, 2015; Gray & Bourke, 2015; Gray & Liotta, 2012; Tylee et al., 2017). There is also evidence that changing the focus of attention moderates amygdalar response (LeDoux & Phelps, 2008; Menon, 2015; Morawetz, Baudewig, Treue, & Dechent, 2010; Nguyen, Breakspear, Hu, & Guo 2016; Nicholson et al., 2016; Xue et al., 2017).

The duration of the exposure is incompatible with extinction

A growing body of evidence points to the temporal dynamics that separate reconsolidation from extinction. In general, brief exposures to the target stimulus invoke reconsolidation. Longer or repeated presentations invoke extinction, while yet longer presentation result in retraumatization (Almeida-Correa & Amaral, 2014; Gray & Liotta, 2012; Kredlow et al. 2016; Lee, 2009; Merlo et al., 2015; Merlo et al., 2014; Nader, 2003; Perez-Cuesta & Maldonado, 2009; Suzuki et al., 2004). Unfortunately, the exact size of the temporal difference separating extinction and reconsolidation effects has not been quantified.

The initiation of labilization requires a novel presentation of the fear stimulus

Memories may be thought of as past lessons which we use to predict the future (Buckner, 2010; Mullally & Maguire, 2014). We also use memories and parts of memories to create new, adaptive responses and fantasies that we may never encounter. We can use the context of a past memory to construct new activities in a familiar scenario, as well as completely new kinds of actions in places unknown to us (Mullally & Maguire, 2014; Nadel & Jacobs, 1998). PTSD is a disorder of memory that predicts and prepares for feared events in contexts where those responses are no longer and may have never been useful.

Novelty and prediction error are essential for the labilization of a target memory. If a trauma memory in PTSD may be thought of as a prediction or a set of predictions, then violation of those predictions should initiate labilization of the fear memory as represented in the BLA (Almeida-Correa & Amaral, 2014; Fernández et al., 2016; Kindt & van Emmerik, 2016; Kindt, Soeter, & Vervliet 2009; Lee, 2009; Pedreira et al., 2004). In general, the presence of a prediction error suggests that there is something to be learned (Krawczyk, Fernandez, Pedreira, & Boccia, 2017; Sevenster et al., 2012). RTM presents multiple opportunities for the violation of such predictions. The first such expectations and their violation, have to do with the trauma narrative.

As noted, when the fear memory is activated, there is an almost immediate activation of the HPA-Axis. The resulting set of physiological changes primes the Insular Cortex to begin registration of fear and to focus attention on the fear memory. Here, the early awakening of the sympathetic nervous system represents the first prediction to be generated by the fear memory: these feelings portend an uncontrollable (Foa & Kozak, 1986) flashback or visitation of the traumatic memory and the expectation of several minutes, hours, or days of incapacitating fear, depression, uncontrollable anger, and other PTS related emotions.

In RTM, the clinician is trained to stop the trauma narrative and to return the client's attention to the present as soon as they observe signs of increased arousal. This violates the first prediction generated by increasing autonomic arousal and the intensity of the trauma memory. By dampening the arousal and returning the client's attention to the present circumstance, two or more predictions generated by the memory are violated.

These are:

1. An uncontrollable emotional episode is about to begin;
2. Most therapists and friends will just make it worse by encouraging or forcing me to continue.

When the therapist interrupts these expectations, a PE is generated, and the trauma memory is (presumably) labilized; it becomes subject to change.

Within the therapeutic procedures (see below), novelty is reinforced by a succession of novel manipulations of the memory that include perceptual modifications of the remembered event (time, distance, color, aspect, clarity, focus, detail, sound quality, sound intensity, reversal, rescripting, etc.). Each provides a new opportunity for dissociation from the trauma memory and other opportunities for labilization of the memory if previous transformations of the experience have not successfully labilized the target trace. In every case, at the onset of observed sympathetic arousal or the client's declaration that they are uncomfortable, the intervention is stopped, the client is reoriented to the present, and the intervention is adjusted to ensure the client's comfort.

The results of the intervention tend to be long lasting

As related to the RTM Protocol, reconsolidation is the neural context in which therapeutic treatments are made. If those treatments are relevant to the target memory then, after the close of the labilization window – after a period of one to six hours (Nader, 2003; Nader et al., 2000; Monfils et al., 2009) – those changes may become permanent parts of the original memory.

The labilization window is the period during which the memory is malleable. Content-relevant information, including information that is evoked by the original (or similar) stimuli, changes in safety information, changes in temporal relations between the CS (or in this case, the narrative, a modified UCS) and the expected reinforcement, the context of evocation, and perceptual modifications of the recalled trauma may all provide relevant information for inclusion in the modified trace.

Consistent evidence indicates that changes to fear memories made in the context of reconsolidation tend to persist over time as compared to extinction memories. Reconsolidation is not subject to the hallmark relapse mechanisms associated with extinction. These include spontaneous recovery, contextual renewal, reinstatement, and rapid reacquisition (Bouton, 2004; Bouton & Moody, 2004; Dillon & Pizzagalli, 2007; Hartley & Phelps, 2009; Massad & Hulsey, 2006; Quirk & Mueller, 2007; Rescorla, 1988; Vervliet, 2008).

There is a small but growing body of evidence that changes made in humans in the context of reconsolidation can persist for a year or more (Björkstrand et al., 2015; Gray, et al., 2019; Gray et al., 2020; Schiller et al., 2010; Tylee et al., 2017). Björkstrand et al. (2015), followed participants 18 months after a fear conditioning experiment performed by the Agren group (2012) in which an electric shock was paired with a previously innocuous stimulus. Half of the group had extinction training 10 minutes after a brief activation trial, while the others received the extinction training six hours after the reactivation (outside the expected labilization period). Subsequent testing included fMRI examinations and reinstatement trials. At 5 days post, the reconsolidation group showed no autonomic reactivity when the CS was presented. fMRI examinations of the BLA showed significantly reduced activity. The six-hour group showed no such change. After 18 months, Björkstrand and colleagues found that those results had persisted. The reconsolidation group showed no amygdalar activity in response to the CS and no autonomic reactivity.

Schiller et al. (2010), in an earlier study, reported a fear conditioning paradigm in which an aversive stimulus (UCS; rubber band snap) was associated with a visual stimulus (CS), so that the visual stimulus evoked a mild fear response. Experimental subjects who received a non-reinforced trial before the end of the labilization period, apparently unlearned the association whereas controls maintained the fear response. Experimental results were maintained for at least one year after treatment. There have been some difficulties replicating the Schiller results (Meir Drexler & Wolf, 2018; Goode et al., 2017; Kredlow, Unger, & Otto 2016).

Both Tylee et al. (2017) and Gray et al. (2020), report one-year follow-ups in trials of the RTM protocol with results holding at one-year post. Tylee, Gray, Glatt, and Bourke (2017) reported that 30 male veterans were randomly assigned to treatment and waiting list control groups. The groups were compared at three weeks post for the experimental group and at an equivalent time for the controls. The controls were unchanged, while the treatment group showed significant losses in symptom scores and more than 60% loss of diagnosis. Post treatment follow-ups at six months and one year indicated that those results were maintained over time. Gray et al. (2020) report similar findings with a waitlist RCT of 30 female victims of mixed trauma including 73% identifying MST as their central issue. Of those contacted one-year post (55% of treatment completers), treatment gains remained unchanged from the two-week measures.

The fear schema and RTM

It has long been understood that fear memories may have multiple elements (Hogberg & Hallstrom, 2018) and from time to time these parts must be dealt with individually. Foa's bio-informational theory (Foa, Keane, &

Friedman 2000; Foa & Kozak, 1986; Foa & Meadows, 1997) points to just such a schema- organization.

Although RTM relies upon the initial interruption of the target memory to open the labilization window, novelty and the disruption of autonomic responses are distributed throughout the intervention (See Table 3.1).

RTM, as an NLP-based intervention may be understood in terms of the structural elements of percepts as described below, in Chapter 11. Memory schemas are multisensory internal images. The sensory data for those internal images appear in idiosyncratic orderings for any event, independent of whether the source is external (the taste of a madeleine dipped in tea) or internal (the memory of that madeleine; Bandler & Grinder, 1975; Dilts et al., 1980; Dilts & DeLozier, 2000; Grinder & Bandler, 1976). The proposition that internal multisensory representations of target stimuli are inseparable from consciousness is commonplace and non-controversial (Clark, 1999; Ottaviani & Beck, 1987; Redies et al., 2020; Wells & Hackmann, 1993).

NLP describes what it terms the submodality structure of internal percepts and natural stimuli. Besides being composed of the more basic data of the individual senses (e.g., seeing, hearing, and feeling; VAK), natural stimuli also have position, size, intensity, complexity, movement, and other dimensions that define their more subtle qualities. Although these distinctions are most directly derived from the discipline of NLP (Andreas & Andreas, 1989; Bandler, 1985; Bandler & MacDonald, 1987), these elements have all been described as individual stimulus qualities in cognitive/perceptual psychology (Gray, Wake, Andreas, & Bolstad, 2013; NLPWIKI, 2014).

The elements of submodality structure are specifically targeted in RTM as the means for restructuring the target memory. These include, as reflected in the indicated submodalities, foreground-background (all modalities), intensity (brightness, volume, pressure), complexity (hue, timbre, texture), contrast (granularity, frequency contrast, textural disparity); frequency (color, pitch, felt distinctions of type: emotions, temperature, hedonic impact), and source movement. These distinctions represent the output of neural filters that encode the importance or salience of individual percepts within a scene (Itti et al., 1998; Kalinli & Narayanan, 2007; Kaya & Elhilali, 2012; White, Berg, Kan, Marino, Itti, & Munoz 2017; Veale, Hafed, & Yoshida 2017). Recent research suggests that multi-modal sensory maps are organized (for mammals) retinotopically in the superior colliculus (Knudsen, 2018; Perrault et al., 2011; White, Berg, Kan, Marino, Itti, & Munoz 2017; Veale, Hafed, & Yoshida 2017). The importance of various stimuli is mediated in a bottom-up manner by external stimulus qualities (typically for unexpected stimuli) and in a top-down manner determined by expectations and subjective motivational states (hunger, thirst, sexual deprivation, present-time outcomes, and personal preferences). Other submodality features including the position in three-dimensional space have correlates in a three-dimensional perceptual schema for understanding perception and consciousness more generally (Derks, 2018; Edelman, 2003,

2004; Jerath, Beveridge, & Jensen, 2019; Jerath, Crawford & Barnes, 2015; Park et al., 2020). These schemas are the personal maps that define individual perception and response systems. It is these structural elements that RTM targets in order to transform emergent, PTSD-related trauma memories, into normal, untroubling, past memories.

Summary and conclusions

We have here reviewed the RTM Protocol. In four published, two as yet unpublished, and two ongoing research projects, RTM is becoming established as an effective intervention for PTSD in both military and civilian populations in a gender-neutral manner. The intervention has been noted as a promising intervention by The International Society for Traumatic Stress Studies ISTSS (2019) and has shown itself superior to more than 30 other interventions for combat PTSD in a Cochrane Systematic Review (2019). It has now shown great promise in the treatment of civilian populations (Gray et al., 2021). We have also spent some time reviewing the evidence connecting RTM with the process of reconsolidation. While this association still requires empirical evaluation, we believe that the above arguments support our hypothesized association.

References

Adams, S., & Allan, S. (2018). Muss' Rewind treatment for trauma: Description and multi-site pilot study. *Journal for Mental Health*, 27(5), 468–474. doi:10.1080/09638237.2018.1487539

Agren, T. (2014). Human reconsolidation: A reactivation and update. *Brain Research Bulletin*, 105, 70–82. doi:10.1016/j.brainresbull.2013.12.010

Agustina López, M., Jimena Santos, M., Cortasa, S., Fernández, R. S., Carbó Tano, M., & Pedreira, M. E. (2016). Different dimensions of the prediction error as a decisive factor for the triggering of the reconsolidation process. *Neurobiology of Learning and Memory*, 136, 210–219. doi:10.1016/j.nlm.2016.10.016

Almeida-Correa, S., & Amaral, O. B. (2014). Memory labilization in reconsolidation and extinction--evidence for a common plasticity system? *Journal of Physiology, Paris*. 2014 Sep-Dec, 108(4–6):292–306M. PubMed PMID: 25173958. Epub 2014/09/01. eng.

American Psychiatric Association. (2000). *Diagnostic and statistical manual of mental disorders* (4th ed., Text Revision). Washington, DC: Author.

American Psychiatric Association. (2013). *Diagnostic and statistical manual of mental disorders* (5th ed.).

Andreas, C., & Andreas, S. (1989). *Heart of the mind*. Boulder, CO: Real People Press.

Baldi, E., & Bucharelli, C. (2015). Brain sites involved in fear memory reconsolidation and extinction of rodents. *Neuroscience & Biobehavioral Reviews*, 53, 160–190. doi:10.1016/j.neubiorev.2015.04.003

Balleine, B. W., & Killcross, S. (2006). Parallel incentive processing: An integrated view of amygdala function. *Trends in Neuroscience*, 29(5), 272–279. doi:10.1016/j.tins.2006.03.002

Bandler, R. (1985). *Using your brain for a change*. Moab, UT: Real People Press.

Bandler, R., & Grinder, J. (1975). *The structure of magic*. Palo Alto, CA: Science and BehaviorBooks.

Bandler, R., & MacDonald, W. (1987). *An insider's guide to submodalities*. Moab, UT: Real People Press.

Bisson, J. I., Roberts, N. P., Andrew, M., Cooper, R., & Lewis, C. (2013). Psychological therapies for chronic post-traumatic stress disorder (PTSD) in adults. *Cochrane Database of Systematic Reviews*, 2013(12). doi:10.1002/14651858.CD003388.pub4

Björkstrand, J., Agren, T., Frick, A., Engman, J., Larsson, E.-M., Furmark, T., & Fredrikson, M. (2015). Disruption of memory reconsolidation erases a fear memory trace in the human amygdala: An 18-month follow-up. *PLoS ONE*, 10(7), e0129393. doi:10.1371/journal.pone.0129393

Bonin, R. P., & De Koninck, Y. (2015). Reconsolidation and the regulation of plasticity: Moving beyond memory. *Trends in Neuroscience*, 38(6), 336–344. doi:10.1016/j.tins.2015.04.007

Bouton, M. E. (2004). Context and behavioral processes in extinction. *Learning & Memory*, 11(5), 485–494. doi:10.1101/lm.78804

Bouton, M. E., & Moody, E. W. (2004). Memory processes in classical conditioning. *Neuroscience and Biobehavioral Reviews*, 28(7), 663–674. doi:10.1016/j.neubiorev.2004.09.001

Buckner, R. L. (2010). The role of the hippocampus in prediction and imagination. *Annual Review of PsychologyMullally*, 61(27-48), C21–C28. doi:10.1146/annurev.psych.60.110707.163508

Clark, D. M. (1999). Anxiety disorders: Why they persist and how to treat them. *Behaviour Research and Therapy*, 37(Suppl 1), S5–S27. doi:10.1016/s0005-7967(99)00048-0

Clem, R., & Huganir, R. (2010). Calcium-permeable AMPA receptor dynamics mediate fear memory erasure. *Science (New York, N.Y.)*, 330(6007), 1108–1112. doi:10.1126/science.1195298

Clem, R., & Schiller, D. (2016). New learning and unlearning: Strangers or accomplices in threat memory attenuation? *Trends in Neuroscience*, 39(5), 340–351. doi:10.1016/j.tins.2016.03.003

Damasio, A. R. (1989). The brain binds entities and events by multiregional activation from convergence zones. *Neural Computation*, 1, 123–132.

Daw, N. D., Gershman, S. J., Seymour, B., Dayan, P., & Dolan, R. J. (2011). Model-based influences on humans' choices and striatal prediction errors. *Neuron*, 69(6), 1204–1215. doi:10.1016/j.neuron.2011.02.027

Derks, L. A. C. (2018). *Mental space psychology: Psychotherapeutic evidence for a new paradigm*. Netherlands: Coppelear b.v. Nijmegen.

Dillon, D. G., & Pizzagalli, D. A. (2007). Inhibition of action, thought, and emotion: A selective neurobiological review. *Applied & Preventive Psychology: Journal of the American Association of Applied and Preventive Psychology*, 12(3), 99–114. doi:10.1016/j.appsy.2007.09.004

Dilts, R., Grinder, J., Bandler, R., & DeLozier, J. (1980). *Neuro-linguistic programming: Volume I. The structure of subjective experience*. Cupertino, CA: Meta Publications.

Dilts, R. , & DeLozier, J. (2000). *NLP Encyclopaedia*. NLP University Press.

Dunbar, A. B., & Taylor, J. R. (2017). Reconsolidation and psychopathology: Moving towards reconsolidation-based treatments. *Neurobiology of Learning & Memory*, 142(Pt A), 162–171. doi:10.1016/j.nlm.2016.11.005

Edelman, G. M. (2003). Naturalizing consciousness: A theoretical framework. *Proceedings of the National Academy of Sciences of the United States of America*, 100(9), 5520–5524. doi:10.1073/pnas.0931349100

Edelman, G. M. (2004). *Wider than the sky. The phenomenal gift of consciousness*. New Haven, CT: Yale University Press.

Erlich, J. C., Bush, D. E., & Ledoux, J. E. (2012). The role of the lateral amygdala in the retrieval and maintenance of fear-memories formed by repeated probabilistic reinforcement. *Frontiers in behavioral neuroscience*, 6, 16. doi:10.3389/fnbeh.2012.00016

Fernández, R., Bavassi, L., Forcato, C., Pedreira, M. (2016). The dynamic nature of the reconsolidation process and its boundary conditions: Evidence based on human tests. *Neurobiology of Learning and Memory*, 130, 202–212. doi:10.1016/j.nlm.2016.03.001

Foa, E., Keane, T., & Friedman, M. (2000). *Effective treatments for PTSD*. New York, NY: Guilford.

Foa, E., & Kozak, M. (1986). Emotional processing of fear: Exposure to corrective information. *Psychological Bulletin*, 99(1), 20–35.

Foa, E., & Meadows, E. (1997). Psychosocial treatments for posttraumatic stress disorder: A critical review. *Annual Review of Psychology*, 48(1), 449–480. doi:10.1146/annurev.psych.48.1.449

Foa, E., Riggs, D., Dancu, C., & Rothbaum, B. (1993). Reliability and validity of a brief instrument for assessing post-traumatic stress disorder. *Journal of Traumatic Stress*, 6(4), 459–473. doi:10.1007/BF00974317

Forcato, C., Burgos, V. L., Argibay, P. F., Molina, V. A., Pedreira, M. E., & Maldonado, H. (2007). Reconsolidation of declarative memory in humans. *Learning & Memory*, 14(4), 295–303. doi:10.1101/lm.486107

Goetter, E. M., Bui, E., Ojserkis. R. A., et al. (2015). A systematic review of dropout from psychotherapy for posttraumatic stress disorder among Iraq and Afghanistan combat veterans. *Journal of Traumatic Stress*, 28(5), 401–409. doi:10.1002/jts.22038

Goode, T. D., Holloway-Erickson, C. M., & Maren, S. (2017). Extinction after fear memory reactivation fails to eliminate renewal in rats. *Neurobiology of Learning and Memory*, 142(Pt A), 41–47. doi:10.1016/j.nlm.2017.03.001

Gray, R., & Bourke, F. (2015) Remediation of intrusive symptoms of PTSD in fewer than five sessions: a 30-person pre-pilot study of the RTM protocol. *Journal of Military, Veteran and Family Health*, 1(2), 13–20.

Gray, R. M., Budden-Potts, D., & Bourke, F. (2017). The Reconsolidation of Traumatic Memories (RTM) Protocol for PTSD: A case study. *Journal of Experiential Psychotherapy*, 20, 47–61.

Gray, R., Budden-Potts, D., & Bourke, F. (2019). Reconsolidation of Traumatic Memories for PTSD: A randomized controlled trial of 74 male veterans. *Journal of the Society for Psychotherapy Research*, 29(5), 621–639.

Gray, R. M., Budden-Potts, D., Schwall, R. J., & Bourke, F. (2020). *An open-label, randomized controlled trial of the reconsolidation of traumatic memories (RTM) in military women*. Psychological Trauma: Theory, Research, Practice and Policy.

Gray, R., Davis, A., & Bourke, F. (2021). Reconsolidation of Traumatic Memories, The RTM Protocol: Albuquerque trainee results. Submitted manuscript.

Gray, R., & Liotta, R. (2012). PTSD: Extinction, reconsolidation, and the visual-kinesthetic dissociation protocol. *Traumatology*, 18(2), 3–16. doi:10.1177/1534765611431835.

Gray, R., Wake, L., Andreas, S., & Bolstad R. (2013). Indirect research into the applications of NLP. In Lisa Wake, Richard Gray, & Frank Bourke (Eds.), *The clinical efficacy of NLP: A critical appraisal* (pp. 153–193). London: Routledge.

Grinder, J., & Bandler, R. (1976). *The Structure of Magic II*. Cupertino, California: Science and Behavior Books.

Hartley, C. A., & Phelps, E. A. (2009). Changing Fear: The Neurocircuitry of Emotion Regulation. *Neuropsychopharmacology*, 35(1), 136–146. Retrieved from 10.1038/npp.2009.121

Hermans, E. J., Battaglia, F. P., Atsak, P., de Voogd, L. D., Fernandez, G., & Roozendaal, B. (2014). How the amygdala affects emotional memory by altering brain network properties. *Neurobiology of Learning and Memory*, 112, 2–16. doi:10.1016/j.nlm.2014.02.005

Hogberg, G., & Hallstrom, T. (2018). Mood regulation focused CBT based on memory reconsolidation, reduced suicidal ideation and depression in youth in a randomised controlled study. *International Journal of Environmental Research and Public Health*, 15(5). doi:10.3390/ijerph15050921

Hoge, C. W., Yehuda, R., Castro, C. A., McFarlane, A. C., Vermetten, E., Jetly, R., & Rothbaum, B. O. (2016). Unintended consequences of changing the definition of posttraumatic stress disorder in DSM-5: Critique and call for action. *JAMA Psychiatry*, 73(7), 750–752. doi:10.1001/jamapsychiatry.2016.0647

Itti, L., Koch, C., & Niebur, E. (1998). A model of saliency-based visual attention for rapid scene analysis. *IEEE Transactions on Pattern Analysis and Machine Intelligence*, 20(11), 1254–1259. doi:10.1109/34.730558.

The International Society for Traumatic Stress Studies ISTSS. (2019). *PTSD Prevention and Treatment Guidelines–Methodology and Recommendations. Author*. Retrieved from http://www.istss.org/getattachment/Treating-Trauma/New-ISTSS-Prevention-and-Treatment-Guidelines/ISTSS_PreventionTreatmentGuidelines_FNL.pdf.aspx

Jerath, R., Beveridge, C., & Jensen, M. (2019). On the hierarchical organization of oscillatory assemblies: Layered superimposition and a global bioelectric framework. *Frontiers in Human Neuroscience*, 13, 426. doi:10.3389/fnhum.2019.00426

Jerath, R., Crawford, M. W., & Barnes, V. A. (2015). A unified 3D default space consciousness model combining neurological and physiological processes that underlie conscious experience. *Frontiers in Psychology*, Aug 27, 6, 1204. doi:10.3389/fpsyg.2015.01204. eCollection 2015.

Johnson, D. C., & Casey, B. J. (2015). Extinction during memory reconsolidation blocks recovery of fear in adolescents. *Scientific Reports*, 5, 8863. doi:10.1038/srep08863

Kalinli, O., & Narayanan, S. S. (2007). *A saliency-based auditory attention model with applications to unsupervised prominent syllable detection in speech*. Paper presented at the INTERSPEECH.

Kaplan, F., & Oudeyer, P. Y. (2007). In search of the neural circuits of intrinsic motivation. *Frontiers in Neuroscience*, 1(1), 225–236. doi:10.3389/neuro.01.1.1.017.2007

Kaya, E. M., & Elhilali, M. (2012). *A temporal saliency map for modeling auditory attention*, 2012 46th Annual Conference on Information Sciences and Systems (CISS), Princeton, NJ: 2012, pp. 1–6. doi:10.1109/CISS.2012.6310945.

Kindt, M., & van Emmerik, A. (2016). New avenues for treating emotional memory disorders: Towards a reconsolidation intervention for posttraumatic stress disorder. *Therapeutic Advances in Psychopharmacology*, May 1, 2016. doi:10.1177/2045125316644541

Kindt, M., Soeter, M., & Vervliet, B. (2009). Beyond extinction: Erasing human fear responses and preventing the return of fear. *Nature Neuroscience*, 12(3), 256–258. doi:10.1038/nn.2271

Kitchiner, N. J., Lewis, C., Roberts, N. P., & Bisson, J. I. (2019). Active duty and ex-serving military personnel with post-traumatic stress disorder treated with psychological therapies: Systematic review and meta-analysis. *European Journal of Psychotraumatology*, 10(1). doi:10.1080/20008198.2019.1684226

Knudsen, E. I. (2018). Neural circuits that mediate selective attention: A comparative perspective. *Trends in Neuroscience*, 41(11), 789–805. doi:10.1016/j.tins.2018.06.006

Krawczyk, M. C., Fernandez, R. S., Pedreira, M. E., & Boccia, M. M. (2017). Toward a better understanding on the role of prediction error on memory processes: From bench to clinic. *Neurobiology Learning & Memory*, 142(Pt A), 13–20. doi:10.1016/j.nlm.2016.12.011

Kredlow, M., Unger, L., & Otto, M. (2016). Harnessing reconsolidation to weaken fear and appetitive memories: A meta-analysis of post-retrieval extinction effects. *Psychological Bulletin*, 142(3), 314–336. doi:10.1037/bul0000034

Kroes, M. C., & Fernández, G. (2012). Dynamic neural systems enable adaptive, flexible memories. *Neuroscience and Biobehavioral Reviews*, 36(7), 1646–1666. doi:10.1016/j.neubiorev.2012.02.014

LeDoux, J. E. (2000). Emotion circuits in the brain. *Annual Review of Neuroscience*, 23, 155–184. doi:10.1146/annurev.neuro.23.1.155

LeDoux, J. E., & Phelps, E. A. (2008). Emotional networks in the brain. In *Handbook of emotions*, 3rd ed. New York, NY, US: The Guilford Press. 159–179.

Lee, J. L. (2009). Reconsolidation: Maintaining memory relevance. *Trends in Neuroscience*, 32(8), 413–420. doi:10.1016/j.tins.2009.05.002

Lee, J. L., Nader, K., & Schiller, D. (2017). An update on memory reconsolidation updating. *Trends in Cognitive Science*, 21(7), 531–545. doi:10.1016/j.tics.2017.04.006

Lewine, J., Gray, R., Paulson, K., Budden-Potts, D., Murray, W., Goodreau, N. Davis, J. T., Bangera, N., & Bourke, F. (2017). A *Pilot Study of Quantitative EEG Markers of Post-Traumatic Stress Disorder*. Submitted manuscript.

Lewis, D. J., Miller, R. R., & Misanin, J. R. (1968). Control of retrograde amnesia. *Journal of Comparative and Physiological Psychology*, 66(1), 48–52. doi:10.1037/h0025963

Liberzon, I., & Abelson, J. L. (2016). Context processing and the neurobiology of post- traumatic stress disorder. *Neuron*, 92(1), 14–30. doi:10.1016/j.neuron.2016.09.039

Liu, J., Zhao, L., Xue, Y., Shi, J., Suo, L., Luo, Y., Chai, B., Yang, C., Fang, Q., Zhang, Y., Bao, Y., Pickens, C. L., & Lu, L. (2014). An unconditioned stimulus retrieval extinction procedure to prevent the return of fear memory. *Biological Psychiatry*, 76(11), 895–901. doi:10.1016/j.biopsych.2014.03.027

Luo, Y. X., Xue, Y. X., Liu, J. F., Shi, H. S., Jian, M., Han, Y., Zhu, W. L., Bao, Y. P., Wu, P., Ding, Z. B., Shen, H. W., Shi, J., Shaham, Y., & Lu, L. (2015). A novel UCS memory retrieval-extinction procedure to inhibit relapse to drug seeking. *Nature Communications*, 6, 7675. doi:10.1038/ncomms8675

Massad, P. M., & Hulsey, T. L. (2006). Exposure therapy renewed. *Journal of Psychotherapy Integration*, *16*(4), 417–428. Retrieved from http://www.sciencedirect.com/science/article/B7588-4MY0M37-3/2/3ecad6f5228e5f3b83b0f2ae8ecab3d0

Meir Drexler, S., & Wolf, O. T. (2018). Behavioral disruption of memory reconsolidation: From bench to bedside and back again. *Behavioral Neuroscience*, 132(1), 13–22. doi:10.1037/bne0000231

Menon, V. (2015). Salience Network. In Arthur W. Toga (Ed.), *Brain mapping: An encyclopedic reference* (Vol. 2, pp. 597–611). Waltham, MA: Academic Press.

Merlo, E., Milton, A., Goozée, Z., et al. (2014). Reconsolidation and extinction are dissociable and mutually exclusive processes: Behavioral and molecular evidence. *Journal of Neuroscience* 2014, 34(7), 2422–2431. doi:10.1523/jneurosci.4001-13.2014

Merlo, E., Milton, A., & Everitt, B. (2015). Enhancing cognition by affecting memory reconsolidation. *Current Opinion in Behavioral Sciences*, 4, 41–47. doi:10.1016/j.cobeha.2015.02.003

Misanin, J., Miller, R., & Lewis, D. (1968). Retrograde amnesia produced by electroconvulsive shock after reactivation of a consolidated memory trace. *Science (New York, N.Y.)*, 160(3827), 554–555. doi:10.1126/science.160.3827.554

Monfils, M. H., Cowansage, K. K., Klann, E., & LeDoux, J. E. (2009). Extinction-reconsolidation boundaries: Key to persistent attenuation of fear memories. *Science*, 324(5929), 951–955. doi:10.1126/science.1167975

Monson, C., Gradus, J., Young-Xu, Y. (2008). Change in posttraumatic stress disorder symptoms: Do clinicians and patients agree? *Psychological Assessment*, 20(2), 131–138.

Morawetz, C., Baudewig, J., Treue, S., & Dechent, P. (2010). Diverting attention suppresses human amygdala responses to faces. *Frontiers in Human Neuroscience*, 4, 226. doi:10.3389/fnhum.2010.00226

Mullally, S. L., & Maguire, E. A. (2014). Memory, imagination, and predicting the future: A common brain mechanism? *Neuroscientist*, 20(3), 220–234. doi:10.1177/1073858413495091

Muss, D. (1991). A new technique for treating post-traumatic stress disorder. *British Journal of Clinical Psychology*, 30(1), 91–92.

Muss, D. C. (2002). The rewind technique in the treatment of post-traumatic stress

disorder: Methods and applications. In C. R. Figley (Ed.), *Brief treatments for the traumatized: A project of the Green Cross Foundation* (pp. 306–314). Westport, CT US: Greenwood Press/Greenwood Publishing Group.
Nadel, L., & Jacobs, W. J. (1998). Traumatic memory is special. *Current Directions in Psychological Science*, 7(5), 154–157. doi:10.1111/1467-8721.ep10836842
Nader, K. (2003). Memory traces unbound. *Trends in Neuroscience*, 26(2), 65–72. doi:10.1016/s0166-2236(02)00042-5
Nader, K. & Einarsson, E. Ö. (2010). Memory reconsolidation: An update. *Annals of the New York Academy of Sciences*, 1191(1), 27–41. doi:10.1111/j.1749-6632.2010.05443.x
Nader, K., Schafe, G., & Le Doux, J. (2000). Fear memories require protein synthesis in the amygdala for reconsolidation after retrieval. *Nature*, 406(6797), 722–726. doi:10.1038/35021052
Nguyen, V. T., Breakspear, M., Hu, X., & Guo, C. C. (2016). The integration of the internal and external milieu in the insula during dynamic emotional experiences. *Neuroimage*, 124(Pt A), 455–463. doi:10.1016/j.neuroimage.2015.08.078
Nicholson, A. A., Sapru, I., Densmore, M., Frewen, P. A., Neufeld, R. W., Theberge, J., & Lanius, R. A. (2016). Unique insula subregion resting-state functional connectivity with amygdala complexes in posttraumatic stress disorder and its dissociative subtype. *Psychiatry Research*, 250, 61–72. doi:10.1016/j.pscychresns.2016.02.002
NLPWIKI. (2014, December 7). NLP Journal Support (1) 12-7-14---v3000.doc. NLPWIKI.ORG. http://www.nlpwiki.org/nlp-research-information-document.pdf
Ottaviani, R., & Beck, A. T. (1987). Cognitive aspects of panic disorders. *Journal of Anxiety Disorders*, 1(1), 15–28. doi:10.1016/0887-6185(87)90019-3
Park, S. A., Miller, D. S., Nili, H., Ranganath, C., & Boorman, E. D. (2020). *Map making: Constructing, combining, and inferring on abstract cognitive maps.* bioRxiv 810051; doi:10.1101/810051
Pedreira, M. E., Perez-Cuesta, L. M., & Maldonado, H. (2004). Mismatch between what is expected and what actually occurs triggers memory reconsolidation or extinction. *Learning & Memory*, 11(5), 579–585. doi:10.1101/lm.76904
Perez-Cuesta, L., & Maldonado, H. (2009). Memory reconsolidation and extinction in the crab: mutual exclusion or coexistence? *Learning Memory*, 16(11), 714–721. doi:10.1101/lm.1544609
Perrault, T., Stein, B., & Rowland, B. (2011). Non-stationarity in multisensory neurons in the superior colliculus. *Frontiers in Psychology*, 2(144). doi:10.3389/fpsyg.2011.00144
Quirk, G. J., & Mueller, D. (2007). Neural mechanisms of extinction learning and retrieval. *Neuropsychopharmacology*, 33(1), 56–72. Retrieved from 10.1038/sj.npp.1301555
Redies C., Grebenkina, M., Mohseni, M., Kaduhm, A., & Dobel, C. (2020). Global image properties predict ratings of affective pictures. *Frontiers in Psychology*, 11, 953. doi:10.3389/fpsyg.2020.00953
Rescorla, R. A. (1988). Pavlovian conditioning. It's not what you think it is. *American Psychologist*, 43(3), 151–160. doi:10.1037//0003-066x.43.3.151
Resick, P. A., Williams, L. F., Suvak, M. K., Monson, C. M., & Gradus, J. L. (2012). Long-term outcomes of cognitive–behavioral treatments for posttraumatic stress

disorder among female rape survivors. *Journal of Consulting and Clinical Psychology*, 80(2), 201–210. doi:10.1037/a0026602.

Sandrini, M., Cohen, L. G., & Censor, N. (2015). Modulating reconsolidation: a link to causal systems-level dynamics of human memories. *Trends in Cognitive Science*, 19(8), 475–482. doi: 10.1016/j.tics.2015.06.002

Schiller, D., & Phelps, E. A. (2011). Does reconsolidation occur in humans? *Frontiers in Behavioral Neuroscience*, 5. doi:10.3389/fnbeh.2011.00024

Schiller, D., Kanen, J. W., LeDoux, J. E., Monfils, M.-H., & Phelps, E. A. (2013). Extinction during reconsolidation of threat memory diminishes prefrontal cortex involvement. *Proceedings of the National Academy of Sciences.* doi:10.1073/pnas.1320322110

Schiller, D., Monfils, M.-H., Raio, C. M., Johnson, D. C., LeDoux, J. E., & Phelps, E. A. (2010). Preventing the return of fear in humans using reconsolidation update mechanisms. *Nature*, 463(7277), 49–53. doi:http://www.nature.com/nature/journal/v463/n7277/suppinfo/nature08637_S1.html

Schnurr, P. P., Friedman, M. J., Engel, C. C., Foa, E. B., Shea, M. T., Chow, B. K.,… & Bernardy, N. (2007). Cognitive behavioral therapy for posttraumatic stress disorder in women: a randomized controlled trial. *JAMA*, 297(8), 820–830. doi:10.1001/jama.297.8.820

Schwabe, L., Nader, K., & Pruessner, J. C. (2014). Reconsolidation of human memory: brain mechanisms and clinical relevance. *Biological Psychiatry*, 76(4), 274–280. doi:10.1016/j.biopsych.2014.03.008

Sevenster, D., Beckers, T., & Kindt, M. (2012). Retrieval per se is not sufficient to trigger reconsolidation of human fear memory. *Neurobiology of Learning and Memory*, 97(3), 338–345. doi:10.1016/j.nlm.2012.01.009

Silverstein, D. N., & Ingvar, M. (2015). A multi-pathway hypothesis for human visual fear signaling. *Frontiers in Systems Neuroscience*, 9, 101. doi:10.3389/fnsys.2015.00101

Steenkamp, M. M., & Litz, B. T. (2014). One-size-fits-all approach to PTSD in the VA not supported by the evidence. *American Psychologist*, 69(7), 706–707. doi:10.1037/a0037360

Steenkamp, M. M., Litz, B. T., Hoge, C. W., & Marmar, C. R. (2015). Psychotherapy for Military-Related PTSD: A Review of Randomized Clinical Trials. *JAMA*, 314(5), 489–500. doi:10.1001/jama.2015.8370

Suzuki, A., Josselyn, S. A., Frankland, P. W., et al. (2004). Memory reconsolidation and extinction have distinct temporal and biochemical signatures. *Journal of Neuroscience*, 24(20), 4787–4795. doi:10.1523/jneurosci.5491-03.2004

Tronson, N. C., & Taylor, J. R. (2007). Molecular mechanisms of memory reconsolidation. *Nature Reviews Neuroscience*, 8(4), 262–275. Retrieved from 10.1038/nrn2090

Tylee, D. S., Gray, R., Glatt, S. J., & Bourke, F. (2017). Evaluation of the reconsolidation of traumatic memories protocol for the treatment of PTSD: A randomized wait-list-controlled trial. *Journal of Military, Veteran and Family Health*, 3(1), 21–33.

VA National Center for PTSD. (2014). *Using the PTSD Checklist for DSM-IV (PCL)* [Internet]. 2014 Jan. Washington, DC: US. Department of Veterans Affairs. http://www.ptsd.va.gov/professional/pages/assessments/assessment-pdf/

PCL-handout.pdf. Published January. 2014. Updated March 2016. Accessed July 4, 2016.

Veale, R., Hafed, Z. M., & Yoshida, M. (2017). How is visual salience computed in the brain? Insights from behaviour, neurobiology and modelling. *Philosophical Transactions of the Royal Society B: Biological Sciences*, 372(1714). doi:10.1098/rstb.2016.0113

Vervliet, B. (2008). Learning and memory in conditioned fear extinction: Effects of D- cycloserine. *Acta Psychologica(Amst)*, 127(3), 601–613. doi:10.1016/j.actpsy.2007.07.001

Wells, A., & Hackmann, A. (1993). Imagery and core beliefs in health anxiety: Contents and origins. *Behavioural and Cognitive Psychotherapy*, 21(3), 265–273. doi:10.1017/S1352465800010511

White, B. J., Berg, D. J., Kan, J. Y., Marino, R. A., Itti, L., & Munoz, D. P. (2017). Superior colliculus neurons encode a visual saliency map during free viewing of natural dynamic video. *Nature Communications*, 8, 14263. doi:10.1038/ncomms14263

Xue, Y. X., Chen, Y. Y., Zhang, L. B., Zhang, L. Q., Huang, G. D., Sun, S. C., Deng, J. H., Luo, Y. X., Bao, Y. P., Wu, P., Han, Y., Hope, B. T., Shaham, Y., Shi, J., & Lu, L. (2017). Selective inhibition of amygdala neuronal ensembles encoding nicotine-associated memories inhibits nicotine preference and relapse. *Biol Psychiatry*, 82(11), 781–793. doi:10.1016/j.biopsych.2017.04.017

4 NLP diagnostics

Dr Richard Gray

Introduction

Classical diagnostics, using the Diagnostic and Statistical Manual of the American Psychiatric Association, (DSM-5; American Psychiatric Association [APA], 2013) and the International Classification of Diseases (ICD-11; World Health Organization [WHO], 2018), are largely based upon the descriptions of patient complaints and their possible biological and neurological mechanisms. They are modeled upon the nearly obsolete Linnaean descriptive strategies of Botany as used in medicine into the late 20th century (Mason & Hsin, 2018). Because of their root in medicine and the descriptive strategies of medicine, the American Psychiatric Association's DSM looks at mental health problems as diseases that must be diagnosed.

One of the outfalls of this approach is a ponderous accumulation of diagnostic categories that often overlap, confuse symptoms and typologies, and provide no targets for intervention (Allsopp, Read, Corcoran, & Kinderman, 2019; Bakker, 2019; Feczko et al., 2019). Bakker (2019) notes the following seven divergent, overlapping, and often contradictory means used by DSM to describe various mental disorders. Not one of them is used consistently for all of the categories listed.

1. A symptom cluster (If you have 5 of these 7 symptoms, the diagnosis is X)
2. A certain level of distress (The patient must be sufficiently upset by the complaint to qualify)
3. The patient must experience a certain level of dysfunction (Because of the problem–drinking, depression, verbal outbursts – the patient can't work, can't perform familial responsibilities)
4. The problem must have a certain kind of etiology (this might include a family history as in schizophrenia or ADD/HD. It may also refer to the progression of a disease over time – consider the classical (but now disproven) progression of drinking problems from alcohol abuse to alcoholism or the distinctions between a depressive episode, chronic recurring depression, and Major Depressive Disorder)

DOI: 10.4324/9781003198864-4

5. The problem represents a statistical deviation from some norm (e.g., length of time to ejaculation; the number of alcoholic drinks in one sitting)
6. The presence of specific chemical markers or systems which indicate the presence of the disorder, or a measure of some neurochemical that appears to drive the problem (the search for biomarkers, the use of SSRIs in the treatment of presumed serotonin insufficiencies in depression)
7. The duration of the complaint (PTSD symptoms must have persisted for at least one month before a diagnosis can be made).

Bakker concludes that "… not a single mental disorder has been established as a discrete categorical entity …" (2019, p.4). He makes the important point that factor analyses of the diagnostic systems indicated that the problems themselves tend to reflect processes and not the categories promulgated in ICD and DSM.

Bakker suggests that rather than calling them diseases or disorders, we should speak more properly of clinical psychological problems (CPPs), a domain of psychology, not medicine. Others have also called for an individualized approach to classification and diagnosis that is uniquely psychological and rooted in individual experience (Bakker, 2019; Braganza & Piedmont, 2015). We believe that NLP can help to provide such an approach.

Recognition of the errors implicit in the topographical approach has led cognitive behavioral psychologists to pursue underlying patterns that can, potentially, identify broad traits or behavioral dispositions. These may include general states of anxiety, fear, or depression, that may be used to understand and treat the roots of multiple diagnoses at once. The search for a deeper level of unifying traits that might be used to understand anxiety disorders (for instance) as a broad trans-diagnostic strategy (Clark & Taylor, 2009; Farchione et al., 2012; Gros, 2014; Newby, McKinnon, Kuyken, Gilbody, & Dalgleish, 2015), or the identification of internally and externally driven species of depression (Zimmerman, Morgan, & Stanton, 2018) are well-meant and move in the right direction. However, these efforts remain bound to the topological descriptors that create even their generalizable classifications, while interventions still tend to be framed at the level of cognitive approaches.

NLP responds to the standard model of diagnosis and treatment by pointing out that such approaches are aimed at the wrong level of analysis. That is, the standard, topological, descriptive nosologies ask the wrong question. Rather than simple descriptive categories – "What does the problem look like?", a working diagnostic must focus upon the subjective structure of the experience – "How do individuals do that?" The answer to this question lies in processes that individuals use to create their own maps of the world, of world-building or map-making, not in trait typologies or invariant models. NLP diagnostics are not typological; every person is a unique, evolving individual. Every person creates their own problems by creating multi-sensory representations, or maps, that fail to represent the real world in one or more areas, thereby creating problems for the map-maker (Korzybski, 1994; Bandler & Grinder, 1975; Dilts, Grinder, Bandler, & DeLozier, 1980).

NLP operates on the assumption that humans are dynamic, evolving systems, who, in their diversity defy classification. Eschewing taxonomies of any kind, NLP takes aim at the structural elements that drive behavior at the level of phenomenal consciousness.

NLP diagnostics begin with the understanding that individuals navigate through the world based upon highly personalized subjective maps. These maps represent the outside world as multisensory images reflecting the individual's personal and cultural history. They frame our expectations of what is in that world and the rules for operating in it. In a very real sense, those maps are our only access to the outside world. When those maps diverge too much from consensual reality, psychopathologies result (Bandler & Grinder, 1975, 1979; Grinder & Bandler, 1976; Korzybski, 1994). Symptoms are reflections of the conflict between the structure of individual maps, the expectations that they create, and the surrounding reality. NLP also emphasizes that maladjustments and rigidities are often rooted in old choices and experiences that can become the target of creative restructuring (Bandler & Grinder, 1975; 1979; Grinder & Bandler, 1981). The NLP focus is on how (not why) people respond and what they can do to change the perceptions that drive their behavior.

NLP-based behavioral analysis does not posit an image apart from its neural representation, nor a disembodied homunculus who views that image. Most modern researchers (Fingelkurts, Fingelkurts, & Neves, 2010; Polák & Marvan, 2018) agree with this position. Symptoms are driven by the way that expectations, driven by the structure of an individual's maps of certain perceptions, actions, and contexts differ from affordances in the "real world". So, changing the structure of internal representations directly impacts both the neural networks that embody each memory and the responses they elicit. When the structure of these representations is changed under the therapist's direction, the client's subjective experience is changed directly.

We note here that the DSM and ICD categories represent the lingua franca of professional change workers, the insurance infrastructures, welfare programs, court systems, and other organizations that employ them. As such licensed clinicians must, for the most part, deal with the standard nosological models for billing purposes, and to ensure that their contracts with other agencies are fulfilled. All of NLP's diagnostics may be applied within the standard frames. Until those frames shift, we need to use them artfully, while our praxis is determined by the following observational strategies.

NLP and the study of the structure of subjective experience

Before setting out on identifying a treatment strategy, every clinician needs to know what they are dealing with. In NLP, as in other approaches, this understanding evolves in dialogue with the client. Crucially, every client interaction begins with an extensive client history. When, however, this is not possible – some NLP practitioners hold that getting to the problem alone is sufficient – collecting information about the problem is essential. Wake (2008), inter alia, suggests the following (adapted from the original):

> How does the client know they have this problem? (Elicit a reality strategy and any diagnosis made.) • When do they do it? • When don't they do it? • How long have they had this problem? • What have they done about it so far? • Was there ever a time when they didn't have this problem? • In each of these events, what is the relationship between the event and the current situation in life? (Elicit every single event and scan for patterns.) • What happened the first time they had this? (for each event) • What has happened since then? (for each event) • What emotions do they have associated with this problem? • What do they believe about the problem? • Pattern of childhood in relation to the problem. • Elicit history to trace the derivation of the problem or problems back to the source. … (pp. 156–57)

Such a history makes an important contribution to understanding the nature and scope of the problem (see also Bolstad, 2002). These are essential elements.

NLP centers diagnosis and treatment upon the underlying sensory sequences and submodality distortions that create the client's current map of the presenting situation and their world more generally. Diagnosis depends less upon predetermined diagnostic categories than on symptoms and the subjective structure, the strategy, that creates them. In so doing, NLP provides an implicitly transdiagnostic means of analyzing behavior.

Consider, for example, two depressed clients (Depression NOS, DSM-5 311). The depression of one is triggered by their recall of their wife's voice criticizing and condemning, always with the same repeated phrase, "You are just a fool, everyone laughs at you". The voice repeats insistently. The client finds it nearly impossible to ignore. As the voice speaks, their stomach sinks, their limbs grow heavy, and they are immobilized. A second client presents with a very similar depressed state, but for them, it is the vision of their dead child that triggers their experience. In their mind's eye, they experience a close, full-color image of the lifeless body of their too-young, much-loved child, their face waxen and pale, their body, stiff and cold. The client sinks into a deep depression from which it seems impossible to emerge. These two clients present with similar DSM-5 diagnoses. NLP practitioners would agree that both problems are rooted in memory, they would, however, focus on the structure of the present-time internal representation of the remembered event, not its content. The content is normal, we often remember bad and sad things that have happened to us. What makes the memory pathological are the structural elements that increase its importance and immediacy to an unmanageable level.

Despite their common diagnoses in topological terms, these two examples reflect very different patterns of subjective experience: what maintains the problems in the present. For one, it is a remembered voice. The voice is recognizable as the wife's voice. The words are experienced as a single string of linked verbal elements: a single emotional event. For the other, it is a remembered visual image. The image presents itself as close and insistent; it zooms quickly into view and blocks the client's capacity to think of anything but the dead child. Both cases are structured in such a way that the clinician believes that standard NLP interventions will work for them. For the internal voice, they choose Kemp's (2009) pattern for slowing internal speech. For the image-driven case, they choose the Visual/Kinesthetic-Dissociation Protocol (V/K-D; Andreas & Andreas, 1989; Dilts & DeLozier, 2000; Gray & Liotta, 2012, and Chapter 6, this volume).

In the first case, where the internal voice is experienced as a single event, an NLP-based therapist might instruct the client to listen carefully to the voice and to repeat what it says using the same tempo, intonation, and volume as the internal voice. Then, in several successive repeats of the phrase, the client is instructed to say the phrase aloud several more times, while, with each repetition, they gradually increase the amount of time between words. At first, they add one second between each word, then two, then more. They continue in this manner until the phrase disintegrates into individual words that no longer evoke the depressive response (Kemp, 2009).

In the second case, the NLP therapist might employ the visual kinesthetic dissociation (VK/D) protocol. The VK/D involves imagining several repetitions of a fast, dissociated, two-dimensional black and white movie of the scene projected on a wall. Modifications are made to the structure of the client's imagined black and white movie by changing its distance, angle, aspect ratio, speed, level of detail, etc. This is followed by vividly reimagining the experience several times in first-person, in full color, in reverse, from end to beginning in under two seconds (Andreas & Andreas, 1989; Dilts & DeLozier, 2000; Gray & Liotta, 2012; Linden & Perutz, 1998). In both cases, the patient's emotional symptoms are resolved by a structurally determined intervention, independent of content. It will be noted that neither case required the naming of the problem – that is, its categorization. They only required the analysis of its dynamic structure.

Levels of NLP diagnosis

NLP diagnostics unfold on several levels. These include strategy analysis and outcome clarification, cognitive interventions: the meta model and reframes, using strategy analysis to determine the use of NLP-based interventions; and problem strategy elicitation and modification.

In the following, it should be noted that NLP diagnostics do not create or identify categories so much as they identify patterns in the structure of the multi-sensory subjective maps that drive symptoms in present time. On some level, diagnosis is merged with the preparation for and execution of treatments. Moreover, diagnosis and treatment work with the assumption that all of diagnosis and treatment is focused upon how the structure of the client's subjective representation of the target event generates the symptom. Once the symptoms are resolved, the problem is resolved. NLP assumes no continuing internal source for further psychological problems.

Level 1: strategy analysis and outcome clarification

The first level of diagnostic analysis is the basic description of the problem state which would be, on a gross level, very much like standard DSM5 or ICD 11 diagnoses. This evocation is usually quickly terminated by the therapist and followed by a probe to determine the desired state or outcome. The outcome state is described in some detail and the client is invited to fully access that state. In some cases, simply knowing what they want and having the experience of having it in imago, is sufficient to change the client's map to complete the needed change. In many cases the enumeration of consciously available resources, already within the client's repertoire, may provide ready solutions.

Here we should recall that NLP incorporates a defined structure for outcomes, derived from the linguistic concept of well-formedness (Bandler & Grinder, 1975, 1979; Grinder & Bandler, 1976; Dilts, Grinder, Bandler, & DeLozier, 1980; Linden & Perutz, 1998), that is generally applicable for any circumstance. This definition includes the following characteristics. The outcome is (minimally):

1. a positively desired action or experience
2. under the client's personal control
3. described in multi-sensory terms
4. tried on in imago
5. analyzed into a number of steps or actions to start the process (Andreas & Andreas, 1989; Bandler & Grinder, 1982; Dilts and DeLozier, 2000; Dilts et al., 1980; Linden & Perutz, 1998).

Level 2: cognitive interventions – the meta model and reframes

A second typical level involves the cognitive tools provided by the Meta-Model of Language and other cognitive-linguistic NLP elements such as reframing (Bandler & Grinder, 1975, 1979; 1982; Grinder & Bandler, 1976). In some cases, these cognitive elements will successfully enlarge the client's map so that they may complete a brief series of interventions needing little further guidance beyond tools for improving motivation and help in designing a plan of action (see well-formed-ness conditions for outcomes).

At this, and the previous level of analysis, clients often identify outcomes that are inconsistent with their own true intentions, having replaced their own internal direction with cultural definitions, family traditions, or religious strictures. In many such cases simple cognitive reframes may be unsuccessful. In such cases, diagnosis moves to level three, where more complex applications such as the Six step reframe (Bandler & Grinder, 1979, 1982), Core Transformation (Andreas & Andreas, 1994), or the Wholeness Work (Andreas, 2018), are appropriate.

At this level, and almost uniquely in NLP, we are concerned with content. More specifically, the metamodel and reframing strategies address missing, or distorted information.

The Meta-model of Language is described in *The Structure of Magic I & II* (Bandler & Grinder, 1975; Grinder & Bandler, 1976) and other foundational NLP works (Lewis & Pucelik, 1990; O'Connor & Seymour, 1990; Tosey & Mathison, 2008). In brief, the Meta-Model is a set of linguistic descriptions designed to reveal and (often) remedy the deletions, distortions, and generalizations that people use in the construction of their subjective reality and that may render their subjective maps self-limiting. It assumes that people's subjective maps are reflected in the way they use language, and that language can, in turn, affect those maps.

The Meta-Model includes linguistic descriptions for specific categories of linguistic deletion, as in the Lost Comparative. This distinction reflects that one arm of a comparison is missing. For example, an acquaintance says, without other reference, that some state or condition is "much better". As we cannot tell from this statement to what improvement the acquaintance is referring, the missing information can be regained by asking, "Better than what, specifically?" Nominalizations represent another category of usage. This one distorts verb forms so that an active verb appears as a static noun. "I had an episode". somewhat common-sensically invites the challenge, "What kind of episode were you having? Where and when were you experiencing this?" Similarly, a species of generalization is revealed in the sentence, "I always fail in relationships". As a Universal Quantifier, the statement would be challenged, in an exaggerated manner, by asking, "Always? Every single time? You mean that you've never, ever, ever succeeded in a relationship in your whole life? Even briefly" (Bandler & Grinder, 1975; Lewis & Pucelik, 1990; O'Connor & Seymour, 1990; Tosey & Mathison, 2008)?

A client comes in for counseling because she believes her partner no longer respects her. The therapist, hearing the statement, "My partner doesn't respect me anymore." recognizes that this sentence has deleted and distorted several pieces of information. They expect that retrieving this information may be useful to the client. Applying the Meta-Model, the therapist begins by challenging the Mind Read (the claim to know what another is thinking) that is implied by the statement "My partner doesn't respect me". To recover the lost information, they ask, "How do you know your partner doesn't respect you?" There is also a statement that meets the criterion for Presuppositions. The statement, "My partner doesn't respect me." presupposes that at some point, they did respect her and invites the challenge, "Does that mean that your partner did respect you at some point? When was that, and how did you know?" The Meta-Model can be used, carefully and respectfully, to uncover the details of a person's understanding of the world.

The Meta-model is also a means for assessing the state of a client's subjective map as they progress through change (Bateson, 1975). Clients who have successfully processed a problem will often spontaneously begin to refer to it in the past tense, they may also now be unable to access the problem.

Although the NLP Meta-Model categories are very much parallel to the list of automatic thoughts promulgated by CBT and REBT (Ellis, 2017; Grohol, 2019), NLP differs in that its Meta-Model categories are non-judgmental; they are merely descriptive and make no judgment about the rationality of the client or their ideations. Their intent is to increase conscious access to currently unknown or inaccessible content and to provide more flexibility in the client's map. Appropriately used, the Meta-Model can produce useful, even revelatory insights into the nature of client complaints.

In addition to the Meta-Model, this level of analysis and intervention includes reframes. Reframes are divided into two broad types, content reframes, and context reframes (Bandler & Grinder, 1979; Grinder & Bandler, 1976, 1981).

Contents only take on meaning with regard to specific frames of reference (Grinder & Bandler, 1981; Watzlawick, Beavin, & Jackson, 1967). Persons with attention deficit disorder often suffer from hyper-focus. They get stuck concentrating on some object, idea, or behavior. Hyper-focus can be reframed when it becomes useful as a way of improving study or is transformed into meditative practice. Used in this manner, the meaning of hyper-focus is transformed from a disability into a useful skill. This is a content reframe; it changes the meaning of some content by changing its scope or target.

Bandler tells the story of working with a schizophrenic patient who suffered from constant visual and auditory hallucinations. After having the patient taken off medication, Bandler suggested that the patient try changing the channel that was playing on his internal television. He suggested that the patient turn the channel to the playboy station and tell no one. Until returned to his medication regimen, the client no longer complained about this internal programming (Bandler, 1993).

Context reframes change meaning by changing the setting of the perceived problem (Bandler & Grinder, 1982). An informant once told the following story about his four-year-old daughter, Elizabeth. Elizabeth was in the kitchen with her mother when it came time for her to take her medicine. The child refused. Despite continued coaxing, threats, and other efforts by her mother, the young girl adamantly refused to submit. The exasperated mother sat the young girl down on a stool in the middle of the kitchen and told her that there she would stay until she took her medicine. Young Elizabeth sat there and made irritating noises for the next hour until her mother, at her wit's end, shooed her from the kitchen. Later that night, the mother, still frustrated by the day's events related the tale of Elizabeth's adamantine stubbornness to her father. Well, he said, when some creep tries something without her permission, we know who's going to win. This is a context reframe, the meaning is changed by placing it in a new frame (Bandler & Grinder, 1982).

It should be noted that from some of the earliest texts, NLP has presented an intervention known as a six-step reframe (Bandler & Grinder, 1979, 1982). While the technique, applicable across multiple standard diagnostic categories, provides new definitions of actions, percepts, or beliefs that ultimately reframe them, this is not a simple cognitive process, but a more complex technique more appropriate to the third level of diagnosis.

Whole life reframes: awakening personal meaning

At this same level, as noted we encounter the problem where the desired outcome is not consistent with the client's positive intentions, or personal developmental pathway. In many such cases, the client has substituted cultural definitions, family traditions, or religious strictures for their own internal direction. This can often be resolved on a cognitive level.

Outcomes may be tested for their propriety by applying the criteria for well-formed outcomes (Bandler & Grinder, 1975, 1979; Grinder & Bandler, 1976; Dilts et al., 1980; Linden & Perutz, 1998) already cited, above. When the outcome is analyzed, it may be discovered that the client has not stated it as a positively desired object. As the brain does not process negation, both stopping doing something and not-doing something are ill-formed by definition. Ill-formed outcomes may also depend upon someone else's action, or pure luck (winning the lottery). Positive futurity relies upon personal action; if my future is not designed in terms of what I can imagine myself doing, it will not happen. Because the brain deals in sensory-based imagery (VAKOG), abstractions must be replaced with image-based outcomes-I'll see the band playing; I'll hear my family shouting; I will shake the Dean's hand; I will smell the flowers in my bouquet. Finally, the client must step into the future that they have designed to test whether it is appropriate to them. The following story is adapted from Gray's, (2011), *Interviewing and counseling skills: An NLP perspective.*

Many years ago, the author was teaching psychology at a local Community College. As part of a lesson on motivation, he asked students to apply the NLP well-formedness criteria to outcomes that they had already set for themselves. These criteria may be used both to test the validity of a current outcome, or to design positively motivating future outcomes. Each individual criterion must be satisfied, else the outcome is ill-formed and will either fail or be dissatisfying over time. An important facet of the exercise was the imaginal experience of the anticipated outcome. That is, after specifying a positive outcome, after determining that the outcome was under their personal control and specifying several sensory-based means by which the student would know that they had attained the desired state or position, they were asked to imagine stepping into the end state and trying it on.

On this occasion there was a young woman in the class who had been working toward a two-year degree in nursing. She had just begun the program and had no idea of what it was that a nurse actually did. When she tried on the imagined experience of the day-to-day realities of nursing, she came rather quickly to the realization that it was not something that she wanted to do. She had never considered that it was about people who were suffering, bleeding, crying, and that filth and death were part of the job. She changed her major soon thereafter. Here, the NLP well-formedness criteria diagnosed an ill-formed outcome that may well have been the foundation of other difficulties.

Where the positive intention or life direction is unclear an intervention such as Core Transformation (Andreas & Andreas, 1994; Braganza, & Piedmont, 2015; Braganza, Piedmont, Fox, Fialkowski, & Gray, 2019) or the Brooklyn Program (Gray, 2011, 2011a, 2008/2013) can be used to clarify those directions and use them to empower change.

Level 3: problem strategy elicitation and modification

Finally, there is the basic strategy elicitation, with experimental manipulation of the structural elements of the driving experience. This is pure NLP elicitation and manipulation that seeks to first model the client's strategy and then modify it. Modeling requires the clinician to engage in dialogue of discovery with the patient in which they tease out the order and qualities of the internal image(s) that drive the problem behavior or cognition. In what order do the senses present themselves and what specific qualities do they have (intensity, frequency, complexity, contrast; foreground-background, etc.)? The modification may consist of having the client imagining turning off one or more of the sensory elements that drive the experience. They may manipulate the source location relative to personal center, or its intensity, distance, amplitude, and other structural elements until a combination is found that reduces the symptom.

In many cases, the combination of the initial descriptive complaint and the specification of the sensory representations that drive it is sufficient to identify an intervention that is appropriate to the client's complaint.

So, a patient comes in complaining of a fear of spiders. During their interview, the clinician notices that at any mention of spiders, the client cringes and flushes. This observation is sufficient to confirm to the therapist that the complaint is real; the client's physiological reaction to the word alone has allowed them to calibrate the presence of a specific phobic response (DSM-5 300.29). While essential for billing, this information is insufficient for specifying an intervention. Further questioning reveals that the mention of spiders, the presentation of their images, or actually encountering a spider, creates in the client's imagination the all-too real image of a giant, looming, hairy spider, rushing toward them with fangs dripping poison. In light of the subjective image's overwhelming visual emphasis (images exist in all sensory systems), the therapist decides that the NLP Visual/Kinesthetic-Dissociation protocol (V/K-D) is appropriate. In response, he asks the client to pick, in an abstract, dissociated manner, either their original terrifying encounter with a spider or their memory of the worst example of a phobic reaction to spiders. The client is reminded to pick one and only one specific memory for today's session. Once the target memory has been chosen, the intervention begins with a brief activation of the memory. Here, the client begins to describe the incident in the first person – as if they were there. The therapist stops them before the fearful response becomes overwhelming – just when the therapist first calibrates the client's fearful response. The client is then reoriented into the present and provided with a short practice of the imaginal techniques to be used (brief black and white movies with structural variations and very fast reversed experiences of the event). They are then asked to imagine that they are in a movie theater with a small screen. Projected on the screen is a still black and white image of the traumatic memory just before the target event begins. They are then to imagine floating out of their body to a position behind themselves (perhaps in the projection booth). Now, as they remain in this position-behind their seated self-in-the-theater, the client imagines a fast black and white movie of the target event running from beginning to end. The client then runs the movie multiple times, while watching their self-in-the-theater as that self watches the movie until the therapist can be assured by watching (calibrating) and asking that the client is comfortable.

When the client is comfortable, they are instructed to return to their seat in the theater and walk up to the screen. At the screen, they are instructed to step into the last scene of the movie, turn on the sound and the colors, and experience that same event in reverse, entirely associated, with everything running backward, seemingly undoing itself. The client repeats this several times. When, by asking and observing, the therapist determines that the client is no longer responding fearfully to the movie of the target event, their phobic response can be tested. To test the phobic response, the client is presented with a spider, a picture of a spider, or they are asked to recount the phobia narrative again. If there is no response, the therapist tests it against other examples of the experience in the past or in an imagined future. If there is still no response, the intervention has worked. If a fearful response remains, the process is repeated (Andreas, 2009, 2012; Andreas & Andreas, 1989; Gray & Liotta, 2012).

The final level of NLP diagnostics involves conversational strategy elicitation identifying the structural elements of the driving experience and then modifies those structures. This is pure NLP. The modification may consist of having the client imagine changing the source, intensity, distance, amplitude, and other structural elements of the evoking stimulus until a combination is found that reduces the symptom.

We note here, that submodality distinctions include not only distance, angle, aspect ratio, speed, level of detail, etc. for each sensory system, but also spatial variables that code for content, valence, and more complex elements of meaning including trustworthiness and value (Connirae Andreas, Personal communication, August 2020; Derks, 2018).

Derks (2018) has described a set of spatial distinctions that enlarge upon both the standard NLP perspective, and Bandler's position as related in the Design Human Engineering (DHE) materials (1999) regarding the distribution of subjective images in 3-dimensional space. This 3-Dimensional mapping accords with observations by modern neuroscience (Edelman, 2003, 2004; Feinberg & Mallatt, 2020; Jerath & Beveridge, 2019; Jerath, Beveridge, & Jensen, 2019; Jerath, Crawford, & Barnes, 2015). Derks posits that the position of an image in subjective 3-dimensional space (independent of sensory system), codes for its current salience, its relationship to other content, and other dimensions. In Chapter 6 he discusses how this schema operationalizes the classical psychodynamic idea of repression.

In conformity with observations by Andreas & Andreas (1989) in the Aligning Perceptual Positions pattern, Derks, in his Social Panorama (2005), points to how elevation in perceptual space equates to influence as power, respect, or authority. The higher the image is above the visual plain, the more influential. The lower they are, the less influential. Persons and things to the front are the center of attention, but things in the rear may represent currently subliminal influences.

Subjective distance in 3-Dimensional space equates to temporal distance so that things that are 20 years old should group together at the same subjective distance as other 20-year-old memories. When they do not, it may be diagnostic of issues with that content. Relationships are also reflected by distance in 3-D space. Emotional distance is reflected by distance in subjective space (Derks, 2018).

Significantly, this submodality of place seems to have a reciprocal relationship between itself and the other submodalities. That is, a change in an image's location in subjective 3-D space affects some or all of the submodalities in a given subjective representation. Just so, changes in submodality structure, both individually and in aggregate, affect the image's location in 3-D space (see, e.g., Andreas, 2021).

Some years ago an informant was working on his dissertation in psychology. Having drawn out the process for several years while seeking, as one committee member put it, "the last citation in Arabic", he began to consider his presentation before the doctoral committee. As he did so, he found that his image of that committee seemed to be represented to the left of center and slightly below eye level. The image was a muted, still picture of a group of oldish men, dressed in brown. They were wearing costumes appropriate to the 17th century and frowning unhappily at the informant. The author was inspired by Bandler's descriptions in the DHE materials (1999) indicating that one could drag a subjective image from a position in subjective 3-D space – where it had a negative meaning – to a place where a personal positive event was represented. The author, having had a considerable background as a musician, recalled the image of an audience at one of his solo performances from years before. The audience was applauding, cheering, and calling for an encore. The image was just to the right of center about at eye level. It was large, in color, full of sound, motion, and in three dimensions. Following the instructions provided by Bandler, the informant reached out with his hand and imagined grabbing the original picture of the dour Dutch-Masters-Cigar-Box-PhD-Committee. He flexed it with his fingers and used a full physical arm movement to drag it, with imagined friction, from the image's original place to the place of the cheering audience. As suggested in the audio, he then "clicked it into place". As he did so the image changed. What had previously been an image of a dour Dutch-Masters-Cigar-Box-PhD-Committee, now came to life as a cheering, full color, moving image of a smiling, waving committee, enthusiastically cheering him on. The image stayed and he completed his Ph.D. successfully.

The position of a content in 3-dimensional space may be used to understand the valence associated with the content, the nature of the content itself, and its meaning in relation to other contents of consciousness. In such cases, the affect generated by the content may be assessed for diagnostic relevance and possibly changed (when ecology permits) by changing its position in subjective space. We note here, that one of the tell-tale signs of client success with the RTM Protocol (Chapter 3), is the spontaneous movement of the trauma content-image from a space directly in front of the client (where it appears as an emergent threat), to a space consistent with older, less relevant past memories (behind the client).

Please note that the actual arrangements of all such contents are to some extent determined by cultural norms. This is especially so regarding time relations (Ouellet, Santiago, Funes, & Lupiáñez, 2010; Santiago, Román, Ouellet, Rodríguez, & Pérez-Azor, 2010; Tversky, Kugelmass, & Winter, 1991; Weger & Pratt, 2008). Although NLPers have argued for a neurological basis for the front to back and left to right organization of subjective temporal imagery (as it appears in normally organized westerners), this appears to be a learned pattern rooted in orthography. In cultures where writing is left to right, the past tends to be leftwards and the future to the right. In cultures reading right to left, the relationship is reversed (Ouellet et al., 2010; Santiago et al., 2010; Tversky et al., 1991; Weger & Pratt, 2008).

Summary and conclusions

Psychiatry and psychology depend upon massive catalogs of psychiatric diagnoses that are largely descriptive and provide little real guidance for treatment. In general, their failure to create useful categories has fed the drive for transdiagnostic interventions and personally relevant diagnoses.

NLP provides a new perspective on diagnosis by moving description from the perspective of the external observer to the structure of the client's internal representations. People operate based upon their unique, subjective maps of the world out there. Those maps consist of multi-sensory images that express the importance (salience), emotional charge (valence) and meaning of the memory percept or action through the presence or absence of sensory elements, the ordering of those elements, and their submodality structure. Psychological problems are expressed and identified by symptoms. Symptoms are driven by mismatches between subjective maps and the predictions they make about the world out there. Diagnosis and treatment depend upon the identification of the subjective elements that drive symptom expression.

References

Allsopp, K., Read, J., Corcoran, R., & Kinderman, P. (2019). Heterogeneity in psychiatric diagnostic classification. *Psychiatry Research*, 279, 15–22. doi:10.1016/j.psychres.2019.07.005

American Psychiatric Association. (2013). *Diagnostic and statistical manual of mental disorders*. (5th ed.). Arlington, VA: Author.

Andreas, C. (2018). *Coming to wholeness: How to awaken and live with ease*. Boulder, CO: Real People Press.

Andreas, C., & Andreas, S. (1989). *Heart of the Mind*. Boulder, CO: Real People Press.

Andreas, C., & Andreas, T. (1994). *Core transformations: Reaching the wellspring within*. Real People Press.

Andreas, S. (2021, February 16). Submodalities Model, Part 2: Mapping Across. *NLP Comprehensive*. https://nlpco.com/submodalities-model-part-2-mapping-across/.

Andreas, S. (2012). The Fast Phobia Trauma Cure Part 1. *NLP Comprehensive*. https://www.youtube.com/watch?v=mss8dndyakQ. Date accessed August 31, 2020.

Andreas, S. (2009). Original NLP Fast Phobia Cure Part 2–25 Year Follow Up. [Video]. *NLP Comprehensive*.https://www.youtube.com/watch?v=TjjCzhrYJDQ.

Bakker, G. (2019). A new conception and subsequent taxonomy of clinical psychological problems. *BMC Psychology*, 7(1). doi:10.1186/s40359-019-0318-8

Bandler, R. (1999). *Introduction to DHE*. Chicago (Audio).

Bandler, R. (1993). *Time for a change*. Capitola, CA: Meta Publications.

Bandler, R., & Grinder, J. (1982). *Reframing: Neuro-linguistic programming and the transformation of meaning*. Moab, UT: Real People Press.

Bandler, R., & Grinder, J. (1979). *Frogs into princes*. Moab, UT: Real People Press.

Bandler, R., & Grinder, J. (1975). *The structure of magic*. Palo Alto, CA: Science and BehaviorBooks

Bateson, G. (1975). Introduction. In: R. Bandler, & J. Grinder (Eds.), *The Structure of Magic* (pp. ix–xi). Real People Press.

Bolstad, R. (2002). *Resolve: A new model of therapy*. Carmarthen, UK: Crown House Publishing.

Braganza, D., & Piedmont, R. L. (2015). The impact of the Core Transformation process on spirituality, symptom experience, and psychological maturity in a mixed age sample in India: A pilot study. *Journal of Religion and Health*, 54(3), 888–902. doi:10.1007/s10943-0150049y

Braganza, D. J., Piedmont, R. L., Fox, J., Fialkowski, G. M., & Gray, R. M. (2019). Examining the Clinical Efficacy of Core Transformation: A Randomized Clinical Trial. *Journal of Counseling & Development*, 97(3), 293–305. doi:10.1002/jcad.12269.

Clark, D. A., & Taylor, S. (2009). The transdiagnostic perspective on cognitive-behavioral therapy for anxiety and depression: New wine for old wineskins? *Journal of Cognitive Psychotherapy: An International Quarterly*, 23, 60–66.

Derks, L. A. C. (2018). *Mental Space Psychology: Psychotherapeutic Evidence for a New Paradigm*. Nijmegen, Netherlands: Coppelear b.v.

Derks, L. A. C. (2005). *Social Panoramas; Changing the unconscious landscape with NLP and psychotherapy*. Camarthen, Wales: Crown House Publishing.

Dilts, R., & DeLozier, J. (2000). *Allergy Process*. http://nlpuniversitypress.com/html/AaAj22.html

Dilts, R., Grinder, J., Bandler, R., & DeLozier, J. (1980). *Neuro-linguistic programming: Volume I. The structure of subjective experience*. Cupertino, CA: Meta Publications.

Edelman, G. M. (2003). Naturalizing consciousness: a theoretical framework. *Proceedings of the National Academy of Sciences of the United States of America*, 100(9), 5520–5524. doi:10.1073/pnas.0931349100

Edelman, G. M. (2004). *Wider than the sky. The phenomenal gift of consciousness*. New Haven, CT: Yale University Press.

Ellis, A. (2017, May 17). *The Essence of REBT*. Retrieved June 18, 2020, from https://www.rebt.ws/albert_ellis_the_essence_of_rebt.htm

Farchione, T. J., Fairholme, C. P., Ellard, K. K., Boisseau, C. L., Thompson-Hollands, J., Carl, J. R., Gallagher, M. W., & Barlow, D. H. (2012). Unified protocol for transdiagnostic treatment of emotional disorders: a randomized controlled trial. *Behaviour Therapy*, 43(3), 666–678. doi:10.1016/j.beth.2012.01.001

Feczko, E., Miranda-Dominguez, O., Marr, M., Graham, A. M., Nigg, J. T., & Fair, D. A. (2019). The heterogeneity problem: Approaches to identify psychiatric subtypes. *Trends in Cognitive Science*, 23(7), 584–601. doi:10.1016/j.tics.2019.03.009

Feinberg, T. E., & Mallatt, J. (2020). Phenomenal consciousness and emergence: Eliminating the explanatory gap. *Frontiers in Psychology*, 11. doi:10.3389/fpsyg.2020.01041

Fingelkurts, A.A., Fingelkurts, A.A., & Neves, C.F. (2010). Natural world physical, brain operational, and mind phenomenal space-time. *Physics of Life Reviews* 7(2), 195–249. doi:10.1016/j.plrev.2010.04.001. Epub 2010 Apr 13.

Gray, R. (2008/2013). *Transforming futures: The Brooklyn program facilitators manual. 2nd ed.* Lulu.com. http://www.lulu.com/content/2267218.

Gray, R. (2011a). Overcoming addiction: A new model for working with drug and alcohol abusers,*Innovations in NLP Volume 1*, Charvet, S., & Hall, L.M. (Eds.). Carmarthen, Wales: Crown Publishing.

Gray, R. (2011). *Interviewing and counseling skills: An NLP perspective.* Raleigh, NC: Lulu Press.

Gray, R., & Liotta, R. (2012). PTSD: Extinction, reconsolidation, and the visual-kinesthetic dissociation protocol. *Traumatology*, 18(2), 3–16. doi:10.1177/1534765611431835.

Grinder, J., & Bandler, R. (1976). *The structure of magic II.* Cupertino, California: Science and Behavior Books.

Grinder, J., & Bandler, R. (1981). *Trance-formations: Neuro-linguistic programming and the structure of hypnosis.* Andreas, C. (Ed.). Boulder, CO: Real People Press.

Grohol, J. M. (2019, June 24). *15 Common Cognitive Distortions.* Retrieved June 18, 2020, from https://psychcentral.com/lib/15-common-cognitive-distortions/

Gros, D. F. (2014). Development and initial evaluation of Transdiagnostic Behavior Therapy (TBT) for veterans with affective disorders. *Psychiatry Research*, 220(1), 275–282. doi:10.1016/j.psychres.2014.08.018

Jerath, R., & Beveridge, C. (2019). Multimodal integration and phenomenal spatiotemporal binding: A perspective from the default space theory. *Frontiers in integrative neuroscience*, 13, 2. doi:10.3389/fnint.2019.00002

Jerath, R., Beveridge, C., & Jensen, M. (2019). On the hierarchical organization of oscillatory assemblies: Layered superimposition and a global bioelectric framework. *Frontiers in Human Neuroscience*, 13, 426. doi:10.3389/fnhum.2019.00426

Jerath, R., Crawford, M. W., & Barnes, V. A. (2015). A unified 3D default space consciousness model combining neurological and physiological processes that underlie conscious experience. *Frontiers in Psychology*, 6,1204. doi:10.3389/fpsyg.2015.01204. PMID: 26379573; PMCID: PMC4550793.

Kemp, N. (2009). Chapter 2: Changing tempo and tonality: Slowing Tempo Exercise Outline. In S. Andreas (Eds.), *Transforming Negative Self-Talk: Practical, Effective Exercises* (pp. 25–43). Real People Press.

Korzybski, A. (1994). *Science & sanity (5th ed.).* European Society for General Semantics. Retrieved from http://esgs.free.fr/uk/art/sands.htm

Lewis, B., & Pucelik, F. (1990). *Magic of NLP demystified. A pragmatic guide to communication and change.* Portland, Oregon: Metamorphous Press.

Linden, A., & Perutz, K. (1998). *Mindworks: NLP tools for building a better life.* NY: Berkley Publishing Group.

Mason, D., & Hsin, H. (2018). 'A more perfect arrangement of plants': the botanical model in psychiatric nosology, 1676 to the present day. *History of Psychiatry*, 29(2), 131–146. doi:10.1177/0957154×18757341

Newby, J. M., McKinnon, A., Kuyken, W., Gilbody, S., & Dalgleish, T. (2015). Systematic review and meta-analysis of transdiagnostic psychological treatments for anxiety and depressive disorders in adulthood. *Clinical Psychology Review*, 40, 91–110. doi:10.1016/j.cpr.2015.06.002

O'Connor, J., & Seymour, J. (1990). *Introducing NLP.* London: Element.

Ouellet, M., Santiago, J., Funes, M. J., & Lupiáñez, J. (2010). Thinking about the future moves attention to the right. *Journal of Experimental Psychology: Human Perception and Performance*, 36(1), 17–24. doi:10.1037/a0017176.

Polák, M., & Marvan, T. (2018). Neural correlates of consciousness meet the theory of identity. *Frontiers in Psychology*, 9(1269). doi:10.3389/fpsyg.2018.01269

Santiago, J., Román, A., Ouellet, M., Rodríguez, N., & Pérez-Azor, P. (2010). In hindsight, life flows from left to right. *Psychological Research/Psychologische Forschung*, 74(1), 59–70. doi:10.1007/s00426-008-0220-0

Tosey, P., & Mathison, J. (2008). *Neuro-linguistic programming: A critical appreciation for managers and developers*. Palgrave-Macmillan.

Tversky, B., Kugelmass, S., & Winter, A. (1991). Cross-cultural and developmental trends in graphic productions. *Cognitive Psychology*, 23(4), 515–557. doi:10.1016/0010-0285(91)90005-9

Wake, L. (2008). *Neurolinguistic psychotherapy: A postmodern perspective*. Routledge

Watzlawick, P., Beavin, J., & Jackson, D. (1967). *Pragmatics of Human Communication: Study of Interactional Patterns, Pathologies and Paradoxes*. NY: W.W. Norton.

Weger, U. W., & Pratt, J. (2008). Time flies like an arrow: Space-time compatibility effects suggest the use of a mental timeline. *Psychonomic Bulletin & Review*, 15(2), 426–430. doi:10.3758/pbr.15.2.426

World Health Organization. (2018). *International classification of diseases for mortality and morbidity statistics* (11th Revision). Retrieved from https://icd.who.int/browse11/l-m/en

Zimmerman, M., Morgan, T. A., & Stanton, K. (2018). The severity of psychiatric disorders. *World psychiatry: official journal of the World Psychiatric Association* (WPA), 17(3), 258–275.

5 Neurolinguistic psychotherapy and complex mental health conditions

Dr Lisa de Rijk and Rob Kamps

Introduction

Neurolinguistic psychotherapy (NLPt) has existed as a recognised therapeutic modality since the 1980s with recognition of this approach by various psychotherapy organisations across the world (The European Association of NLPt (EANLPt), 2021).

There is some emerging evidence that suggests good therapeutic outcomes can be facilitated with clients presenting for psychotherapy.

In this chapter we review the existing research literature on NLPt in the treatment of complex mental health problems. The authors then present a case series of clients presenting with just such conditions. Complex Mental health conditions are defined by DSM-V as follows:

- B – psychotic disorders – schizophrenia
- C – mood disorders – bipolar disorder
- H – dissociative disorders – depersonalisation disorder; dissociative identity disorder
- K – eating disorders – anorexia nervosa; bulimia nervosa

Cases are considered in the context of actual or perceived diagnosis and presenting symptomatology. We present the cases through the lens of NLPt, bringing other theories and approaches in where they are relevant to the case.

The authors conclude by critiquing the use of NLPt to support those with complex mental health conditions and make recommendations for future research in this area.

NLP and psychotherapy

Although NLP was modelled by therapists Satir, Perls, and Erickson, with the models of linguistic process tested by therapists, it was never intended to be presented as a psychotherapeutic model. Erickson noted this in his comment on the early work of the NLP founders.

DOI: 10.4324/9781003198864-5

> Although this book by Richard Bandler and John Grinder… is far from being a complete description of my methodologies, as they so clearly state it is a much better explanation of how I work than I, myself, can give. I know what I do, but to explain how I do it is much too difficult for me… While I would like still further analyses of the complexities of communication for hypnotic purposes, which would require much more than this book by Bandler and Grinder can encompass, I would also like an analysis of how and why carefully structured communications can elicit such extensive and effective patient responses, often not actually requested. (Bandler & Grinder, 1975, p. ix).

Erickson continued his own self-reflection, noting that he was making intuitive note of the many layers of conflicting messages that a client might communicate verbally and non-verbally. Bandler and Grinder posited that these intuitions were a conscious bio-feedback mechanism (1975) yet Erickson begged to differ. Erickson's view was that a two-way process existed between client and therapist with both responding to the non-conscious material of the other. If this was understood and used, then this would lead to an improvement in the client's condition (1975, pp. 44–45). This is highlighted in Bandler and Grinder's work through an exploration of Erickson's work with Aldous Huxley on unconscious processes (pp. 59–126). Huxley presents an identity confusion between himself, his infant self, and Erickson (pp. 107–118), in what appears to be an attachment response to Erickson with Huxley responding as an infant to Erickson.

Unfortunately, the field of psychotherapy has not benefited from this early example of NLP-modelling which, had it continued, may have highlighted the psychodynamic processes at play. Instead, Bandler and Grinder referred to these as fuzzy functions and then focussed on the linguistic patterns and used these to train other therapists, who were then unable to replicate the same level of result as Erickson, Satir, and Perls (Bandler & Grinder, 1975). Bateson reinforces this view that Bandler and Grinder missed an important element, "*it never occurred to us to ask about the effects of modes upon interpersonal relations*" (Bateson in Bandler & Grinder 1975, p. x). Bandler and Grinder continue this observation in a subsequent publication (1979) where they refer to therapist intuition as "*doing what they do without knowing how they do it. They do it by the 'seat of their pants'–that's another way to say 'unconscious mind*'". (1979, p. 6). Here Bandler and Grinder are contradicting their own earlier observation that all therapist observations are conscious and are consciously used in their interaction with their clients

> they may, from long experience, have an intuition about what the missing piece is……..his intuition may be based upon previous therapy or upon his recognition of a particular body posture or movement he has seen the client use……..if this new Surface Structure containing the

> therapist's intuition about the identity of the deleted portion of the clients original Surface Structure fits the client's model, he will typically experience a certain sensation of congruity or recognition. (1975, p. 42).

NLP started to return to the field of psychotherapy in the 1980s. By 1996, a formal therapy body for Neurolinguistic Psychotherapy (NLPt) developed as an off-shoot of the Association of NLP. Therapists McDermott and Jago (2001), Lawley and Tomkins (2000), Gawler-Wright (2004, 2007), and Wake (2008) began to integrate the NLP in their therapeutic work. As a result, NLP is now recognised as brief psychotherapy by the UK's voluntary regulatory body for psychotherapy, the UK Council for Psychotherapy (UKCP). NLPt is seen as a goal-oriented therapy (The European Association of NLPt EANLPt, 2021; Kostere & Malatesta, 1990; McDermott & Jago, 2001; Neurolinguistic Psychotherapy and Counselling Association, 2021). More recently, there has been a greater focus on the early critique of Erickson and a movement back towards the emphasis on the therapeutic relationship (Gawler-Wright, 2007; Wake, 2008, 2010).

Psychotherapy research studies

This chapter reviews the use of NLPt with clients presenting with complex mental health conditions. The use of NLP with other mental health conditions is discussed in other chapters in this edition, reviewed as a general psychotherapy modality in Chapter 2, and discussed extensively in the first edition.

The recently published DSM-5has moved away from the historical model of coding personality disorders on a separate axis from other mental health conditions. Instead, it has adopted a hybrid personality model that focuses on impaired personality functioning and five areas of personality traits:

- Borderline Personality Disorder
- Obsessive-Compulsive Personality Disorder
- Avoidant Personality Disorder
- Antisocial Personality Disorder
- Narcissistic Personality Disorder

We conducted an on-line search for reports of the use of NLP in the treatment of these disorders using the following databases, CINAHL, MEDLINE, PSYCHINFO. Search terms used included:

> nlp OR neurolinguistic programming OR neuro-linguistic programming
>
> AND
>
> personality disorder OR borderline personality disorder OR emotionally unstable personality disorder OR eupd OR bpd

AND/OR complex mental health

AND/OR

mental health OR mental illness OR mental disorder OR psychiatric illness

A total of 3 papers were identified. All were excluded as they referred to Natural Language Processing (NLP), not Neuro-Linguistic Programming. To date, there are no credible research studies evidencing the use of NLPt with clients presenting with severe and enduring mental health conditions.

Case series

In this section we present a series of case studies that highlight how we have worked with clients presenting with long-standing mental health conditions. These conditions range from Anorexia Nervosa, to Bipolar Disorder necessitating hospitalisation, and Dysthymic Disorder.

Bipolar disorder (C00 – DSM-v)

Julia presented in her middle years. She had experienced 4 significant episodes of mania with psychosis and on each occasion had required hospitalisation and was given a diagnosis of Bipolar Disorder. Julia had an extensive history of adverse childhood experiences including sexual abuse, emotional neglect, and physical abuse. She had also been a witness to domestic violence from a young age. Julia reported her experience of care within the health and social care system as varying from abusive, to neglectful, to uncaring and occasionally good. By the time she presented for therapy she had worked with her own family doctor and regular psychiatrist and had agreed to be medication free. My first experience of Julia was of a delightful, intriguing, and intelligent woman. Her story was difficult to grasp as she would go off onto different story tangents that appeared to be unrelated to the previous story. The slightest questioning of her thought processes would take her into yet a different story as she tried to explain her own process to me. Julia was keen that I should be aware of her previous hospitalisations and her early adult diagnosis of bipolar disorder and unstable personality disorder. The notion of labelling runs counter to the NLP presupposition that *People are not their behaviours* (Dilts & DeLozier, 2000, p. 1002). I thanked Julia for sharing her history with me and asked her what she wanted from therapy – establishing a well-formed outcome (Wake, 2008, pp. 118–121). This question took her off into many different storylines and she appeared to be somewhat reluctant to be pinned down to a specific goal or set of goals for therapy. I recognised that pacing Julia was the best way to gain a useful therapeutic relationship with her. Her speed of processing was much faster than mine and she reflected an amazing ability to make links between subjects that I found challenging to grasp.

Erickson had long been a therapist whose skill I admired. I was minded to consider his strategic approach to therapy (Haley, 1993) and decided that the only way I could realistically work with this lady was to stay present in the here and now and offer her reflections on her own processing. Asking questions of her took her into degrees of distraction that at times appeared to be delusional and hallucinatory. Taking her back into the stories of early childhood traumas triggered dissociative episodes.

I have worked with this client for more than 6 years. In NLP terms, that is extensive therapy. Yet in her world view, she has developed a lasting attachment relationship with me. NLP as a modality although utilising rapport as a core component of developing a relationship of trust and responsiveness with the client, does not hold any theory regarding a developmental and attachment-based therapy encounter (Schore, 2003), preferring instead to see the presupposition that everyone has all the resources they need (p. 1002, Dilts & DeLozier, 2000) indicating that the client does their 'getting better' on their own, they are in charge of their own mind and their own results (2000, p. 1001). Yet it is this deep attachment process over time that has enabled her to explore some deep traumas from her childhood. From within the safety of the attachment relationship with me, we have over time been able to utilise her long meandering stories as metaphors that hold significant meaning for her. For example, she has been able to reframe her own experiences of prejudice and discrimination by utilising political discourse as an alternative perspective. These meanings have become more conscious as she has trusted and shared more of her internal subjective world with me. We have been able to reframe aspects of her experience where she has started to see her dissociative episodes as taking her away from past memories that are triggered as if they were here and now experiences. She has been able to anchor the past memories in the past and stay fully present in the here and now, again using anchoring techniques to keep her in the here and now. We have also experienced ruptures within the relationship where I have inadvertently violated one of her values. She has also tested our relationship with 'acting out' behaviours, for example for a time, she would claim to be confused with a plea that I help her work things out, a behaviour that she observed between her parents that created a shift in their relational dynamic. Throughout these times, I have looked for the positive intention in her behaviour (Dilts & DeLozier, 2000, p. 1002), and recognised that she has been doing the best she could with her available resources (Dilts & DeLozier, 2000, p. 1002). This has enabled her to reflect on these moments of acting out behaviour. Over time, and working very carefully and sensitively, I have encouraged her to wonder at her younger self and what must have been going on for that self that had possibly limited her behavioural options. I have been at times extremely concerned about her mental health and have chosen to adopt the presupposition that she does have all the resources she needs and that she is in charge of her mind and her results (Dilts & DeLozier, 2000, p. 1001).

Her recent presentation, after several years in therapy, is as someone who has developed psychological maturity. She has now learned to channel her 'manic' episodes into the pursuit of specific intellectual interests rather than acting out with risky behaviours. This frequently results in a series of emails to me with her latest thinking e.g., on the use of language in political discourse. My contract with her has been that I will read but not reply to her emails between sessions. We then utilise the pattern of the content of these emails as a reflection of her own state over time. She reports that she can now take a meta perspective on her 'abusers' from the past and see the positive intention behind their behaviour. This highlights Bateson's (1972) theory of schizophrenia (psychosis) being resolved by depth therapy through the NLP lens.

The attachment relationship with me continues and Julia uses this to reflect on elements of 'good enough' (Winnicott, 1971) mothering that she did experience in childhood and through NLP modelling processes (Dilts & DeLozier, 2000, p. 790) uses these to resolve some of current family dynamics.

Anorexia nervosa and orthorexia

Sam came to me as a client from a coach within the NLP world. At 52, Sam had been battling with Anorexia since the age of 9. She had adopted a career choice in health care that gave her an opportunity to focus most of her time and energy on food, nutrition, and weight. Her initial presentation was a very lively, bubbly, and friendly woman. She was of medium build and looked considerably younger than her years.

Sam's history was complex with a parent with an eating disorder, an older sibling with an alcohol problem, and another sibling who was physically and emotionally abusive towards her from a very young age. Neither of Sam's parents was able to deal with the family problems and as Sam entered her teenage years she began to engage with older adolescents who also developed abusive relationships with her. Sam was sexually abused during her teen years by peers and also by adult family friends. She has had very few intimate personal relationships and had been in a controlling marriage for most of her adult life. As Sam matured into adulthood, she developed creative ways of managing her weight and body image. This included orthorexia – an unhealthy and obsessive focus upon healthy eating. Her body image remained poor and she had multiple plastic surgeries.

Sam's awareness of her eating disorder began at 9 years. She reported that her abusive sibling regularly used to call her fat and other body-shaming names. These were often associated with mealtimes and she quickly developed a strategy of not eating with the family or hiding food for later to preempt any name-calling. We used modelling (Dilts & DeLozier, 2000, p. 790,) to understand how she did her anorexia rather than focusing on her diagnosis. The first stage was to map the patterns around food, body image and self-esteem in herself, her parents and her other close family members. This in itself highlighted some clues to her pattern of behaviour, with her recalling her mother's obsession with her own body image from Sam being a young age, and consistent negative body images from her brother at mealtimes. We took this a step further and also mapped her patterns of relating with others and particularly where Sam felt safe. This became a theme that Sam wanted to explore further. We used symbolic modelling (Lawley and Tomkins, 2000) to explore the theme of safety. This process resulted in a significant shift in Sam's self-concept. More traditional forms of therapy for eating disorders would have focused in on the problem state. The NLPt approach is focused more towards the goal and solution states (Wake, 2008, pp. 118–121). By building on Sam's self-concept and a series of resource states, Sam was then able to identify the 'not' solution state. She became very aware that certain relationship patterns in her marriage signalled that she would quickly revert to either binging or excluding certain food groups. I worked with Sam to elicit her strategy (Dilts, 1995) for the doing of the problem. Using strategy redesign principles (Wake, 2010) we worked together to put in place an alternative step within her current strategy that gave her an option to exit.

With Sam having developed a new and more useful strategy and a stronger self – concept, she started to experience aspects of her personality that had hitherto been hidden. She saw these as controlling her or not being her, referring to them specifically as the 'beast', 'toad', 'goblin' and 'the naughty one'. My approach to working with multiplicity has always been to be supportive and inclusive. I am in disagreement with the NLP principle that fewer parts are better than more parts and the notion of a parts integration (Dilts & DeLozier, 2000, pp. 926–927) for clients with psychotic processes. These clients already dissociate in response to trauma, particularly when abuse and control by others are at the root of the problem state. In my experience, trying to integrate these parts using parts integration or six-step reframe can make the parts feel more threatened, resulting in further splitting, with the client developing further dissociative identities. In some instances where a parts integration has been utilised with someone with a pre-existing dissociative identity process in play, I have witnessed this process resulting in an acute psychotic state, necessitating hospitalisation for their own safety. Instead, I encouraged Sam to develop a relationship with these parts that were controlling her and give them voice as suggested by O'Hanlon and Bertolino (1998) and Gilligan (1997). Over time Sam has experienced spontaneous integration of these aspects of her personality sometimes through metaphor.

For example, when I asked her to describe 'toad', she said she could not because he was hidden in a dark wood, under a tree stump that she could not see. She told me that the 'naughty little one' was the only one who knew where the tree stump was, but that 'toad' would not come out if the 'naughty little one' was there. I asked her what the relationship was between 'toad' and the 'naughty little one' was. Her reply was "*there isn't one, it's just that the 'naughty little one' has turned the light off*". I asked her what might happen if she turned the light back on again. Her reply was "*well, she'd just turned it on and 'toad' now knows his way out from under the stump. He just needs me to dig down through the soil and help him come out*". Sam sat with this metaphor for around 15 minutes and I observed in silence as Sam's hands made digging movements. Sam's face gradually changed to a smile and when she opened her eyes, she said she was now holding 'toad' in her hand. She did not refer to him again for some weeks until one day she came into therapy and told me that toad had found a pond one day when she was out running, had hopped out of her pocket into the pond. She had not seen him since, but the aspect he was controlling was no longer a feature in her life. Because the metaphor structurally resolved the needs of the part and its relationship with Sam's larger part, its meaning, as content was immaterial to the process. What is important is that Sam had found a way to relate to an aspect of her psyche that had previously led to problem states and behaviours, and it was no longer a problem to her.

As I worked with Sam over time, we gradually developed a strong therapeutic alliance and Sam was able to explore with me her experiences of safe and not safe. She increasingly began to test the relationship of what she could bring into it without being judged. As we got to around 2 years of working together Sam started to share some profound experiences that she had not shared with anyone else. These were described as shaming events and I assured her that I would remain respectful of Sam's model of the world and encouraged her to be at choice with how she wanted to process these.

Four years on, Sam has now developed a strong self-concept. Her eating disorder has faded into the background. She now allows herself to make mistakes, she challenges and questions her relationships, and particularly the boundaries around them. Sam still experiences an obsessive side to her range of behaviours and has chosen to embrace these and use them for a different career choice. Interestingly this new direction was her preferred career choice as an adolescent that got squashed for being thought of as silly by her parents.

At this time, Sam and I are still working together. Recently we have started to explore our relationship and the bond that we have built over time. Sam is now using this to reflect on what was missing in her own childhood and is starting to explore with her partner their respective attachment styles. She has expressed that she wants to use what she is learning about her relationship to help her develop healthier relationships with other significant people in her life.

Dysthymia I (F 34.1)

Joyce was 32 years old when I first had contact with her. According to her, she had been struggling with a persistent form of chronic mild depression for more than 14 years. Characteristic of her undesirable situation was that she spoke out about her gloomy mood, which filled most of the day. She also indicated that this took place over several days of the week. She said that she often got up with a feeling as if there was a heavy blanket over her and that she could not shake it during the day. Joyce had seen 15 different professional therapists in her life between the ages of 18 and 32 who had done their utmost to alleviate, reduce, or remedy her problem. When her symptoms began, several care providers started working with her. Unfortunately, after making various diagnoses such as anorexia or depression, they were ultimately unable to offer the solution Joyce needed to change her problem situation.

Joyce eventually came to my practice, on the recommendation of a friend who referred her, after she had successfully completed a treatment for eating disorders.

Joyce felt a great need to be able to fully tell her story. From a strict NLP perspective, coaches or NLP therapists are fairly quick to put a stop to this process of going into too much depth. This is rooted in the idea that the structure of a process is more important than the content of a process (Dilts, Grinder, Bandler, & DeLozier, 1980). I have found that there are some things that seem to work well for people who have a problem they want to get rid of: that is that they need to put their problem into words and be heard. A wonderful side effect of listening to a story, contextualised by the therapeutic relationship, is that when someone gives a lot of information, their process becomes clearly visible through their linguistic patterns. Terms like: "I can't do this", and "I don't want this", indicate the fact that someone experiences a situation as permanent instead of temporary. They also reflect that someone is more focused on what they do not want and have little or no insight into what they do want. This seems like a simple observation, perhaps even a language game, but within the field of NLP these are crucial signals about how the thinking patterns are structured, and in turn how they experience the world. By listening to this and getting a picture of the story both in terms of content and process, it becomes easier to make a distinction between the two. This makes it easier later on to become aware of the processes that ultimately cause the symptoms, to understand them, and ultimately transform them. Joyce was also very eager to tell which therapist she had had and how these people had failed to help her. Through her facial expressions and paraverbal cues, she unconsciously indicated that there was enormous significance in the importance of her problem. Several therapists had told Joyce that she suffered from depression, that her problems were caused by sleep problems, and that she had a mild form of anorexia. Joyce has also been told several times that she was resisting the treatments and that she was not really cooperating with her own recovery. It would later turn out that the problem with these earlier therapeutic approaches was that they all reinforced Joyce's problem. Because Joyce had a persistent feeling of not meeting the wishes or demands of others, the therapists had unconsciously and unintentionally contributed to a perpetuation and confirmation of her problem.

From Joyce's story a number of things emerged that together formed a clear picture that was reminiscent of symptoms within a dysthymic disorder. (It should be noted here that NLP therapists do not assume labelling or nominalisation of processes, nor do they attach real value to the labelling as it exists in DSM-5. Rather, they look at psychological or neurological processes that lead to undesirable results.) For the brain, however, the results are very realistic and are perceived by the individual as reality.

In general, dysthymic disorder involves a low mood, loss of interest and pleasure. In addition, there are complaints such as:

- Sadness or feeling of dread, or the inability to feel intense emotion
- Marked decrease in interest in pleasurable activities (also feelings of pleasure are suppressed).
- Changing appetite and marked weight gain or weight loss (this is where the misperception of anorexia can arise).
- Disturbed sleep patterns or insomnia or sleeping more than usual
- Mental and physical fatigue
- Feelings of guilt, failure, not belonging, not being good enough, helplessness, anxiety and/or fear
- Greatly reduced self-esteem
- Persistent Depression

Major events can create a lot of tension. This applies to negative experiences such as divorce, the death of a loved one or loss of work, but also positive events such as the birth of a child or getting a promotion. Tension can also be created by prolonged exposure to negative criticism from key figures in childhood, or prolonged exposure to a narcissistic love partner.

In people who are sensitive to it, a large amount of tension over a longer period of time can lead to dysthymia. Furthermore, a mentally painful event does not have to be recent. For example, a person may not become depressed until adulthood if they have been abused or sexually abused in their youth, Not be confused with PTSD, which is mostly caused by a singular, severe traumatic experience, rather than milder and long-lasting exposure, which may lead to dysthymia.

Another important indicator is social life. People with good friends, a stable relationship and satisfying work are less likely to suffer from depression and recover faster if they do become depressed. People who are not able to solve problems, process grief, or ask for support are more likely to become dysthymic. Lack of self-confidence, perfectionism, fear of failure, and a strict conscience also increase the risk of a dysthymic disorder.

After giving Joyce the opportunity to tell her story, I explained to her that telling her story was only a one-time exposition in the journey I would take with her. We would occasionally come back to specific moments and specific details of the story, without having to retell the story and relive it at some moments. Because Joyce felt heard, she opened herself up to be curious to discover what she previously did not know about her problem, about her own contributions to that problem and the unconscious need to keep re-visiting undesirable situations.

The feedback Joyce gave, after finishing the therapy, is that she liked the fact that she wasn't being judged again, and that she felt like she was talking to someone who understood her without judgment. One of the most important basic structures of an NLP focused approach is that we assume that the client is an expert in creating their own results. The fact that those results may have undesirable consequences does not in any way mean that the underlying process is wrong. As strange as it may sound to some people, from an NLP perspective, we view a symptom as a successful outcome of a well-functioning strategy. That this is experienced as undesirable by the person in question only means that there is motivation and room for change. For the first time in a long time, Joyce heard that she could do something really well and she actually had to laugh because she had never realised that she was successful in creating unwanted situations. That was also the first time in the conversation that I saw Joyce smile. I immediately pointed this out to her, and she indicated that it was one of the first times in months that she laughed out loud.

Now that her story had been told and heard, the actual therapy could begin. Through a combination of focused questions, guided thought processes, and awareness techniques, I invited Joyce to tell her story again, with the difference that I could interrupt her at any time with a question or a comment when I thought it mattered. She could also interrupt the story at any given time, when she would become aware of important information that could help support her improvement.

An important part of an NLP therapeutic session can be to have the client's information divided into small chunks so that each part can be examined for any unconscious information that is often missed in the big story.

Working back from Joyce's symptoms, it emerged that she had an almost permanent sense that she did not matter, and whatever she did always resulted in her not being good enough. Thinking back to an earlier statement by Joyce: "that she had enjoyed it so much that she was not judged again", along with her permanent feeling of not being good enough, gave me a possible entrance to the early origins of her current problems.

Joyce shared that she had felt for a long time that she was somehow not good enough. I asked, "What is very long for you and in what way exactly, not good enough?"

Joyce answered, "As far as I can remember, that goes back to my early childhood". In response, I asked, "How early?"

Joyce said that as a child of 4 she had apparently really enjoyed listening to German lessons on records using headphones. Her father would then question her about the lessons and kick her if she did not give the right answers. It became apparent that listening to the German lessons was not her idea at all but was imposed by her father. Several similar examples followed. This was the start of a process that slowly revealed the story that Joyce saw as her reality. In every image she described, the father was present with assignments that were too demanding for her abilities at that age. When she failed to meet his expectations, he punished her. A pattern of permanent failure in the eyes of one of the most important people in her life was born.

Her father died when she was 16. In a continuing need to gain his approval, she continued to do her best for him. Now, however, he was completely unable to approve of her, so she began to criticise herself instead. This was a completely unconscious process. After Joyce became aware of this story that she had imposed on herself, there was a great emotional release.

Starting from the NLP idea that every experience has a gift that we have not yet unpacked, Joyce came to the decision that her father, from his limited worldview, wanted to provide her with knowledge and an edge in the world. However, the result turned out to be the opposite.

We then discussed the reverse reality structure: we are all raised to believe that what others think of us is about us and what we think of others is about the other. NLP shows through the structural differential, a concept originated by Korzybski (1994), that this is a fallacy. What you think of others is about you. What others think of you is not about you.

This understanding was the basis of a breakthrough that ultimately led to her being able to function optimally on her own behalf, no longer needing the approval or permission of others. She also learned that the criticism of the other person (in this case her father) was about the other person (her father) and not about Joyce. Following this, we did an intervention that gave Joyce the opportunity to use the knowledge and emotions gained here and now to transform how she perceives herself. I invited her to make a mental journey back into her childhood through guided imagery using Ericksonian hypnotic patterns to integrate the new beliefs. By making the child inside her aware that whoever she was and whatever she did was always good enough, she was able to install the new process into her system as an adult as well.

The sessions with Joyce ultimately had a total duration of nine months. This was metaphorically interesting because that is also the time from conception to birth. Joyce and I are still in regular contact. Joyce completed therapy 4 years ago. At the time of this writing, she is married with a daughter and a second on the way. She is happy with her life and will be careful not to pass on her old experiences to her children.

Dysthymia II

Robin came to my practice with a question that he and his wife had, related to a relationship problem. Robin and his wife had been together for ten years and the relationship had suffered quite a few cracks during their marriage. The core of Robin's wife's complaints was that she found him insensitive and emotionally inaccessible. He was often verbally aggressive, sharply sarcastic, and cynical.

I wanted to see Robin individually besides the regular relationship counselling. In couples counselling it is advisable to also speak to both partners individually, this gives both parties the space to speak freely about their own experiences free from judgment by their partner or spouse.

Robin indicated that he did not recognise Melinda's complaints at all and had a whole list of complaints about her. From an NLP perspective, supported by a Socratic model of discourse, it is not desirable to let people talk about each other. I explained to Robin that within this moment it was about his own experience of his problems and his interpretations and perceptions of what was going on. It was logical that Melinda was an incidental subject of the conversation, but I insisted that I would not discuss her personal content with him. That was her story to tell. It soon became apparent that Robin had suffered from depressive feelings over a longer period of time than originally suspected. However, he experienced this as normal, as a part of who he was, and explained that he was not really a sensitive person. When I asked how that came about, he explained that he did not really know that, but couldn't remember a time when it had been any different.

When I asked about his memories, he said that he could not remember them very well and burst into tears. Emotions not related to the present context, often are a way for the subconscious mind to communicate information. As sadness is an emotion of loss, it gave information about how to proceed and in what direction: what is the loss related to, in what way, with what intensity, and when did that occur?

Regarding his feelings of grief, he related them to the death of his father two years before. He quickly recovered and went back into computer mode. With some further questioning, a number of intra-psychological processes came to the surface. According to Robin, he did have internal conflicts, but they were not related to the relationship problem with Melinda. I invited him to tell his story anyway. A therapeutic relationship was thus initiated with Robin. This is the first step in NLP for change work: contact first, contract second.

Robin said that he regularly suffered from chronic fatigue, that he was less effective at work and at home, and that he generally had a rather pessimistic view of life. He preferred to be more socially withdrawn, and has acted like this actually for as long as he could remember. The pattern of ailments gave me reason to identify Robin as someone who falls within a dysthymic disorder pattern. Dysthymia can only be diagnosed post-hoc, after at least two years for adults and one year for adolescents and children. Dysthymia usually starts in early adulthood. The symptoms Robin described fell within the criteria of the DSM-5 for dysthymia. Robin indicated that his ailments went back as far as he could remember. When I asked what it actually was that went so far back in his experience, it quickly emerged that his father, who had died two years earlier of a heart condition, had emphasised to him from about age seven that he (the father) would not grow old and could die at any moment. Robin, then seven years old, was told at least weekly, and sometimes daily by his father that he would die because of his heart condition. After a few months, little Robin, unconsciously, decided not to get attached to a parent who probably was about to die at any moment. The best and therefore, the only way for Robin to respond at that time was to suppress his feelings of love, friendship, affection and connection for his father. This would insulate him from the permanent pain that he anticipated when his father would inevitably die. Robin got remarkably good at this. For thirty-two years he cultivated this strategy and subconsciously shaped it to perfection. He became a star at suppressing feelings and expressing them in surliness, rudeness, verbal aggression, and social withdrawal. These expressions extended to his marriage and also to his children.

At first, when Robin became aware of this information, he didn't want to assume that this could be causally related to his current feelings and behaviour. After long conversations and deepening NLP Meta-Model questions about these processes, he began to develop a sense of guilt about the years in which he exhibited his behaviour and the results it had brought. In NLP we work with the law of requisite variety, that originally states: the larger the variety of actions available to a control system, the larger the variety of perturbations it is able to compensate. NLP adapted the law and states: the system with the most choices has the most possibilities, the system with the most possibilities has the most choice (Ross Ashby's Law of Requisite Variety (Ashby, 1956). The system that holds the most choices and possibilities is in control of the context and unconsciously will always respond from the best choice available within that context. The bottom line of this principle is that a human system always makes the best available choice within a context and that will always be the better choice that provides competitive advantages and more options to thrive causes the least pain. When Robin began to understand this, a mental door opened that gave him the space to explore possible options for making better choices.

As he was given the space to investigate his thought process, and through the artful use of the Metamodel questions, more and more pieces of information surfaced that had previously been subconsciously programmed into his system. The most important message of all that Robin had internalised was: don't attach yourself to a person you love, because they will die anyway. You can imagine how devastating this program can be for relationships. After many question and answer processes, the most important thought process emerged in the form of a lost performative: "Don't get attached to people; they will die anyway". Now, a lost performative language pattern (Grinder & Bandler, 1976) has three elements that need to be examined and resolved:

1 The (lost) performer: who said/did it?
   Robin became aware that his father had a central part in the program that he had been running successfully for thirty-two years.
2 The (lost) standard of performance: what is the rule here? What is the standard is used to judge the behavior?
   The standard by which he learned to look at people was: if you get attached to someone, he/she dies.
3 The (lost) subject: who is this concerning/is being judged.

The subject was Robin and not the other people in his life.

This awareness caused a landslide in his thinking and emotions. He was upset about this for a full week. Now and only now, the needed healing could begin. This was the work of creating new definitions and building new beliefs. Robin discovered that the gift (NLP positive intention) from his father was to protect him from the pain of the impending loss. Not knowing that this could take decades, Robin developed a coping strategy that helped him suppress his emotions. In order to maintain this strategy, he started a permanent pattern of cognitive dissonance, where he equalled 'love' to keeping your distance. Another process that helped perpetuate the situation for years was his acceptance that he would never really get what he needed. He did this by telling himself that the minimal connection with his father was enough for him because it was the best he could expect (a form of secondary gain). With this, he had also unconsciously created a circle of reasoning: if you want to love someone, they will die, therefore it is better to not love someone. Life is apparently designed so that you should not love anyone. Therefore, you can have contact with people but no connection, because if you connect, someone will die.

These were the awakenings that caused the aforementioned mental shift. The healing had begun.

Robin and I developed a healing process in which he first created an outcome frame for himself. In that frame, which he saw himself as he would like to be, as an emotionally mature person, in relationship with himself and others. We went through various processes that contained elements of insights that were developed using NLP patterns. Robin first made a clear picture of what he wanted to experience, do, and be. He was able to discover distinctions in sensory experience (NLP modalities and submodalities) so that a clear contrast analysis was created between the current undesirable situation and the new desired situation.

By exploring different techniques with Mental Rehearsal, Robin envisioned his dreamed future situation and "stepped in" by associating himself, making this future mentally real. We used resource emotions as anchors to give Robin the opportunity to fill the memories of the strongest negative situations he remembered, with uplifting feelings. In NLP, we see successful transformation as an unconscious redefinition (or restructuring) of the perception of the remembered experience.

In the continuing sessions, Robin became quite experienced in associating and dissociating at will, so that he could adjust his internal pictures to his liking. He was now able to add new images to his existing memories. He used the resources that we had identified together so that past-Robin learned to look at the same life-determining situations in a different way, thereby reshaping how he sees the world. After about twenty sessions over a period of 6 months, Robin's depressive moods faded and were eventually non-existent. He said he could not recall having felt so good in his life. It was as if a foggy pair of glasses had been removed. Now it was time to mourn the death of his father, and he could continue to carry on with his life.

After about six months of intensive therapy sessions, Robin's symptoms were resolved in a mild and non-invasive way. His life is more fun, his relationship is emotionally mature, and he sees life a lot sunnier since completing the therapy sessions.

Due to occasional contact, I have monitored Robin for a longer period of time. The changes are stable. Sometimes he says he *still acts like an asshole*, but that is because he's human. Don't we all from time to time?

Summary and future research directions

From the four case studies above, it is clear that both of the therapists have worked intensively within the therapeutic relationship. Literature (Stiles, Barkham, Twigg, Mellor-Clark, & Cooper, 2006) consistently suggests that it is the therapist, not the therapy that makes a difference. This reinforces the studies (Stipancic, Reiner, Schütz, & Dond, 2010; Genser-Medlitsch, & Schütz, 1997, 2004) conducted by EANLPt colleagues. Each of these studies describes a flexible NLP approach to those presenting for general psychotherapy. Yet the NLP field has been able to develop protocolised models such as those utilised for PTSD, psychoneurological and immunological conditions, and phobias.

Following the success of the clinical research studies of the RTM protocol for PTSD, we propose that clinical protocols should be developed and tested for specific complex mental health conditions such as anorexia, building on the eating disorder work of Heemskerk (Chapter 9); depression and anxiety.

References

Ashby, W. R. (1956). *An introduction to cybernetics*. Oxford, England: John Wiley and Sons.

Bandler, R., & Grinder, J. (1975). *The Structure of Magic*. Palo Alto, CA: Science and BehaviorBooks.

Bandler, R., & Grinder, J. (1979). *Frogs into princes*. Moab, UT: Real People Press.

Bateson, G. (1972). *Steps to an ecology of mind: Collected essays in anthropology, psychiatry, evolution and epistemology*. University Of Chicago Press.

Dilts, R. (1995). Strategies of Genius.3, Cupertino, CA:Meta Publications.

Dilts, R., & DeLozier, J. (2000). *Allergy Process*. http://nlpuniversitypress.com/html/AaAj22.html

Dilts, R., Grinder, J., Bandler, R., & DeLozier, J. (1980). *Neuro-linguistic programming: Volume I. The structure of subjective experience*. Cupertino, CA: Meta Publications.

Gawler-Wright, P. (2004). *Intermediate contemporary psychotherapy volume 2*. London: BeeLeaf Publishing.

Gawler-Wright, P. (2007). *Intermediate contemporary psychotherapy. Volume 2*, 2007 Edition. London: Beeleaf Publishing.

Genser-Medlitsch, M., & Schütz, P. (1997, 2004). *Does Neuro-Linguistic psychotherapy have effect? New Results shown in the extramural section*. Martina Genser-Medlitsch; Peter Schütz, ÖTZ-NLP, Wiederhofergasse 4, A-1090, Wien, Austria/Nowiny Psychologiczne Psychological News. issue 1

Grinder, J., & Bandler, R. (1976). *The structure of magic II*. Cupertino, California: Science and Behavior Books.

Gilligan, S. (1997). *The Courage to Love: Principles & Practices of Self-Relations Psychotherapy*. New York: W.W. Norton & Company.

Haley, J. (1993). *Uncommon therapy: The psychiatric techniques of Milton H. Erickson, M.D.* New York: W.W. Norton.

Korzybski, A. (1994). *Science & sanity* (5th ed.). European Society for General Semantics. Retrieved from http://esgs.free.fr/uk/art/sands.htm

Kostere, & Malatesta. (1990). *Maps, models and the structure of reality. NLP technology in psychotherapy*. Portland, Oregon: Metamorphous Press.

Lawley, J., & Tomkins, P. (2000). *Metaphors in mind. Transformation through symbolic modelling*. UK: The Developing Company Press.

McDermott, I., & Jago, W. (2001). *Brief NLP Therapy*. London: Sage.

Neurolinguistic Psychotherapy and Counselling Association. (2021). NLPtCA - Neuro-Linguistic Psychotherapy. Date accessed:16/06/2021

O'Hanlon, B., & Bertolino, B. (1998). *Even from a broken web. Brief, respectful solution-oriented therapy for sexual abuse and trauma*. New York: W.W. Norton & Company.

Schore, A. N. (2003). *Affect regulation and the repair of the self*. London: W.W. Norton.

Stiles, W. B., Barkham, M., Twigg, E., Mellor-Clark, J., & Cooper, M. (2006). Effectiveness of cognitive-behavioural, person-centred and psychodynamic therapies as practiced in UK National Health Service settings. *Psychological Medicine*, 26, 555–556.

Stipancic, M., Reiner, W., Schütz, P., & Dond R. (2010). Effects of neuro-linguistic psychotherapy on psychological difficulties and perceived quality of life. *Counselling and Psychotherapy Research*, 10(1) – Routledge: 39–49.

The European Association of NLPt (EANLPt). (2021). EANLPt - European Association for Neuro-Linguistic Psychotherapy accessed 10/06/21

Wake, L. (2008). *Neurolinguistic psychotherapy: A postmodern perspective*. Routledge.

Wake, L. (2010). *NLP principles in practice*. St. Albans, Hertfordshire, UK: Ecademy Press.

Winnicott, D. (1971). *Transitional objects and transitional phenomena. Playing and reality*. London: Tavistock.

6 Anxiety, depression, and phobias

Dr Lucas Derks and Dr Richard Gray

Introduction

Depression and anxiety are two of the most common categories of psychological maladies. Anxiety disorders and phobias are differentiated in terms of their time focus. Anxiety is an emotional response to some anticipated future event. Phobias represent immediate fearful responses to specific or generalized objects or situations (whether real or imagined) rooted in past experience (DSM-5). DSM-5 describes 8 varieties of depression with more than 100 different subcategories. Anxiety disorders involve about 12 different diagnoses with considerably fewer features.

The current trend in biological psychiatry is toward seeing these disorders as caused by physiological and genetic determinants. That makes a further shift from psychotherapeutic treatments toward pharmacological treatments a logical one.

NLP approaches these disorders, their diagnosis and treatment in a distinctive fashion (see Chapter 4 for a complete analysis). Understanding that there is reciprocal feedback between the immediate biological roots of symptoms and their behavioral expression, NLP looks to the capacity of behavioral interventions to affect the underlying neurological base of the problem. NLP emphasizes the internal imagery (from any or all sensory systems but usually in an integrated manner) that is believed to drive these problems and looks to modify the structure of those images and by so doing, eliminate the symptoms and with them, the disorders.

In this chapter we present two applications of NLP, one to models of depression, and a second, phobias. The first presentation by Derks, is an expansion of the submodality elements of NLP's structural axioms (Derks, 2018). The second, by Gray, outlines reports on NLP-based treatments for phobias in peer-reviewed literature with suggestions for future research.

Derks demonstrates how he has expanded the NLP frame, emphasizing the submodality of location in 3D space to identify a major determinant of depressive disorders. He redefines the classic idea of repression in terms of the presence and structure of dark places in the imaginal 3D space. Within these parameters, he describes an approach to the treatment of depression

DOI: 10.4324/9781003198864-6

with unknown precursors. Derks describes the development of this approach, its fundamental theoretical positioning, how it operates in practice, and the results of his own clinical research into the use of this model in the context of depression.

Gray continues by describing current research into NLP-based treatments for phobias and integrates the emerging clinical evidence of using NLP with phobic reactions. He discusses the imbalance between the large body of research evidence for methods that have partial, short-lasting results (exposure) and the little research done on the less well-established NLP-treatments that seem very reliable and lasting in practice (fast phobia cure). This weaves in with the wider case discussion presented by Derks for the treatment of and diagnosis of depressive disorders.

A brief conclusion provides an overview of how these insights help to point to new directions for NLP in the context of clinical practice and specifically for the context of the treatment of anxiety and depression.

Toward a mental space paradigm of depression

Language versus space

Psychology inherited a strong focus on language from its roots in Philosophy. Some psychologists went as far as equating all thought with inner speech (Sokolov, 1972; Tversky, 2019). From the 1960s onward, social science began to appreciate non-verbal communication, bodily experience, unconscious representations, emotional expression, spatial behavior, states of consciousness, and imagination in all senses. As a result, the NLP community was able to find research support for a host of their practical tools that use these kinds of subjective phenomena (Bolstad, 2002; Gray, 2008/2012, 2011; Gray, Wake, Andreas, & Bolstad, 2013).

Crucial for the development of the mental space paradigm was Bandler's (1985) clinical work with the sub-divisions of sensory experience (light-dark, colored-black and white, hot-cold, far away-close by, moving-still, etc.). He called them "sub-modalities". Reflecting on that work, several authors mentioned the prominent role of the sub-modality of location; that is, where in a sphere of awareness around a person memory images appear (Bandler, 1985; Bandler & MacDonald, 1987; Derks & Hollander, 1996). They also noticed that location is a critical quality for all senses. Although only a few members of the NLP community were aware of the existing academic interest in "location", this recognition helped to link spatial psychotherapy with the growing academic field of "spatial cognition" (Derks, 2016; Tversky, 1991, 1997, 1999, 2009, 2019; Spivey et al., 2010). Spatial cognition builds on a growing realization that cognition is grounded in the capacity, found in all moving creatures, to navigate through their three-dimensional environment. This broad insight funnels into one solid conclusion, which is: the brain is a navigation device (Burgess, 2014; Bellmund, Gärdenfors, Moser, &

Doeller, 2018). In other words, all moving animals create 3-dimensional models of their surroundings, that is, spatial maps (O'Keefe & Nadel, 1978). These navigational skills are essential for organisms to find food, safety, and mates.

This unconscious navigational activity is consistent with a background of spatial thinking of all sorts. Memories appear somewhere in the field of awareness around the person, as do the fantasized projections of future events. Finding the way in a building or city requires spatial maps, the spatial organization of those maps is similar in structure to the way that a person organizes the categories within a field of knowledge or someone creates their hierarchy of values. Even the most abstract logical concepts depend on spatial relations to determine their meaning and importance as these are created by the mind in the space in and around the person (Tversky, 1997, 2020). From there, it follows by logical implication that all manner of conscious and unconscious thought is located/projected somewhere in the space in and around the person (Fauconnier, 1997; Groh, 2014). In the mental space paradigm, this spatial reference structure is understood as the foundation on which even the most complex forms of cognition are built (Lakoff & Johnson, 1999; Gallese, 2015). Three-dimensional cognitive maps help us to orient ourselves in the world and allow us to create abstract mappings of anything. They are essential elements of our capacity to discriminate, recollect, organize, store, and manage all manner of memory (Derks, 2016).

Despite a growing interest in subjective space among cognitive scientists, only a few psychologists with clinical backgrounds have taken notice of the spatial nature of cognition. In the NLP community it surfaces most notably in psychotherapeutic techniques like the *personal timeline* (James & Woodsmall, 1988), and the *social panorama* (Derks, 2005). In both systems, clients are guided to locate and relocate memory images somewhere in the field of awareness that surrounds their bodies. In timeline therapy they are imagined linearly, in Mental Space Psychology they are imagined in a sphere centered around the locus of consciousness. In both, the images – or their affects – may be moved to new locations. Although this moving and shifting of images was clearly described in the *personal timeline* and *social panorama* models, it was also recognized that memories change their positions automatically whenever psychotherapy alters the client's lived experience. Any significant change in cognition necessarily implies some relocation of the relevant concepts in subjective 3D space. For instance, when a client suffers from intimidation by a person they consider to be an authority figure, the image in the social panorama of this authority figure, as if by a law of nature, will be located high up, above eye level, in the field of awareness. The authority will be looking down on the client and the corresponding self-image of the client tends to be smaller than the image of the authority figure. In brief, the image of the authority figure may have a very prominent location high-up in front and close to the client. Any psychotherapeutic intervention that helps to change the client's experience of intimidation toward something better, will be accompanied with the shifting down, and moving away, of the image of the authority figure. A lower, more distant position that is more to the side will necessarily be the major indicator of the change: even if neither the therapist nor the client is aware that this is happening. However, when the therapist is aware of these spatial phenomena, as when using the social panorama, the results will probably come in a predictable manner.

Besides explicit and implicit movements of the problem concepts during therapeutic imagery like imagery, as in the above example with authority, the ability to represent or move cognitions from location to location in subjective space is also essential for structuring psychotherapeutic processes as in spatial anchors; walking over timelines and in the Gestalt hot-seat work; Dilts' pieces of paper as context markers in the Disney Method (Dilts, 1995) and his restructuring beliefs (Dilts, 1993); Satir's family sculptures and constellations, sand play and spatial grids. Together, all of these reveal the crucial role of space in human cognition, emotion, and experience in an unequivocal way (Derks, 2016).

A paradigm shift

Some authors have opined that Neuroscience without reference to its embodiment in a three-dimensional world is no longer tenable (Kelly, 2007; Gallese, 2015). For psychologists to make the move from the currently dominant topological-descriptive, neuro-scientific/linguistic perspective to the mental space paradigm, human behavior must be studied in its relationship to the surrounding space. One needs to see that the brain, as an organ, extends into the empty space and projects its activity there. Without this context, the brain is just a piece of neurological tissue (Graziano, 2018; Derks, 2016; Derks & Wilmsig, 2018). At the same time, one needs to see how language, and in particular the language of spatial relationships, helps to communicate the meanings of concepts and memories from one person to another (Lakoff, 1987; Barsalou, 2012). In the mental space paradigm, as in NLP more generally, the subjective experience of space provides more fundamental data than the language that describes it; it is a primary determinant of meaning.

Subjects (in psychological experiments) can usually tell nothing about what is going on in their brains, but they can explain rather clearly WHERE something is experienced in the imaginary space around them. The emerging research paradigm in mental space psychology tends to use questions like: *Point out where you notice your favorite food? Point out where you sense your loved one? Where is your trauma located? Where is grammar school in your memory?*

Perception and memory need to be understood as inseparable. Indeed, the brain processes both raw perception and the sensory images associated with memories in nearly the same manner (Kiverstein, & Gangopadhyay, 2009).

From the Buddhist perspective, and from the perspective of modern neuroscience all of our experiences are records of past events.

When we first perceive an object or event, our immediate experience reflects it in the same spatial relationship to other elements of the percept as we encountered it in the environment (James, 1890). After processing, however, it will typically assume a position in subjective 3-dimensional space that accords with its content and its valence. Its post-processing subjective position is determined by its meaning to the percipient (Derks, 2002, 2016).

The locations of memory images projected into subjective 3-D space can be easily pointed out by anyone. When we imagine that our conscious experience is a central point in the middle of our heads and that this point is centered within a sphere upon which is projected memory images, we may then ask any client: *Where is your trauma located*? Or even as we will see: *Where is your depression located?*

The next step on the way to the mental space paradigm is the understanding that the mind is capable of transforming and morphing (e.g., moving, relocating, rotating, coloring, abstracting, and generalizing, scaling up and down, etc.) all mental content in all sensory modalities, simply by the power of intentionality. In other words, the mind can voluntarily reach out to a concept or percept and change its subjective representation.

Tversky (2019) came to equate "thinking" with the movement of concepts in mental space. It is suspected that this process is preceded by inner speech (I want it bigger) or suggestions made by someone else (make it more important), however, this may be only in a minority of instances (Mckellar, 1957). The movement of concepts and their relocation in subjective space may be seen as the core of cognitive processes like composing, designing, schematizing, and of reasoning when combined with inner speech (Bandler, 1985; Tversky, 2019).

The full mental space paradigm also depends upon the very basic recognition that organisms strive to create stable (fixed, solid, sturdy, inflexible) maps of their worlds. However, to keep sufficient grips on the world, the dynamic nature of reality forces the creature to update its maps regularly. The updating of older, more rigid 3-D maps that reflect earlier experiences and expectations requires the movement and relocation of their components. Thus, just as in psychological problem solving and psychotherapy, thinking generally requires the shifting, rearranging, and morphing of the "frozen" maps that we have already created. This last view parallels the philosophies of Peirce (1982), Korzybski (2010) and Buddha (in the Abidhamma Pitaka, see Bodhi, 1995). Grinder & Bandler (1976) point to inflexibility as a major problem in mental health. Preferred representational systems become liabilities when they limit the mind's ability to perform flexibly in other sensory systems. Old answers appropriate to other ages and other contexts become pathologies when we find ourselves unable to adjust them. Just so, our spatial maps, and the worlds they define, require appropriate and timely adjustment.

The mental space paradigm prioritizes location/space over the other aspects of experience. In NLP terms location is identified as the most influential sub-modality. This has also pragmatic grounds. It is an efficient, simplified focus for researchers and therapists alike. But one should remember that there exist cognitive processes in which other sensory qualities than location stand out. Bandler's (1985) concepts of "driving sub-modalities" and "critical sub-modalities" include the possibility that color, size, brightness, etc., can overrule the emotional impact of location. Beside the top rank given to the sub-modality location, one should realize that the distinct sensory qualities as experienced in our imagination (with eyes closed) like temperature, size, color, distance, etc., function as one interacting system. A shift in location may automatically also shift color, size, and brightness, and vice versa.

A new presupposition for NLP

NLP was built upon a strong pragmatism that is reflected most notably in the NLP presuppositions.

In light of the above considerations, we propose the following new presupposition for NLP: *Space is the primary organizing principle in subjective* experience.

This means:

1. each person's *model(s) of the world* is represented in a 3-D manner in the space in and around the person (O'Keefe & Nadel, 1978; Thomas & Tsai, 2011)
2. loci in subjective space code for content including category (simple category as kind of thing, emotional category as trusted, untrusted, safe, dangerous, etc.), valence, and salience (both present and historical)
3. loci in subjective space exist in a reciprocal relationship with the sub-modality features of the percept – i.e., changes in the structure of the percept change its location in subjective space, changes in subjective space, change the percept's sub-modality structure
4. language is secondary to structure and as such, cognitive-linguistic interventions are often insufficient for the restructuring of personal, spatial maps
5. experience, as encoded in our 3-D maps requires a new spatial vocabulary *and grammar* (Lakoff, 1987).

Depression in mental space

Zones of darkness

While applying the mental space paradigm to clients with depressive symptoms, mental space-informed therapists have observed that clients reported zones of darkness, that is, spaces where the content was dimmed or darkened to such an extent that the content of the memory was unavailable or difficult to ascertain (Derks, 2016; Beenhakker & Manea, 2017). In hindsight these same therapists observed gestures, postures, and eye movements that indicated the position of these darkened locations in mental space. When clients were asked to point to these darkened areas in the subjective space around them, they could do that swiftly, confirming their previous unconscious indicators.

It is typical for the NLP tradition to explore such descriptions as being literal (not metaphorical) components of inner sensory experience. Clients had always given clear signals when describing their misery by using words like black, dark, shady, misty, somber, and gloomy. The variety in the shapes of *zones of darkness* – their size, opacity, and locations – was quite wide. Many clients described their *zones of darkness* (Beenhakker & Manea, 2017) as all manner of black and heavy things like rocks, burdens, walls, clouds, or animals like "black dogs" (remember Churchill's Black Dog). Most researchers and therapists, therefore, saw this darkness as metaphorical rather than a literal description of subjective experience. The NLP-trained therapist may assume that when a client speaks about "dark" that there will be some "really" dark subjective elements. When the therapist is informed with the spatial paradigm, they may ask the client: "Where exactly do you sense this darkness?"

Mental Space therapists have observed the following primary patterns in the zones of darkness:

1. The zones of darkness tend to be outside of the center of attention (thus not straight in front of the clients' eyes)
2. The darkness appears without clear edges, cloudlike
3. The zones of darkness reduce the clarity, brightness, and coloring of that image
4. The zones of darkness function like a sort of gray filter over parts of the field of experience
5. When treated, the darkness over the memory content is reduced proportionally with the reduction of symptom intensity.

These patterns made the link between depression and the zones of darkness a compelling hypothesis (Derks, 2016: Beenhakker & Manea, 2017).

Repression

For NLP therapists, the logical approach to disturbing zones of darkness would be to adjust their sub-modality structure. This might entail suggesting to the client that they make these zones lighter or let them move away, shrink, or entirely disappear. Any attempt to change the structure of the memory by direct manipulation of its sub-modality structure, inevitably entails exposing the client to the sudden and often unwanted experience of re-emerging memory-content. This violates the supposed positive intent of the zone itself and makes the task more difficult. This traumatic re-emergence of the blocked content was so frequently observed that the value of the zones of darkness was reassessed in terms of the client's world-maps and safety concerns.

"Blocking out" describes the intentional forgetting of certain mental contents to exclude it from awareness and thereby reducing its negative emotional impact. In psychoanalysis this was called *repression* (Freud, 1914; Singer, 1990). In neuroscience researchers may speak of *dissociative amnesia*, a process associated with the inhibitory actions of the prefrontal cortex and the anterior cingulate gyrus (Kikuchi et al., 2010). In other words, when the person cannot cope with certain life-issues, they may try to stop thinking about them.

A later analysis of therapy sessions with depressed clients supported the hypothesis that the zones of darkness reflected the active repression of difficult or traumatizing life issues. However, since these very difficult issues were blocked out of awareness clients often did not mention them during anamnesis (Freud, 1914; Brown & Van der Hart, 1998; Singer, 1990; Derks, 2016; Beenhakker & Manea, 2017). Clients seemed to remain unaware of these issues until they were uncovered, for instance by imagining sunlight shining on the darkness and by moving the zones of darkness toward the center of attention. These suggestions help to "melt" the zones of darkness and make them transparent. With the zones of darkness reduced in size and density it was easy to bring the hidden issues to awareness by asking: "What was the zone of darkness hiding?".

A logical next step for NLP-trained therapists was to treat these *uncovered* issues with classical NLP-techniques *(Change personal history, new behavior generator, or reimprinting)*. Therapeutic progress, in the sense of the client showing a positive change in mood, appeared to correlate with a reduction in the density and size of the zones of darkness. This led to the observation, that *zones of darkness* occurred when clients were depressed and did not know why, and that these zones faded after the hidden issues were resolved (Derks, 2016; Beenhakker & Manea, 2017).

New diagnostic category of depression

In Chapter 4 we addressed the problem of diagnosis and how NLP-trained therapists approach psychological problems and change in terms of sensory structure and how that structure maintains the problem in present experience. Here we suggest a new diagnostic category for depressions characterized by the masking of the associated content locations in subjective 3-D space. These zones of darkness render their content unavailable to conscious access.

From the above we may abstract the symptoms of *depression with an unknown cause*. In these cases a dark veil interferes with access to the underlying issues. The same darkness dampens the luminosity of experience like a gray filter. Repression taxes the capacity of the fronto-cortical inhibitory system that is also needed for concentration and learning (Singer, 1990; Kikuchi et al., 2010). When these inhibitory frontal faculties are exhausted the affected systems produce symptoms of tiredness, tension, and heaviness. Their overuse leads to impaired concentration, sleep issues, reduced short-term memory, bad mood, and agitation (Bogousslavsky & Cummings, 2000). Secondary symptoms like overeating, impulsive behaviors, and suicidal thoughts, often result from the client's desire to escape toward better feelings.

A clinical test of treating depression in mental space

In 2017 we began an experiment to test the theory of zones of darkness and whether psychotherapists in private practice could make use of the spatial diagnostics, and the implied therapeutic interventions. We treated 47 clients who were regular patients visiting private practices for the treatment of depression. Participants were assigned in a pseudo-random manner to treatment and waitlist control groups (Derks et al., 2020).

There were *47 participants, 34 women and 13 men, varying in age between 16 and 71 years.* The immediate treatment group consisted of 27 persons, 18 female and 9 males ranging in age from 18 to 71. The duration of their depressive complaints varied from 4 months to 35 years. Twenty persons were assigned to the waiting list control group: 16 female and 4 male participants ranging in age from 19 to 68. The duration of the depressive complaints varied from 2 months to 40 years.

We required that participants were not currently receiving other treatments for depression. We used the Beck Depression Inventory (BDI) to measure depression. The standard interpretation of the BDI is as follows:

0–9: no or minimally depressed
0–14: marginally
15–20: light
21–30: moderate
31–40 severely depressed.

Persons with extremely high and low scores on the BDI, below 10 and above 30, were originally appointed to be excluded, however, for ethical and practical reasons all clients were taken into treatment. Therapists were asked to not to look at the completed BDIs before treatment, but this was difficult to control in the context of private practice.

At intake therapists collected client demographics including gender, age, the duration of the depressive complaints, and explained the steps of the therapeutic process. They administered a 10-point self-report Likert-style semantic differential scale that recorded the participants' subjective levels of depression. All clients completed the 21-item Dutch BDI. Therapists also sketched the location and size of the areas of darkness in a printed, step-by-step protocol (not provided here; Derks et al., 2020) before and after the interventions.

Each therapist treated 4 clients. Two, the first and third, were to be treated immediately and two others, the second and fourth, were assigned to a 30-day waiting list and would receive the same treatment after the 30 days had expired. All clients returned 30 days after treatment (±2 days) for post testing. One person dropped out of the treatment group and 2 from the control arm.

The ten-point semantic differential scale in the treatment group ($N = 27$) yielded a mean pre-treatment depression score of **5.74** (±1.868; *se 0*.359). At 30 days post, the score was **4.20** (±2.03; *se 0*.391). The individual scores showed a positive paired sample correlation of .628. A dependent samples t-test showed a $t = 4{,}735$, $p < .00005$ at a confidence level of 95%. An effect size calculation yielded a pre–post Hedge's g = 0.56 (95% CI [0.01−1.10]). Conclusion: there was a moderate but **significant relief in symptoms** after the treatment after 30 days.

The ten-point semantic differential scale measures for the waiting list group ($n = 20$) *yielded a* mean depression score at intake of **5.50** (±2.194; se .491). After the 30 day wait period, without treatment, the score was **5.30** (±2.029; *se 0*.454). The individual scores showed a positive paired sample correlation of .833. A dependent samples t-test showed a $t = 0{,}728$, $p < .05$ at a confidence level of 95%. An effect size calculation yielded a pre- post-wait Hedge's g = 0.09 (95% CI [−0.53–0.71]). Conclusion, there was **no significant relief in symptoms** after waiting without treatment for 30 days.

For the immediate treatment group ($N = 27$) the mean pre-treatment BDI score **21.96** (±8.716; *se* 1.677) compared to a mean post treatment level after 30 days of **15.04** (±10.204; *se* 1.964). The individual score showed a positive paired sample correlation of .791. A dependent samples t-test showed a $t = 5{,}735$, $p < .000005$ at a confidence level of 95%. An effect size calculation yielded a pre--post Hedge's g = 0.72 (95% CI [0.16–1.27]). Conclusion, there was a **significant relief in symptoms** after the treatment after 30 days.

For the waiting list group ($n = 20$) the mean pre-treatment score for the level of depression was **22.15** (±8.331; *se* 1.863) and after the untreated 30-day wait-period, **18.95** (±8.703; *se* 1.946). The individual score showed a 7positive paired sample correlation of .812. A dependent samples t-test showed a $t = 2.732$, $p < .05$ at a confidence level of 95%. An effect size calculation yielded a pre—post-wait Hedge's g = 0.37 (95% CI [−0.26–0.99]). Conclusion, there was a moderate but **significant relief in symptoms** after waiting for 30 days without treatment. This was attributed to a **placebo or expectancy effect** (spontaneous remission).

The semantic differential scale for the immediate post wait and 30-day post-treatment measures were as follows. The mean post waiting score ($N = 18$: 2 dropped out) was **5.00** (±2.390; se .845) compared to a mean post-treatment level after 30 days of **3.44** (±2.259; *se* .799). The scores showed a positive paired sample correlation of .291. A dependent samples *t*-test showed a $t = 1.563$, $p < .05$ at a confidence level of 95%. An effect size calculation yielded a post-wait – post-treatment Hedge's g = 0.66 (95% CI [−0.01–1.33]). Conclusion, there was a **significant relief in symptoms** after the treatment after 30 days.

The BDI for the immediate post wait and 30-day post-treatment measures were as follows. The mean post-wait BDI score ($n = 18$: 2 dropped out) was **18.78** (±9.143; *se* 2.155) compared to a mean post-treatment level of **12.17** (±9.147; *se* 2.156). A dependent samples *t*-test showed a $t = 3.313$, $p < .05$ at a confidence level of 95%. An effect size calculation yielded a pre--post Hedge's g = 0.71 (95% CI [0.03−1.38]). Conclusion, there was **a significant relief in symptoms**.

Our primary finding was that the method of treating *depression in awareness space* was technically demanding by itself but even more so in the constrained environment of a clinical trial. However well-trained and experienced therapists could accomplish a significant number of successful treatments with this approach. This study supported what was already anecdotally reported in the practical application of the method for several years in clinical practice.

Other researchers are invited to explore the clinical utility of mental space diagnosis, especially as it describes the relationship between perceived zones of darkness in subjective 3D space, and depression. A large-scale clinical trial to further assess the evidence for the effectiveness of depression through awareness space needs an academic environment for completion.

A design for the experimental evaluation of the Visual Kinesthetic Dissociation Protocol (V/K-D)

DSM 5 classes phobias as anxiety disorders. Phobias, and fear itself, are related to present-time threats, whether real or imagined. Anxiety, on the other hand, refers to the anticipation of future threats, real or imagined. Social anxiety disorder, panic disorder, agoraphobia, and generalized anxiety disorders are also listed under the rubric (American Psychiatric Association, 2013).

Specific Phobias are characterized by unreasonable or excessive persistent fear triggered by a specific object or situation. They are characterized by immediate, involuntary, and disproportional responses to the phobic stimulus. The feared object or situation is avoided at all costs. If the feared object is encountered it causes great distress. Phobias and fear responses generally, imply flight or movement (Alcaro, Carta, & Panksepp, 2017; Ohman & Mineka, 2001). Phobias may interfere with the patient's work, education, or family life. DSM5 reports that 75% of phobics fear more than one object and may include three or more objects or situations.

Incidence and prevalence

Wardenaar et al. (2017) reported cross-national lifetime and 12-month prevalence rates for specific phobias of 7.4 and 5.5%, respectively. The prevalence is higher in females than in males. The median age of onset is 8 years but decreases after age 60. Among patients reporting any phobia in the last 12 months, 18.7% reported significant role impairment. Of those, 23.1% sought treatment. More patients from higher-income countries seek treatment than those from lower-income countries.

The lifetime comorbidity for any specific phobia is 60.2%. In 72% of phobics, phobia symptoms begin before the co-occurring diagnosis. Specific phobias predict a higher occurrence of depression, anxiety, and eating disorders, but they are not associated with substance use disorders. Most persons diagnosed with specific phobias have more than one subtype. Multiple co-occurring subtypes are associated with more impairment, comorbidity, and increased treatment-seeking (Wardenaar et al., 2017).

Among specific phobias, animal fears (spiders, snakes, dogs) are the most common with a lifetime prevalence of 3.8%. They are followed by blood injury and medical phobias (needles, the sight of blood) at 3.0%, fear of heights at 2.8%, still water and weather phobias at 2.5%, and fear of flying at .6 to 1.6%. Fear of flying occurs mostly in high-income countries (Wardenaar et al., 2017).

Front-line treatments

There is a near-universal consensus that in-vivo exposure is the treatment of choice for specific phobia (Craske, Hermans, & Vervliet, 2018; Lebois, Seligowski, Wolff, Hill, & Ressler, 2019; Thng, Lim-Ashworth, Poh, & Lim, 2020; Wechsler, Kümpers, & Mühlberger, 2019; Wolitzky-Taylor, Horowitz, Powers, & Telch, 2008). Imaginal exposure, systematic desensitization, Cognitive Behavior Therapy, and Eye Movement Desensitization and Reprocessing are also used to lesser effect (Thng et al., 2020).

Wolitzky-Taylor et al. (2008) report that exposure techniques result in initial symptom reductions of 70% to 85%. Lebois et al. (2019) report that imaginal or interoceptive exposure is best for panic disorder, with in-vivo best for Social Anxiety Disorder. According to Wechsler and colleagues (2019) for specific phobias, in vivo exposure is slightly better than other exposure-based treatments. Observed differences for virtual and in-vivo exposure for the treatment of agoraphobia and social phobia were non-significant. Suso-Ribera et al. (2019) report that although in-vivo exposure is best for animal phobias, virtual reality has a lower refusal rate.

Craske and colleagues (2014), reviewing behavioral treatments for phobias indicate that the reduction of fear in session does not predict reduced fear levels either for the patient's next visit or for long-term outcomes. These authors report that 27% of patients treated with exposure-based interventions who were panic-free immediately post-treatment returned for more treatments. They also report (Craske et al., 2014; Craske et al., 2018) substantial treatment failure and return of fear post-treatment. Only about 5% of those treated achieve normal functioning after 10 to 20 treatments. Fear returns in 19% to 62% of persons treated with exposure-based techniques. Wolitzky-Taylor et al. (2008) report that exposure techniques result in initial symptom reductions of 70% to 85%.

These observations suggest that although exposure is the intervention of choice, it is far from perfect. The literature repeatedly echoes that the hallmarks of extinction haunt all manner of extinction-based protocols. Extinction models are characterized by four specific effects that drive relapse, these are spontaneous recovery, contextual renewal, reinstatement, and rapid reacquisition (Craske et al., 2014; Craske et al., 2018; Lebois et al., 2019).

NLP-based interventions

As early as 1979 Bandler and Grinder (Bandler & Grinder, 1979) suggested that the most popular treatments, including exposure, (flooding, emotional extinction) and reciprocal inhibition, often failed to achieve lasting results and all require many treatment sessions. As noted above this has not changed (Craske et al., 2014; Craske et al., 2018; Wolitzky-Taylor et al., 2008).

NLP has produced several interventions that have been effective for the treatment of Phobias. These include, most notably collapsing anchors/counterconditioning; the six-step reframe; Core Transformation; and the Visual/Kinesthetic Dissociation protocol (V/K-D; Gray & Bolstad, 2013). Unfortunately, and as noted elsewhere (Please see Chapters 2 and 10, this volume), NLPers have been notoriously resistant to empirical evaluation, claiming that client satisfaction was a sufficient index of success, and that the predominance of variable patterns in NLP made statistical inference impossible (Bandler & Grinder, 1975, 1979; Dilts, Grinder, Bandler, & DeLozier, 1980; Grinder & Pucelik, 2013). It should also be noted that the academic world has been unsympathetic to NLP, its founders, and its continuing validity as an approach to psychological phenomena (Heap, 1988; Witkowski, 2010; Wikipedia, 2021).

The most significant NLP application for the treatment of phobias is the NLP Fast Phobia Cure, also known as the Visual/Kinesthetic Dissociation Protocol (V/K-D). The procedure was originated by Bandler and first appeared in *Using Your Brain for a Change* (1985). An expanded version of the procedure appeared in Andreas and Andreas' *Heart of the Mind* (1989), while Dilts and DeLozier (2000) provided another version.

Bandler (1985) reported that he had interviewed persons who had recovered from phobias. He found that all of them had learned to create dissociated images of the phobic stimulus, and so were freed of their fear. In response he created the V/K-D. This, he claimed, could deliver lasting results within the span of a single session. However often this result may have been realized in clinical practice, and however convinced NLP-therapists may have been about its superior efficacy and efficiency, these results were never established in the peer-reviewed literature. The claimed speed of the intervention has also been the target of criticism (Wikipedia, 2021)

Neurological considerations

There is evidence to suggest that

1. phobias are, to a certain extent, prepotent regarding certain classes of biological and environmental stimuli. This implies that they are more easily learned than other associations (Ohman & Mineka, 2001), and that these experiences are initially associated with specific contexts where the stimuli are most likely to occur (Ohman & Mineka, 2001)
2. the experiences have often been reinforced in multiple contexts and have generalized sufficiently to present themselves as present time emergent dangers in multiple contexts
3. those fears are maintained through the process of reconsolidation as the fearful memory is renewed with every phobic response (Agren, 2014; Fernández, Bavassi, Forcato, & Pedreira, 2016; Lee, 2009; Schiller & Phelps, 2011; Schiller, Kanen, LeDoux, Monfils, & Phelps 2013)
4. phobias are largely problems of stimulus salience; their negative aspects are accorded overwhelming and unwarranted importance (Lebois et al., 2019).

Reliance on the extinction mechanism, as noted, carries with it the caveat that extinction is a temporary fix. Its predictable decay is a continuing liability and appears throughout the literature (Craske et al., 2014; Craske et al., 2018; Wolitzky-Taylor, Horowitz, Powers, & Telch, 2008). As a result we underscore the importance of reconsolidation-based approaches.

In reconsolidation, after an activation of the fearful response that is too brief to support either extinction or retraumatization, the target memory is believed to become malleable and new information, relevant to the perceived threat, can be incorporated into its structure (Fernández et al., 2016; Suzuki et al., 2004; Tylee, Gray, Glatt, & Bourke, 2017). We hypothesize that reconsolidation may be used to change structural elements of the memory related to its perceptual salience and, by reducing the impact of the memory, render it non-traumatizing (Tylee et al., 2017).

Research into the treatment of phobias has confirmed the efficacy of reconsolidation-based interventions. Although the effect sizes are often moderate they have drawn the attention of the field. Recent studies have used both pharmacological and behavioral interventions to prevent reconsolidation of the fear response (for a review see Walsh, Das, Saladin, & Kamboj, 2018). We believe that the V/K-D provides a more effective alternative.

The literature on reconsolidation has exploded during the last 20 years and the body of RTM research has expanded significantly. A recent search for "reconsolidation" on Science Direct returned more than 3500 references.

Previous reports hypothesize that the RTM protocol relies upon the reconsolidation mechanism (Gray, Budden-Potts, Schwall, & Bourke, 2020; Gray & Liotta, 2012; Tylee et al., 2017; and Chapter 3, above). Although lacking in direct empirical evidence, that attribution was made based upon strong parallels in the syntax, timing, and results of the intervention as compared with observations of the neurological mechanism. Elements leading to the identification included:

1. a presentation of the triggering stimulus (whether the conditioned trigger or a narrative of the problem itself) that is too brief to support extinction or re-traumatization
2. interruption of the subjective response to the evoking stimulus
3. a brief waiting period during which non-problem-related programming may occur
4. the introduction of new information about the nature of the triggering stimulus
5. the passage of 24 hours
6. behavioral testing.

Insofar as RTM is based upon V/K-D (see Chapter 4 for the process), we suggest that that intervention also depends upon memory reconsolidation.

NLP research

A review of online databases including PsycInfo, Science Direct, and Medline using the search terms "NLP AND phobia", "Phobia AND Bandler", "Dissociation AND Phobia", and "fast phobia" from 2013 (just after the publication of Wake, Gray, & Bourke, 2013) to the present found no new records reported for the V/K-D.

Although it did not appear in the literature searches, there was one published study, Arroll et al. (2017), "A brief treatment for fear of heights". These authors reported (Arroll & Henwood, 2017) that academic publishers were so reluctant to handle anything related to NLP, that they felt compelled to strip any mention of NLP from the title before a reputable journal would publish it.

Arroll and colleagues completed the first RCT of the Visual/Kinesthetic Dissociation Protocol to be published in a major Medical Journal. The study used a convenience sample of 106 medical patients who scored above 29 on the Heights Interpretation Questionnaire (HIQ; Steinman & Teachman, 2011), a self-report inventory. The survey and treatment were provided during regular visits to participating physicians in Auckland, New Zealand. Patients were randomly assigned to either a single session of scripted V/K-D or a 15-minute meditation. Randomization and study condition were not revealed to subjects. Eight-weeks post-treatment, subjects were reassessed and the proportion of those scoring below 26 on the HIQ (the presumptive cutoff for a diagnosis of acrophobia) was determined.

Ninety-eight persons (92%) responded and were included in an intent to treat (ITT) analysis. Eighteen of 52 persons in the intervention group scored below 26 (34.6%) while 7 of 46 control participants (15.2%) scored below cutoff. This led to a Risk Ratio of 2.26 (95% CI [1.05, 4.95]; $p = .028$). HIQ score differences were non-significant at eight weeks. Successful participants reported improvement in their fear of heights.

Future research

While the current lack of published, peer-reviewed evaluations of V/K-D is apparent, we strongly encourage members of the research community to begin working to fill this lack. This new research would require several steps beginning with standardization of the protocol.

Gray and Bolstad (2013) reported that many of the published studies purporting to examine the V/K-D tested an ad hoc method, only loosely related to the protocol under consideration. V/K-D when standardized should reliably produce results consistent with reconsolidation. These are fast, relatively permanent changes to the phobic memory that reduce its perceived importance (salience) and with that, reduce its capacity to evoke the phobic reaction.

For some NLP practitioners standardization represents a problem. NLP is a strongly humanistic and person-centered endeavor. As such the ability to customize treatments to the client is a highly valued trait of the system. This is a point made by Arroll and Henwood (2017) in their narrative of how they came to grips with the need to supply a scripted intervention for the creation of a randomized controlled study.

NLP solves this problem with the understanding that even in scripted interventions, each client supplies highly personal data making the intervention uniquely their own (Gray, 2008/2013). The scripts allow for the systematic exploration of the process in a replicable manner. In the V/K-D script the client begins with their own experience of the phobic target. They create a unique, imaginal movie theater with details from personal experience. Modifications to the structure of the movie, its distance, size, speed, etc., are all subjectively determined by the patient and are chosen and modified based on the client's intuition as to what kinds of changes would be most useful. Thus the scripted protocol becomes highly individualized.

There is also a need for the field of NLP to frame its investigations in terms of standard psychological concepts, such as reconsolidation. Many of the classic and current NLP texts are un-referenced, and when referenced, frame their discussion in 20- to 30-year-old concepts. Part of the job of serious NLP investigators is to match their reality with the language of standard psychology.

Finally this will also require a willingness by NLP researchers to accept a standard theoretical base as suggested by Tosey and Mathison (2008) and others (infra, Chapters 2 and 10). NLP exponents have resisted such formalization despite its tacit embrace in the presuppositions and structural analysis (modeling) that form an acknowledged base for NLP and the applications that flow from it (Grinder & Bandler, 1976; Dilts et al., 1980; Dilts & DeLozier, 2000; Grinder and Pucelik, 2013).

Summary

In this chapter we have looked at the identification and treatment of depression and phobias from seemingly disparate perspectives. Together, however, they illustrate the systemic perspective of NLP and its capacity to meet the patient's problem at multiple possible levels of integration.

Derks provided a refinement of submodality structure, focusing on depression from unknown causes and a more general need for a 3-dimensional appreciation of imaginal space. His analysis points us toward the spatial dimension that codes for content and valence. Here, he provides an operational definition of the classical Freudian concept of repressed content as darkened spaces in subjective 3-D space. These spaces are positively identified with the felt reality of the underlying trauma even though declarative memory of the specific trauma is not normally accessible to consciousness in these cases. He outlines the process of discovering these darkened regions of subjective space and points to how to work with them so that their intensity is decreased, and the underlying traumas can be dealt with.

Gray describes the classic NLP V/K-D intervention and interprets its mechanism in terms of the reconsolidation of long-term memories as applied to the transformation of the salience, the importance, of the phobic stimulus. He outlines a program for a systematic approach to its study. Like Derks, he focuses upon the structure of the experience on a subjective level.

Interestingly both approaches incorporate the idea of place. For Derks, place appears as the submodality of the location of content. Gray finds place in the V/K-D protocol as one of the submodality dimensions that can redefine the meaning of phobic stimuli and whose transformation is diagnostic of treatment success. In general, both approaches also point us to our internal self-relationships as space opens to the resources and structures that are situationally necessary in our personal maps of the world. We also note that both hold forth the possibility of transforming space, by generalizing across narrower contexts to extend learnings by abduction to more generalized place responses.

References

Agren, T. (2014). Human reconsolidation: A reactivation and update. *Brain Research Bulletin*, 105, 70–82. doi:10.1016/j.brainresbull.2013.12.010

Alcaro, A., Carta, S., & Panksepp, J. (2017). The affective core of the self: A neuro archetypical perspective on the foundations of human (and animal) subjectivity. *Frontiers in Psychology*, 8. doi:10.3389/fpsyg.2017.01424

American Psychiatric Association (2013). Diagnostic and statistical manual of mental disorders, (5th ed.).

Arroll, B., & Henwood, S. M. (2017). NLP research, equipoise and reviewer prejudice. *Rapport*, 54, 24–26.

Arroll, B., Henwood, S. M., Sundram, F. I., Kingsford, D. W., Mount, V., Humm, S. P., Wallace, H. B., & Pillai, A. (2017). A brief treatment for fear of heights: A randomized controlled trial of a novel imaginal intervention. *The International Journal of Psychiatry in Medicine*, 52(1), 21–33. doi:10.1177/0091217417703285

Bandler, R. (1985). *Using your brain for a change*. Moab, UT: Real People Press.

Bandler, R., Delozier, J., & Grinder, J. (1975). *Patterns in the hypnotic techniques of Milton H. Erickson, MD (Vol. 1)*. Capitola, CA: Meta Publications.

Bandler, R. , & Grinder, J. (1979). *Frogs into princes*. Moab, UT: Real People Press.

Bandler, R., & MacDonald, W. (1987). *An insider's guide to submodalities*. Moab, UT: Real People Press.

Barsalou, L. W. (2012). The human conceptual system. In: M. Spivey, K. McRae, & M. Joanisse (eds.). *The Cambridge handbook of psycholinguistics* (pp. 239–258). New York: Cambridge University Press.

Beenhakker, C., & Manea, A. I. (2017). Dark matter: mental space and depression – a pilot investigation of an experimental psychotherapeutic method based on mental space psychology to reduce the distress of moderate depression. *Journal of Experiential Psychotherapy*, 20, 21–26.

Bellmund, J. L. S., Gärdenfors, P., Moser, E. I., & Doeller, C. F. (2018). Navigating cognition: Spatial codes for human thinking. *Science*, 362.

Bodhi, Bhikku (1995). *A comprehensive manual of Abhidhamma: The Abhidhammattha Sangaha of Acariya Anuruddha*. Kandy, Sri Lanka: Buddhist Publication Society.

Bogousslavsky, J., & Cummings, J. J. (2000). *Behavior and mood disorders in focal brain lesions*. Cambridge University Press, 2000–2554.

Bolstad, R. (2002). *Resolve: A new model of therapy*. Carmarthen, UK: Crown House Publishing.

Brown, P., & Van der Hart, O. (1998). Memories of sexual abuse: Janet's critique of Freud, a balanced approach. *Psychological Reports*, 1998(82), 1027–1043.

Burgess, N. (2014). *The 2014 nobel prize in physiology or medicine: A spatial model for cognitive neuroscience*. Institute of Cognitive Neuroscience and Institute of Neurology, University College London.

Craske, M. G., Hermans, D., & Vervliet, B. (2018). State-of-the-art and future directions for extinction as a translational model for fear and anxiety. *Philosophical Transactions of the Royal Society, London, B, Biological Science*, 373(1742). doi: 10.1098/rstb.2017.0025

Craske, M. G., Treanor, M., Conway, C. C., Zbozinek, T., & Vervliet, B. (2014). Maximizing exposure therapy: an inhibitory learning approach. *Behaviour Research and Therapy*, 58, 10–23. doi:10.1016/j.brat.2014.04.006

Derks, L. A. C. (2018). *Mental space psychology: Psychotherapeutic evidence for a new paradigm*. Netherlands: Coppelear b.v. Nijmegen.

Derks, L. A. C. (2016). *Clinical experiments: what cognitive psychotherapies – like CBT, NLP and Ericksonian hypnotherapy – reveal about the workings of the mind. A theoretical analysis over 35 years of clinical experimentation.* Nicaragua: Dissertation, Universidad Central de Nicaragua.

Derks, L. A. C. (2005). *Social Panoramas; Changing the unconscious landscape with NLP and psychotherapy*. Camarthen, Wales: Crown House Publishing.

Derks, L. A. C. (2002). S*ociale Denkpatronen: NLP en het veranderen van onbewust sociaal gedrag*. Utrecht, Netheralnds: Servire.

Derks, L. A. C., & Hollander, J. (1996). *Essenties van NLP*. Utrecht: Servire.

Derks, L. A. C., Masselink, R., Beenhakker, C., van Wijngaarden, D., Heemskerk, J., & Wilimsig, C. (2020). Depression treated within the mental space paradigm: effectiveness and training requirements. *Newsletters*, 16A(17), 18, on www.somsp.com/news, Society for Mental Space Psychology.

Derks, L. A. C., & Wilmsig, C. (2018). Mental Space Psychology-a Review of Some Clinical Experiments and their Neuroscientific Background. ResearchGate.

Dilts, Robert. (1995). *Strategies of genius (3 vols.)*. Cupertino, CA: Meta Publications.

Dilts, R. (1993). *Changing belief systems with NLP*. Cupertino, CA: Meta Publications.

Dilts, R., & DeLozier, J. (2000) *NLP encyclopaedia*. NLP University Press.

Dilts, R., Grinder, J., Bandler, R., & DeLozier, J. (1980). *Neuro-Linguistic Programming: Volume I. The Structure of Subjective Experience*. Cupertino, CA: Meta Publications.

Fauconnier, G. (1997). *Mappings in thought and language*. New York: Cambridge University Press.

Freud, S. (1914). Zur Geschichte der psychoanalytische Bewegung.

Fernández, R., Bavassi, L., Forcato, C., & Pedreira, M. (2016). The dynamic nature of the reconsolidation process and its boundary conditions: Evidence based on human tests. *Neurobiology of Learning and Memory*, 130, 202–212. doi:10.1016/j.nlm.2016.03.001

Gallese, V. (2015). *Embodied simulation and the space around us: The perspective of cognitive neuroscience*. Keynote at the ICSC Rome, September 9, 2015.

Gray, R. (2008/2012). *Transforming futures: The Brooklyn program facilitators manual*. 2nd ed. Lulu.com. http://www.lulu.com/content/2267218.

Gray, R. (2011). *Interviewing and counseling skills: An NLP perspective*, Raleigh, NC: Lulu Press.

Gray, R., & Bolstad, R. (2013). Phobias. In Lisa Wake, Richard Gray & Frank Bourke (Eds.), *The clinical efficacy of NLP: A critical appraisal* (pp. 7–31). London: Routledge.

Gray, R., & Liotta, R. (2012). PTSD: Extinction, reconsolidation, and the visual-kinesthetic dissociation protocol. *Traumatology*, 18(2), 3–16. doi: 10.1177/1534765611431835.

Gray, R. M., Budden-Potts, D., Schwall, R. J., & Bourke, F. (2020). *An open-label, randomized controlled trial of the reconsolidation of traumatic memories (RTM) in military women*. Psychological Trauma: Theory, research, practice and policy. https://doi.org/10.1037/tra0000986

Gray, R., & Liotta, R. (2012). PTSD: Extinction, reconsolidation, and the visual-kinesthetic dissociation protocol. *Traumatology*, 18(2), 3–16. doi:10.1177/1534765611431835.

Gray, R., Wake, L., Andreas, S., & Bolstad R. (2013). Indirect research into the applications of NLP. In Lisa Wake, Richard Gray & Frank Bourke (Eds.), *The Clinical Efficacy of NLP: A critical appraisal* (pp. 153–193). London: Routledge.

Graziano, M. S. A. (2018). *The spaces between us. A story of neuroscience, evolution, and human nature*. New York: Oxford University Press.

Grinder, J., & Bandler, R. (1976). *The structure of magic II*. Cupertino, California: Science and Behavior Books.

Grinder, J., & Pucelik, F. (2013). *Origins of neuro linguistic programming*. Bancyfelin: Crown House Publishing.

Groh, J. M. (2014). *Making space how the brain knows where things are*. Harvard: Harvard University Press.

Heap, M. (1988). Neurolinguistic programming: An interim verdict. In M. Heap (Ed.), *Hypnosis: Current clinical, experimental and forensic practices* (pp. 268–280). London: Croom Helm.

James, W. (1890). *The principles of psychology*. New York: Dover Publications, Inc.

James, T., & Woodsmall, W. (1988). *Timeline therapy and the basis of personality*. Cupertino, CA: Meta Publications.

Kelly, E. F. (2007). *Irreducible mind: Towards a psychology for the 21st century*. United Kingdom: Rawman & Littlefield Publishers Ltd.

Kikuchi, H., Fujii, T., Abe, N., Suzuki, M., Takagi, M., Mugikura, S., Takahashi, S., & Mori, E. (2010). Memory repression: Brain mechanisms underlying dissociative amnesia. *Journal for Cognitive Neuroscience*.

van der Kolk, B. (2015). *The body keeps the score: Brain, mind, and body in the healing of trauma*.

Kiverstein, J., & Gangopadhyay, N. (2009). *Enactivism and the unity of perception and action*. ResearchGate

Korzybski, A. (2010). *Selections from Science and Sanity: An introduction to non-Aristotelian*

Lakoff, G. (1987). *Woman, fire and dangerous things*. Chicago: University of Chicago Press.

Lakoff, G., & Johnson, M. (1999). *Philosophy in the flesh*. New York: Basic Books.

Lebois, L. A. M., Seligowski, A. V., Wolff, J. D., Hill, S. B., & Ressler, K. J. (2019). Augmentation of Extinction and Inhibitory Learning in Anxiety and Trauma-Related Disorders. *Annual Review of Clinical Psychology*, 15, 257–284. doi:10.1146/annurev-clinpsy-050718-095634

Lee, J. L. (2009). Reconsolidation: Maintaining memory relevance. *Trends in Neuroscience*, 32(8), 413–420. doi:10.1016/j.tins.2009.05.002

Mckellar, P. (1957). *Imagination and thinking: A psychological analysis*. Oxford: Basic Books.

Ohman, A., & Mineka, S. (2001). Fears, phobias, and preparedness: Toward an evolved module of fear and fear learning. *Psychology Review*, 108(3), 483–522. doi:10.1037/0033-295x.108.3.483

O'Keefe, J., & Nadel, L. (1978). *The Hippocampus as a cognitive map*. Oxford University Press.

Peirce, C. S. (1982). *The Writings of Charles S. Peirce: A Chronological Edition*, (eds.M. Fisch, C. Kloesel, E. Moore, N. Houser et al.). Bloomington, IN: Indiana University Press.

Schiller, D., & Phelps, E. A. (2011). Does reconsolidation occur in humans? *Frontiers in behavioral neuroscience*, 5. doi:10.3389/fnbeh.2011.00024

Schiller, D., Kanen, J. W., LeDoux, J. E., Monfils, M.-H., & Phelps, E. A. (2013). Extinction during reconsolidation of threat memory diminishes prefrontal cortex involvement. *Proceedings of the National Academy of Sciences*. doi:10.1073/pnas.1320322110

Singer, J. L. (1990). Preface: A fresh look at repression, dissociation, and the defenses as mechanisms and as personality styles. In *Repression and Dissociation*. University of Chicago Press.

Sokolov, A. N. (1972). *Inner speech and thought*. New York: Plenum Press.

Spivey, M., Richardson, D., & Zednik, C. (2010). Language is spatial, not special: using space for language and memory. In L. Smith, K. Mix, & M. Gasser (Eds.), *Spatial foundations of cognition and language* (pp. 16–40). Oxford: Oxford University Press.

Steinman, S. A., & Teachman, B. A. (2011). Cognitive processing and acrophobia: validating the Heights Interpretation Questionnaire. *Journal of Anxiety Disorders*, 25(7), 896–902. doi:10.1016/j.janxdis.2011.05.001

Suso-Ribera, C., Fernández-Álvarez, J., García-Palacios, A., Hoffman, H. G., Bretón-López, J., Baños, R. M.,... & Botella, C. (2019). Virtual reality, augmented reality, and in vivo exposure therapy: A preliminary comparison of treatment efficacy in small animal phobia. *Cyberpsychology Behav Soc Netw*, 22(1), 31–38. doi:10.1089/cyber.2017.0672

Suzuki, A., Josselyn, S. A., Frankland, P. W., et al. (2004). Memory reconsolidation and extinction have distinct temporal and biochemical signatures. *Journal of Neuroscience*, 24(20), 4787–4795. doi:10.1523/jneurosci.5491-03.2004

Thng, C. E. W., Lim-Ashworth, N. S. J., Poh, B. Z. Q., & Lim, C. G. (2020). Recent developments in the intervention of specific phobia among adults: A rapid review. *F1000Research*, 9. doi:10.12688/f1000research.20082.1

Thomas, M., & Tsai, C. I. (2011). Psychological distance and subjective experience: How distancing reduces the feeling of difficulty. *Journal of Consumer Research*, 39, 324–340.

Tosey, P., & Mathison, J. (2008). *Neuro-linguistic programming: A critical appreciation for managers and developers*. Palgrave-Macmillan.

Tversky, B. (2019). *Mind in MotionLakoff, how action shapes thought*. New York: Basic Books.

Tversky, B. (1999). Talking about space. *Contemporary Psychology*, 44, 39–40.

Tversky, B. (1991). Spatial mental models. In: Bower, G.H. (ed.), The Psychology of Learning and Tversky, B., (1997). Spatial constructions. In N. Stein, Ornstein, B. Tversky & C. Brainerd (Eds.), *Memory for emotion and everyday events* (pp. 181–208). Mahwah, N. J.: Erlbaum.

Tversky, B. (1997). Spatial constructions. In: Stein, N., Ornstein, Tversky, B. , & Brainerd, C. (Eds.). *Memory for emotion and everyday events*, (pp. 181–208), Mahwah, N. J: Erlbaum.

Tversky, B. J., Heiser, L. P., & Daniel. M. P. (2009). Explanations in gesture, diagram, and word. In K. R. Coventry, T. Tenbrink, & J. A., Bateman (Eds.), *Spatial language and dialogue* (pp. 119–131). Oxford: Oxford University Press.

Tylee, D. S., Gray, R., Glatt, S. J., & Bourke, F. (2017). Evaluation of the reconsolidation of traumatic memories protocol for the treatment of PTSD: A randomized wait-list-controlled trial. *Journal of Military, Veteran and Family Health*, 3(1), 21–33.

Wake, L., Gray, R. M., & Bourke, F. S. (Eds.). (2013). *The clinical effectiveness of neurolinguistic programming: A critical appraisal.* Routledge.

Walsh, K. H., Das, R. K., Saladin, M. E., & Kamboj, S. K. (2018). Modulation of naturalistic maladaptive memories using behavioural and pharmacological reconsolidation-interfering strategies: a systematic review and meta-analysis of clinical and 'sub-clinical' studies. *Psychopharmacology*, 235(9), 2507–2527. doi:10.1007/s00213-018-4983-8

Wardenaar, K. J., Lim, C. C., Al-Hamzawi, A. O., Alonso, J., Andrade, L. H., Benjet, C., ... & de Jonge, P. (2017). The cross-national epidemiology of specific phobia in the World Mental Health Surveys. *Psychological Medicine*, 47(10), 1744–1760. doi:10.1017/s0033291717000174

Wechsler, T. F., Kümpers, F., & Mühlberger, A. (2019). Inferiority or even superiority of virtual reality exposure therapy in phobias? -A systematic review and quantitative meta-analysis on randomized controlled trials specifically comparing the efficacy of virtual reality exposure to gold standard in vivo exposure in Agoraphobia, specific phobia, and social phobia. *Frontiers in psychology*, 10, 1758–1783. doi:10.3389/fpsyg.2019.01758

Wolitzky-Taylor, K. B., Horowitz, J. D., Powers, M. B., & Telch, M. J. (2008). Psychological approaches in the treatment of specific phobias: a meta-analysis. *Clinical Psychology Review*, 28(6), 1021–1037. doi:10.1016/j.cpr.2008.02.007

Wikipedia. (2021). https://en.wikipedia.org/wiki/Neuro-linguistic_programming

Witkowski, T. (2010). Thirty-five years of research on Neuro-Linguistic Programming. NLP research data base. State of the art or pseudoscientific decoration? *Polish Psychological Bulletin*, 41(2), 58–66.

7 Grief and bereavement

Przemysław Turkowski

Introduction

In this chapter is presented a model of working with grief created as a result of a two-year project 'Lifelong learning – Leonardo da Vinci', which was implemented by psychotherapists and coaches from Germany, Catalonia, France, and Poland. This chapter also discusses NLP concepts in coping with grief.

The first NLP schema for coping with grief was presented by Andreas and Andreas (1989). They found that those who get stuck in grieving, did something that could be described in one of two ways: they recall the end (of relation or somebody's life) and/or they recall the loving relationship, in a distant way, so they experience the feeling of emptiness, rather than the fullness that the person experienced in the loving relationship. This was observed whether the grieving process was long or short. The first step in resolving grief in this strategy was to identify how the client represents a person in presence. Because peoples experiences will vary considerably from one person to another, it is important to elicit out how each particular client does it (Barrett, 2017). The next step was to find out how the client represents the deceased who is the object of grief and mourning. It is important to switch the client's perception from thinking about the end of the relationship to a time when things were particularly good between them and the dead person or the relation was in the best period. Andreas and Andreas used information about individual "templates" to transform the grief experience into one of "felt presence", enabling the grieving client to enjoy the positive feelings of the relationship with dead person as if this person were still alive. However, they found that this step sometimes caused temporary increase of the loss feeling, because the image of the loved dead person was still perceived in a separate or dissociated way. Andreas and Andreas identified that it was important to guide the client, using the template of felt presence, into an associated position from which the client can re-experience the feelings of love, connection, belonging, etc. They also utilised submodalities changes in this step e.g., making images larger and closer, changing still picture into a living movie, etc. Whatever was indicated by the "template" experience of

DOI: 10.4324/9781003198864-7

this particular client. This was identified as the moment when reconsolidation of the memory occurs – creating the possibility to experience tears or melting mood (Ecker, Titic, & Hulley, 2012). By reuniting with the lost experience, the client regained access to all the feelings they had with that person and became able to think of the experience of loss from a resourceful position. This model was created as a very elegant, quick, and efficient process that was quickly adopted by experienced NLPt psychotherapist or counsellors. Additionally, the model identified ways to work with some difficult challenges that may arise, e.g., working with limiting beliefs or social patterns or traumatic circumstances of death or grief about the person who was committed abuse or violence.

The aim, therefore, of this chapter is to utilise NLP modelling to create a coherent strategy to deal with grief, building on Andreas and Andreas work.

Using the neuro-linguistic methodology of modelling success strategies (Dilts, 1998), a team of psychotherapists and coaches involved in the "Dying and death" project asked a series of questions about peoples experiences of the grief process

- how did people who successfully went through the various, and sometimes complicated mourning process do this?
- How did they successfully embrace the experience of loss and/or experience of accepting their own dying?
- What were the success factors described from the perspective of various cultures, clients and supporters?

The group commenced by modelling the processes of going through mourning, by asking questions, talking to hospice employees, physicians, psychologists and volunteers, and confront their experience with contemporary researchers, psychological theories in the field of constructivism and existential approach and then integrate the results and fill with techniques derived from NLP and various NLP models like Social Panorama, Core Transformation, Time Line Therapy. From this emerged a comprehensive model whose milestones are listed below as the four steps for handling mourning and bereavement. The length and intensity of each of them depends on the individual situation of the client/patient in psychotherapy. They can be applied both in long- and short-term work, as illustrated by the three case studies discussed in this chapter. It was important for the research clinicians to develop a robust model that would be easy to understand and learned by non NLP psychologists, coaches, and psychotherapists and possible to use as a self-care process for those who are not able to take advantage of professional support.

The four steps of dealing with bereavement

1. Building rapport and work with beliefs and emotions.

2. Finding a meaning and defining a key message.
3. Experiencing a turning point – transition 'from survival to personal development'.
4. Integration of life experience.

Step 1. Beliefs and emotions

Focusing on individual beliefs about death and dying enables us to check the consistency or dissonance between our emotions and thoughts (Gillies & Neimeyer, 2006; Hall, 2014).

The purpose of step 1 is to explore the client's/patient's system of values and beliefs. In this way, one can gain a better understanding of their way of thinking and the feelings that this way of thinking generates (Dilts, 1998). Following the principle of neuro-linguistic psychotherapy that good communication is a meeting in the client's world map (Korzybski, 1958; McDermott, & Jago, 2001), it was assumed that without understanding and empathetic accompanying the client in discovering how their thoughts, system of assumptions, beliefs and values, i.e., their inner world affects their state (emotions, feelings, well-being) and behaviour, it is not possible to move on from grief.

From a psychological point of view, there is a relationship between the feeling of pain, illness, and sadness, because people think that what happens to them should not have happened. Exploring social perception of grief in various European countries, the researchers found that nowadays humans very often do not perceive death as a natural part of life and even do not accept its existence (Dąbrówka et al., 2011).

To move on with grief it is required that one accepts the fact that dying is a natural part of life. If one assumes that dying is an inseparable part of life, it becomes easier for one to cope with loss (Gillies, Neimeyer, & Milman, 2013; Andreas & Andreas, 1989).

Working with beliefs, apart from getting to know oneself and creating an atmosphere of acceptance and a therapeutic alliance, includes a phase in which it is possible to reformulate the client's cognitive and emotional perspective and make it more flexible and help them find a new reference point that will help them accept the reality in a more gentle way (Stipancic, Reiner, Schütz, & Dond, 2010; Huflejt-Łukasik & Peczko, 2011).

It is important to create a space for client's emotions completely and without self-censoring, i.e., I should respond this way, I must not, I should, etc. This is important because the death of a close person is often accompanied by ambivalent feelings (relief and sadness, anger and regret, guilt and despair). It happens sometimes that they remain 'frozen' for years because people do not allow themselves to feel and express them freely (Perls, 1981; Sills, Fish, & Lapworth, 1999). This step creates a chance to discover that there are different parts of unconscious processing that may be involved in inner conflict. NLP techniques (parts reframe) are utilised that lead the client towards inner peace.

The therapy process involves techniques and exercises making it possible to:

- discover the client's representation related to dying, death, and bereavement (Current State),
- identify the main limiting beliefs that maintain the state of bereavement,
- explore convictions about death and develop supportive beliefs,
- discover and express feelings and emotions related to death and their function,
- discover if there are any inner conflicts (conscious and unconscious) and resolve them,
- define the Desired State, i.e., how the client wants to feel, behave, think when mourning is over.

Step 2. Finding a meaning and defining the key message

When the client is able to accept dying and death as a natural part of life, the client moves from a painful perspective of survival to the perspective of personal development and the use of the gift of life. This idea is based on the assumption that 'in every experience there must be a meaning that can be discovered!'. Making this assumption, even the process of dying that is full of suffering may be a life chance for personal development – the last chance for the dying person or emotionally deep opportunity for their family and friends (Fuller, 2009).

Finding a meaning in a painful experience of one's own life allows one to integrate it with their entire personal story (Currier, Holland, & Neimeyer, 2006). This in turn will positively influence the beliefs and emotions and will support the process of ending grief (Fuller, 2009; Andreas & Andreas, 1989). As clinicians one can support clients in establishing communication with the dying (or deceased) person about their life message, so that they can appreciate life experiences from different perspectives (Walter, 1996; Stroebe, 1997). In addition, experiencing this kind of conversation and sharing emotions is a gift and life-celebrating experience. If such a conversation is not possible because this person has already passed away, there is nothing simpler but to recall the memories associated with this person and the impact they had on one's life. What have I learnt from him/her? What do I value him/her for / what do I value in him/her? What am I proud of? There is always something one can learn from relationships and experiences with a dying or deceased person. If the client is able to appreciate this and integrate it as a message directed to one's present and future, it will support the grieving process and help them cope with their loss. Even if one perceives the behaviour or life of the deceased as a bad example (as in case studies below), one can always find something in it that one will define as a message. This life message will be a legacy that will support one's life (Frankl, 2008; Stroebe, & Schut, 1999; Neimeyer, 1999).

This step is also a chance to switch from a dissociated memory perspective which may cause suffering, feeling of loss or being abandoned into a resourceful perspective of association with positive memories from the relation with a loved person (see the case study below). There is also opportunity to deal with traumatic memories before doing that.

From a psychological perspective, it is important in this step to:

- assign existential meaning to the personal relationship with the deceased,
- notice the positive intentions of their actions (i.e., separate for example the abusive ways of fulfilling their needs or ways of coping with deficits, from their needs and intentions themselves, which is important especially in dealing with bereavement over people for whom the client has ambivalent feelings, who, for example, used violence or were addicted, etc.),
- externalise experiences by changing the perspective of perceiving the experience from 'I' to 'observer', which automatically affects the change in the intensity and quality of emotions felt, and from "observer" into "associate" if necessary and possible – which is important for clients, because it restores them control over how they can manage their memory and helps on emotional way,
- formulate the 'key message' from the deceased or dying person,
- open for a change of perspective from 'survive' to 'grow'.

Step 3. Transition from the state of survival after a loss to personal development – a turning point

After the stage of finding a meaning and defining the key message, the client is usually ready to turn towards personal development. At this stage, it is possible to accept death emotionally (not only as someone else's but also client's own) and experience emotions thanks to creating space for various thoughts and fears about reality. Expressing attitudes and emotions such as denial, anger, sadness, pain, and desperation is usually an expression of deep love and bond. NLP tools and techniques provide a range of ways of working with positive intentions or deep states. Loss causes emotional chaos because the deceased is no longer able to enter into physical interaction and it is impossible to close the situations which may not have been closed completely during their life. And yet, in the mind and memory, the close person who has passed away still exists. The therapist can help the mourner overcome this internal confusion by supporting process of maintaining memories and relationships through the joyful continuation of one's own life. Coping with a loss requires harmonizing and balancing one's values and beliefs. The main goal here is to find a way to deal with a loss by recognizing and appreciating client's past, present, and future life experiences. This leads one to personal development (Hall, 2014). Mourning can be painful, because families and friends very often are afraid to get in contact with a person in grief, because they feel helpless and uncertain. Moreover, the phenomenon of cultural support is increasingly disappearing from the social tradition and spiritual/religious space. This makes people feel left alone with their emotional pain. Under these conditions, it is difficult to open up to new perspectives. And only this 'turning point' can one make a new, joyful life, respectful of the loved one who passed away, possible (Walter, 1996; Libby & Eibach, 2002).

The first two steps: working with beliefs and emotions, finding a meaning and defining the key message, should have prepared an atmosphere of readiness for the turning point. Now the client is ready to find new perspectives in the present and the past as well as the chance to discover new opportunities for the future.

In the third step, it is important to:

- shift from the perspective of fear of death to saying 'yes' to life,
- shift from dependence on the deceased person (or the fact of their death) to autonomy,
- solve the problems resulting in a sense of guilt towards the deceased/dying person,
- change the psychological perception of time from 'past-oriented' to 'here and now' and 'future-oriented'.

Step 4. Integrating life experience by harmonizing the bereavement panorama

The bereavement panorama is a constructivist model that mirrors the social reality. In order to feel safe, confident, and to define their identity, people enter images of other people into their inner mental map of relationships (Derks, 2005). They need, either in a conscious or unconscious way, to 'know' their place in relationships with other people. The bereavement panorama shows the relationships they have, used to have and want to have.

The grieving process shows that there is a bond with people who are gone physically. Each mourning, therefore, creates a natural need to reconstruct the inner mental landscape of a person. Integrating dying, death and grief as a reconstruction of the relationship, which is reflected in the bereavement panorama, actively supports the client on their way towards full life (Marwit & Klass, 1996).

Exploration of the bereavement panorama helps one understand how deeply suffering people got lost in the process of mourning. Finding a new place for the deceased persons may, together with their entire legacy, love and respect, find a new space in the mind of a bereaved person, bring them a sense of security, trust and peace. People hope that this will happen unconsciously over time, which may deepen the suffering of weak and sad people and make them go through an unnecessarily prolonged grieving process (Gort, 1984; Jordan & Litz, 2014). The model of bereavement panorama assumes that most people perceive their relations with others by placing them in their internal social image of other people. This internal representation of a person determines one's real attitude to a particular relationship and affects one's feelings and behaviours. A person who died does not disappear from one's thoughts but the body is gone. The images in one's imagination hurt and at the same time are a sign of love and keeping the deceased in one's heart (Derks, 2005; Trope & Liberman, 2010).

Bereavement panorama helps one to see how clients assign places in the internal representation (in imagined space or using figures) to the deceased persons. This insight will let them appreciate the life experience associated with the deceased person and rearrange their representation of social reality. In practice, this means that one designs representations of dead and living people in the space around one. The place one assigns to them in this mental area determines the relationship and its emotional significance for one. The emotional influence of these mental images supports the natural process of grieving or causes its pathologisation (Gillies & Neimeyer, 2006).

The advantage of applying the bereavement panorama model is that client does not have to wait, hoping that time will successfully heal the wounds. It is possible to work through the structure of mental relationship and the mourner may harmonise it by changing its location and sub-modality associated with the image of the deceased. Grieving is a process that one does not choose, but one can support it and catalyse it going through particular stages. A mental representation of a particular person is something different from the real person, but it is their picture that affects clients' emotions and social reality.

What is more, people can be completely unaware of the social ideas embedded in them. However, emotions related to relationships arise from them, which results mainly from the pattern imprinted in early childhood or during some later experience. There is no need to end a relationship with the deceased, but it must be re-structured (Klass, 1992).

Independently or as extension of a bereavement panorama, the therapist can use techniques allowing people to move from the physical absence to the internal presence in the heart. In order to connect with the simple love, (if it's not there directly) one has to travel through other feelings, emotions that could be hiding it e.g., sadness, guilt, anger. These techniques are based on the ideas of Andreas & Andreas (1987).

In step 4, it is important to:

- become aware of one's internal social representations and create a graphic representation of the bereavement panorama,
- understand one's own system of social relationships and the impact of bereavement,
- strengthen the constructive mechanisms of coping with own perception of a deceased person,

- create a new representation of social relations and support development,
- move clients from the feeling of physical absence to the internal felt presence.

In a similar way, it is possible to use this path when working with other types of loss (job loss, illness, failure).

Each of the steps reflects the stages of mourning described classically already by Kubler-Ross and Kessler (2005). However clinical practice shows that these stages do not have to be experienced linearly, i.e., in the order described by the author. There may be fluctuations, relapses, the client may not notice or go through certain stages. Undoubtedly, Kubler-Ross's works are a very good theoretical foundation for looking at grief. Entering the constructive discourse with this model, we have created its complementation and extension by selecting psychotherapeutic tools so that it would be possible to support clients who start therapy at every stage.

Case study 1 – "she did not give me enough"

The client was a 15-year-old boy Kris (the name were changed for the purposes of the case description in all cases below). When making the appointment and during the initial interview, the father, who brought him to the psychotherapist, did not address the topic of death. He describes the condition of his son at the level of symptoms, mainly related to the school context and apathy. He mentions the death of his wife and the boy's mother parenthetically when he was asked about the current family situation. At the same time, it can be seen that he maintains non-verbal contact with his son, e.g., he is touching his shoulder, although he avoids eye contact. During the conversation about the death of his wife, there are signs of a stronger arousal, tears in his eyes, a trembling voice. It turns out that the father and son had not talked insightfully about the death of the boy's mother until then.

The first session reveals the main belief Kris had about the death of his mother 'and I fear that I will not cope without her because I do not know if she managed to give me everything I should have in order to be successful in life…'. It seems to be the key conviction causing anxiety and affecting his assessment and perception of the whole event.

In the first session he has told the whole story about mother's death for the first time. I used this as an opportunity to reorient him from the moment of her death for the rest of life. The subject of positive intention of emotions was also revealed.

In the second session we started talking about memories related to his mother. For this purpose, a neuro-linguistic concept of working with a timeline was used as a structure. The client was asked to draw significant positive memories of the relationship with his mother using symbols on sheets of paper and arrange them in a timeline, starting from the earliest memories and finishing on the present.

In the next step (the third session), I led the client through the process of associating memories and then, from the perspective of an observer, looking at the symbols on the pages, Kris formulated a 'key message' from the deceased mother for the rest of his life. It was the result of the emotional experience gained from the memories of the relationship with the mother (and experiencing these memories from the perspective of an 'actor' followed by reflection from the perspective of an 'observer'). The client said that it gave him the feeling and conviction that what he got from the relationship with his mother was enough for him to survive in the world and develop and that he would never lose it, it would always be in his heart. What is important, it was the moment in the course of work in which the client created some space to set himself a goal: to be able to live without fear that she is not there, using what she had already given him.

The fourth session was dedicated to bridging the future and embedding the experience of previous sessions in the relationship map. For this purpose, the social panorama technique was used. The client rearranged the sensual representation of his relationship with his mother and also found a new, more supportive place for his father. It allowed him to perceive his father as the one who could support him in growing up and going through life.

The last session was devoted to summing up the whole process. The client was asked to look at all this period of time, at himself at the beginning and at the end of the process, describing changes in the area of emotions and well-being as well as thoughts and behaviour.

A short-term structured intervention led to measurable changes described by both the client and his father. These changes concerned both his behaviour (initially: apathy, staying in bed all day, lack of contact with peers, worse school performance, lack of out-of-school activities) and emotional state (initially: sadness, even dismay, freezing emotions, lack of feeling, and the ability to name emerging emotions) and on the level of beliefs (initially: I am alone, I cannot cope, I have nothing, others have it, it should be different, it should not have happened). The end result of the whole process was greater peace and faith that the client can develop and grow up without the physical presence of his mother. In addition, according to the model of neuro-linguistic influence of emotions on thoughts and of thoughts on behaviour, cascade changes occurred involving various areas of the young man's life.

The main tool during this process was the timeline. Timeline made it possible both to organise memories and broaden the cognitive perspective, experience both from the association (position of an actor) and dissociation (observer's perspective) (Libby & Eibach, 2011). The key intervention, including two sessions, allowed us to formulate a new assumption, which concerned not only the fact of the mother's death, but also his picture of himself and his future opportunities. A turn towards the future thus occurred (while previously attention had been focused mainly on the past).

Case study 2 – "when they all disappear"

This is the story of 23 year old woman Monica. She started therapy because of depression and anxiety. She presented with a lot of compulsive behaviours and furthermore compulsive thoughts about being in danger. Frequent episodes of derealisation occurred as well. At the beginning she said that she used to be in therapy 5 years ago, but she quit because she believed that her mother's death did not affect her actual state, as the therapist suggested. We commenced therapy from this point using the Core Transformation process. I asked her what her anxiety wants for her and going through the outcome chain she discovered, which was no big surprise, safety. The first part of therapy was focused on describing her thoughts, feelings and behaviours in the perspective of positive intention. This helped her sort out her "symptoms" and enter the perspective of cooperation rather than fighting and internal struggle.

Just after dealing with understanding of beliefs and emotions we moved on into the next stage of therapy related to mom's death and the events that followed. The main traumatic events were of course her mother's death, but the final hit was when her father moved to another woman a few weeks after his wife's death. She was living with her granny, who passed away a year later. Although her father was taking care of financial and living standards, he seemed to be completely absent emotionally. There were two important aspects of the therapeutic work: key message from mother and building up a sense of connection with her love and female strength. She discovered that her mother cared for everyone around her but not herself, which, in the opinion of the client, led to health negligence and starting treatment too late, that caused her death. It is a good example of the key message which is a warning rather than supporting in a straight way, but you can still stay connected and feel love to the important deceased person.

So "turning point" for that client was a moment of cognitive and, what is most important, emotional insight that her symptoms are the sign of her own body and mind self-care and attempt of dealing with the fear of being abruptly abandoned (as has happened in the past) rather than signal of any danger in present time. That was possible thanks to step one: working with beliefs and emotions, then aligning perceptual positions, working with timeline (of her and her parents). After "key message" next steps were more accessible for her.

Case study 3 – "mourns a violent father and a passive mother"

The client, aged 43, was referred to psychotherapy by a psychiatrist. She sought his advice because of constant bouts of fear and crying after her mother died in a car accident. Despite the tranquilisers administered temporarily, she decided not to start pharmacotherapy. The client practically did not leave home for the last six months (12 months had passed since her mother's death). She did shopping after dark and always in the same well-known store. She was afraid of moving to unknown places. She had difficulty coming to the initial sessions. She stopped working (she was on sick leave for some time), although earlier her professional activity was close to workaholism. Psychotherapy lasted for 8 months in this case. During this time, 32 sessions were held. For the purpose of this chapter, we will mainly describe the part of the process related to work with grief and loss.

At the beginning of her story, the mother was very idealised and her loss was depicted as a loss of everything. The father has been dead for years and absent in clients' narration. She claimed that she was not waiting for anything anymore, that she had nothing to live for, that there were absolutely no plans that she would believe would come true. A symbiotic relationship with her mother (called by her client 'mummy') emerged from her story. It turned out that the last 4–5 years was actually the first period in which she experienced being loved by her mother. This was interrupted by the deadly accident. What preceded it was the story of escapes and struggles for survival from an early age. At some point the client began to say that from early school age to the moment of leaving home for college, she was a victim of her father's physical abuse. From the time of her father's death the relationship with her mother began to improve gradually. By talking about her parents, the client feared strongly that she was crossing a taboo. It was connected with a strongly internalised belief, instilled by her parents, that 'they deserve respect'. So even now, after more than 20 years since moving out (and despite the fact that both parents died), the conviction really worked on the client. A picture of the father who constantly humiliated and beat her under any pretext and a passive mother, who, being next door, did not react, emerged from her story. At this initial stage it was very important for the client that the therapist accepted her with her story, that she was allowed to tell her story and reassured that she was allowed, like every human being, to experience ambivalent feelings, that on the one hand she can miss her mother and her love, and at the same time feel angry that she showed this love for her so late and that she did not defend her. That she may grieve because of the feeling of loss, that she does not need to feel guilty, that no one is allowed to hurt a child. At this stage, a foundation was laid for further work related to the confrontation and rebuilding of the assumption system, which, until then, was a trap. Moreover, the assumptions connected with death were also discussed. This concerned not only death in general, not only the death of the mother in an accident, but also very important assumptions about what one is and is not allowed to think and say about a deceased person – in accordance with the Roman principle 'speak well about the dead or say nothing at all'.

Thanks to visual-kinaesthetic dissociation techniques we can switch from associated position in memories leading to regret, pain, anger and guilt that 'she was imperfect and it was probably her fault', and with the conviction that 'after all, parents always want something good for their children' into more distant and relaxed mode. The client was able to look at the traumatic situations from the perspective of an observer, it resulted with no flashbacks or ruminations (e.g., when she entered the parents' apartment). The "turning point" was when the client was able to separate herself from the family system in the story of her life and using the timeline technique she could provide support to herself from the past. The key message was 'you survived, you did it' and 'you have the right to think about what happened from your own perspective'. Thanks to this, the client experienced a release from constantly trying to justify her parents and blaming herself.

It enabled her to separate love for the mother from grief and the feeling of harm and, consequently, experience each of these emotions and free herself from the need to continually go deeper into brooding over them.

The social panorama allowed us to work with the 'kinaesthetic self', which the client has experienced very little of so far. The kinaesthetic self is the embodiment of 'self'. People who are victims often have problems with feeling themselves, especially in social situations, which leads to a feeling of insecurity. We focused on the 'kinaesthetic self' enabling the creation of a new representation of the relationship within the social panorama model (Derks, 2005). Other topics addressed were related to new friendships and a personal relationship. It was the moment when it became possible for her to close the inheritance cases od turn into the future.

Final conclusions and need for research

The presented model of work with grief and loss shows great potential as a concept of supporting people in bereavement, and at the same time as a practical set of techniques to be used. A pre-pilot quantitive research study is in progress at the time of writing. In this study we have observed significant improvement of clients' state in several scales of the General Functioning Questionnaire (GFQ-58) (Styła & Kowalski, 2020):

- Malfunction at work and home,
- Lack of entertainment,
- Depressive disorder,
- Sleep disorders,

and slightly less significant in scales of:

- Sexual disorders,
- Somatic symptoms.

This early study proves promising and demonstrates that the structure of the model allows both work in a form similar to crisis intervention and to undertake deeper work at the level of personality disorders. The experience of the authors of the project shows that pathological mourning often gives symptoms similar to those observed in post-traumatic stress: avoiding places associated with the deceased person, obsessive thoughts, flashbacks, intrusions, emotional instability. Staying in such a condition for a long time leads to personality changes, even if they do not qualify for a specific diagnostic category of ICD or DSM (Horowitz et al., 2003). The developed model of work with bereavement is even more promising as it enables effective work at a sufficiently deep level and at the same time allows one to quickly get rid of symptoms that hinder day-to-day functioning or make it impossible. By inviting the client to strengthen them and showing how to do it, the therapist can simultaneously maintain their motivation to work and develop after the symptoms they originally reported disappear (this applies in particular to long-term processes).

At the same time, the model provides a road map that allows both the client to take up challenges suitable for a given moment in their life, their potential, etc. In methodology presented, we can treat the successive steps as both milestones and checkpoints, which allows us to diagnose the cause of the client's condition quite quickly.

Acknowledgements

I would like to thank my friends, participants of the Leonardo da Vinci partner project 'Dying and Death in Europe', thanks to whom the subject of work with mourning appeared in my life, and with whom we modelled the methodology From the perspective of neuro-linguistic psychotherapy, the '4 steps for handling bereavement' model is also an attempt to face the question arising in this approach: to what extent is it a phenomenological approach to a process, Erickson's 'following the client' and to what extent is it a kind of procedure that will lead to a specific point (Wake, Gray, Bourke, 2013). of work with grief and loss, often touching our deep personal experiences: Łukasz Dąbrówka, Marian Gonzales, Sophie Haas, Magdalena Mastalerz, Josep Soler, Michelle Vinot-Coubetergues, and Dr. Klaus Witt (2011) in particular. Klaus, your passion and commitment are a great contribution to the world!

References

Andreas, C., & Andreas, S. (1989). *Heart of the mind*. Boulder, CO: Real People Press.

Andreas, S., & Andreas, C. (1987). *Change your mind—and keep the change*. Boulder, CO: Real People Press.

Barrett, L. (2017). The theory of constructed emotion: An active inference account of interoception and categorization. *Social Cognitive and Affective Neuroscience*, 12. doi:10.1093/scan/nsx060.

Currier, M. J., Holland, J. M., & Neimeyer, R. A. (2006). Sense-making, grief, and the experience of violent loss: Toward a mediational model. *Death Studies*, 30(2006 - Issue 5). doi:10.1080/07481180600614351

Dąbrówka, Ł., Gozales, M., Hass, S., Mastalerz, M. M., Soler, J., Turkowski, P., Vinot-Coubetergues, M., & Witt, K. (2011). *Manual to support professionals during their work with dying and bereaved persons*. Bargteheide: Psymed-Verlag.

Derks, L. A. C. (2005). *Social panoramas; changing the unconscious landscape with NLP and psychotherapy*. Camarthen, Wales: Crown House Publishing.

Dilts, R. (1998). *Modeling with NLP*. Cupertino, CA: Meta Publications.

Ecker, B., Titic, R., & Hulley, L. (2012). *Unlocking the emotional brain: Eliminating symptoms and their roots using memory reconsolidation*. Routledge.

Frankl, V. E. (2008). *Man's searching for meaning*. London: Rider.

Fuller, A. A. (2009). The unexpected gifts of loss. *Bereavement Care*, 28(2009 - Issue 3). doi:10.1080/02682620903355291

Gillies, J., & Neimeyer R. A. (2006). Loss, grief, and the search for significance: Toward a model of meaning reconstruction in bereavement. *Journal of Constructivist Psychology*, 19(2006 - Issue 1).

Gillies, J., Neimeyer R. A., & Millman, E. (2013). The meaning of loss codebook: Construction of a system for analyzing meanings made in bereavement. *Death Studies*, 38(2014 - Issue 4): Meaning and Spirituality in Grief. doi:10.1080/07481187.2013.829367

Gort, G. (1984). Pathological grief: Causes, recognition, and treatment. *Can Fam Physician.*, 1984 Apr, 30, 914–916. 919-[920], 923-[924].

Hall, C. (2014). Bereavement theory: Recent developments in our understanding of grief and bereavement. *Bereavement Care*, 33, 2014. doi:10.1080/02682621.2014.902610

Horowitz, M.J., Siegel, B., Holen, A., Bonanno, G.A., Milbrath, C., & Stinson, C.H. (2003). Diagnostic criteria for complicated grief disorder. *FOCUS The Journal of Life Long Learning in Psychiatry*, 1(3), 290–298.

Huflejt-Łukasik, M., & Peczko, B. (2011). Neurolingwistyczna psychoterapia. In: L. Grzesiuk, H. Suszek (Eds.), *Psychoterapia. Szkoły i metody* (pp. 299–323). Warszawa: ENETEIA.

Jordan, A. H., & Litz, B. T. (2014). Prolonged grief disorder: Diagnostic, assessment, and treatment considerations. *Professional Psychology: Research and Practice*, 45(3), 180–187. doi:10.1037/a0036836

Klass, D. (1992). The inner representation of the dead child and the worldviews of bereaved parents. *Omega-Journal of Death and Dying*, 26, 255–272. 10.2190/GEYM-BQWN-9N98-23Y5.

Korzybski, A. (1958). *Science and sanity*. Lakeville, Conn.: International Non–Aristotelian Library Pub. Co.

Kubler-Ross, E., & Kessler, D. (2005). *On Grief and Grieving: Finding the Meaning of Grief Through the Five Stages of Loss*. New York: Scribner.

Libby, L. K., & Eibach, R. P. (2002). Looking back in time: Self-concept change affects visual perspective in autobiographical memory. *Journal of Personality and Social Psychology*, 82, 167–179.

Libby, L.K., & Eibach, R.P. (2011). Visual perspective in mental imagery: A representational tool that functions in judgment, emotion, and self-insight.

In: Zanna, M.P., & Olson, J.M. (Eds.). *Advances in Experimental Social Psychology*, 44, (pp. 185–245). San Diego: Academic Press.

Marwit, S. J., & Klass, D. (1996). Grief and the role of the inner representation of the deceased. In D. Klass, P. R. Silverman, & S. L. Nickman (Eds.), *Series in death education, aging, and health care. Continuing bonds: New understandings of grief* (pp. 297–309). Philadelphia: Taylor & Francis. (Reprinted in modified form from "Omega—Journal of Death and Dying," 30(4), 1994/1995, pp. 283–298).

McDermott, I., & Jago, W. (2001). *Brief NLP Therapy*. London: Sage.

Neimeyer, R. A. (1999). Narrative strategies in grief therapy. *Journal of Constructivist Psychology*, 12(1999 - Issue 1). doi:10.1080/107205399266226

Perls, F. (1981). Cztery wykłady, In K. Jankowski (Ed.), *Psychologia w działaniu*, Warszawa: "Czytelnik"

Sills, C. H., Fish, S., & Lapworth P. (1999). *Pomoc psychologiczna w ujęciu Gestalt*. Warszawa: Instytut Psychologii Zdrowia PTP.

Stipancic, M., Reiner, W., Schütz, P., & Dond R. (2010). Effects of Neuro-Linguistic Psychotherapy on psychological difficulties and perceived quality of life. *Counselling and Psychotherapy Research*, 10(1) - Routledge: 39–49.

Stroebe, M. (1997). From mourning and melancholia to bereavement and biography: An assessment of Walter's New Model of Grief. *Mortality: Promoting the Interdisciplinary Study of Death and Dying*, 2(1997 - Issue 3). doi:10.1080/714892787

Stroebe, M., & Schut, H. (1999). The dual process model of coping with bereavement: rationale and description. *Death Studies*, Apr–May, 23(3), 197–224. doi:10.1080/074811899201046

Styła, R., & Kowalski, J. (2020). Psychometric properties of the General Functioning Questionnaire (GFQ-58) used for screening for symptoms of psychopathology and overall level of functioning. *Psychiatria Polska*, 54(1), 83–100. doi:10.12740/PP/99564

Trope, Y., & Liberman, N. (2010). Construal-level theory of psychological distance. *Psychological Review*, 117(2), 440–463. doi:10.1037/a0018963

Wake, L., Gray, R. M., & Bourke, F. S. (Eds.). (2013). *The clinical effectiveness of neurolinguistic programming: A critical appraisal*. Routledge.

Walter, T. (1996). A new model of grief: Bereavement and biography. *Mortality: Promoting the interdisciplinary study of death and dying*, 1(1996 - Issue 1). doi:10.1080/713685822

8 Psychoneuroimmunology – research on Lightning Process

Dr Phil Parker

Introduction

The developing field of psychoneuroimmunology (PNI) considers how three important body systems interact and influence each other.

1. Psychological: the mind, thoughts, cognitions, biases, beliefs, and emotions, etc.
2. Neurological: the brain and the network of nerve fibres that control body functions and convey information concerning the internal and external environment
3. Immunological: the vast array of cells and substances, fluids and vessels which monitor the wellness of cells and the internal environment and mounts a defence against threats it detects.

Those working in the field of PNI research investigate how the mind can affect the way the nervous system works and how that, in turn, can influence physiological process and affect health. As a result, the PNI is also often referred to as the Mind-Body Connection (MBC).

The Lightning Process (LP) is a PNI training program, developed in part from NLP and grounded in PNI research. It is designed to help individuals develop conscious influence over their neurological function and affect change in physiological processes (Parker, Aston, & Finch, 2018). It has been applied to a range of issues such as Multiple Sclerosis, Chronic Fatigue Syndrome/Myalgic Encephalomyelitis (CFS/ME), Complex Regional Pain Syndrome (CRPS), Chronic Pain and Fibromyalgia, as well as to emotional and cognitive issues such as anxiety, depression, and substance use disorders.

This chapter focuses in detail on the LP, as it is a PNI/NLP based approach that has a quite well-developed evidence base, something that is not too common for NLP based approaches.

DOI: 10.4324/9781003198864-8

PNI research

An extensive evidence base has been developed that underpins the field of PNI. One commonly used research approach is the study of placebo effects, where the effects of the administration of inert substances (such as dummy pills) on health are evaluated. Nocebo studies, placebo's less well known 'evil twin', research into the negative effect on health that also can occur when receiving inert substances. A large range of physiological responses has been recorded. To highlight the potential for PNI to affect physiology, a few key studies are included below.

Dopamine production

The symptoms of tremor, muscle stiffness, and difficulties with movement in Parkinson's disease are caused by an inability to produce enough of the neurotransmitter dopamine. One treatment is the injection of apomorphine, a dopamine agonist, which stimulates dopamine receptors and reduces symptoms, however, the effects last for less than 12 hrs. In a study (Benedetti et al., 2004) patients with Parkinson's reported improvement in symptoms each time they received apomorphine on four consecutive days. This was despite the fact that on the fourth day the apomorphine was swapped for inactive saline. This utilised the conditioning technique of having a positive response to the injection on the previous three days evoking a similarly positive response on the fourth day.

To address the issues of whether this was a perceived change in symptoms, rather than a genuine change in neural function, the patients underwent electrode implantation to evaluate the firing of neurones in the subthalamic nucleus (STN) of the brain (the area that is a target of surgical treatment of Parkinson's). The study found that in placebo responders there was a significant change in the firing patterns in the STN, which was not seen in the control group or those whose symptoms were unresponsive to the placebo injection. The study concluded these changes were likely to be due to the placebo-activated dopamine.

Immune responses

A study established conditioned responses in participants by giving capsules of the immunosuppressive drug cyclosporin A at the same time as a distinctly favoured drink (Goebel et al., 2002). On the fourth day, after repeated pairings, the cyclosporin A capsules were substituted with inert dummy capsules. As a result of the conditioning, the inert capsules now produced the same suppression of immune functions with changes in IL-2 and IFN-γ mRNA expression, intracellular production, and in vitro release of IL-2 and IFN-γ, and lymphocyte proliferation.

Further studies have developed this response. One paired antihistamine with a distinctly flavoured beverage for those with hay fever. Delivery of the placebo on day four along with the distinctly flavoured drink resulted in less severe subjective symptoms and a reduced skin response (including less basophil activation) to the skin prick test (Goebel, Meykadeh, Kou, Schedlowski, & Hengge, 2008). Another study paired immunosuppressive drugs with a distinctly flavoured beverage, twice daily for three days. On day four, delivery of the distinctly flavoured beverage alone reduced immune response and T-cell proliferation in those having kidney transplants and suggests the potential for dose reduction in immunosuppression drug regime (Kirchhof et al., 2018).

Open-label and deceptive placebos

Further understandings of the nature of placebo responses and how they impact PNI have been developed by the use of open-label placebo studies. It had been thought that placebos worked through deception, that the participant had to believe they are getting a real drug, and this was essential for its effect. This has been challenged by studies in which the placebo is given with the full knowledge of the participant and, surprisingly, produces similar results to deceptive placebos (Kaptchuk et al., 2010; Meeuwis et al., 2019). Studies have attempted to understand the mechanics of this effect. They conclude that if there is an understandable and believable rationale for why the placebos work – for example, explaining how our expectations can affect our responses to medical interventions (response expectancy [Kirsch, 2018]) and providing evidence from other studies as to how placebos impact physiological function – then the open-label seems to work as well as deceptive placebos (Locher et al., 2017).

Language

Another area of PNI research that is of particular interest to clinicians and those interested in NLP is language. A good quality therapist/patient relationship has long been acknowledged as central to supporting positive treatment effects. One core component of this is effective communication skills. However, it is only more recently that the effect of the specific use of words and metaphors on neurological and immunological function has become the subject of research. Studies into the importance of combining a placebo with positive or negative suggestions as to its effect have emphasised the importance of language content on immunological function. For example, in one study (Meeuwis et al., 2019) a placebo cream was applied to irritated skin and symptoms and skin temperature increased or decreased depending on whether suggestions were given about the cream's irritant or helpful effects.

The development and use of fMRI technology have also demonstrated how being exposed to specific symptom-based words, such as 'pain', activate the areas that process the experience of those symptoms (Eck, Richter, Straube, Miltner, & Weiss, 2011; Richter et al., 2010).

Metaphors, often used by practitioners to explain conditions and interventions also affect physiology, choices, and expectations. One systematic review noted that different terms to describe a fracture affected patients' expectations and preferences for more or less invasive procedures. More medicalised descriptions of injuries were related to expectations of more invasive procedure, with 58% of patients expecting an invasive procedure for the terms describing 'broken bone', 42% for 'fracture', 28% for 'greenstick fracture', and 26% for hairline fracture (Nickel, Barratt, Copp, Moynihan, & McCaffery, 2017). Another study measured pupillary responses to words that represented a sense of brightness, such as 'day' or darkness, 'night'. It found that pupil size increased with the 'darkness' words and reduced with 'brightness' words, suggesting an involuntary neurological response to the metaphorical meaning of words (Mathôt et al., 2017).

These findings raise the importance of how thoughtful both practitioner and patients should be about the use of language around prognosis, diagnosis and symptoms in, and out of, the therapeutic encounter as suggested by others (Hansen & Zech, 2019; Parker, 2011, 2013).

The findings from this small selection of the research suggest how well-evidenced the PNI connection is. As a result of such studies, it is now recognised that *all* interventions are likely to have specific effects (predictable and due to the active components of the interventions) and non-specific effects (less predictable, positive or negative responses due to any other factors other than the intervention; suggestion, expectation, therapeutic relationship, time of day, colour of pill, warmth of the room, etc.), further raising the significance of PNI in treatment options. The output of this research can be applied in two major ways. First to inform how health care practice can be developed to reduce any negative effects on health, and second to help develop clinical applications, such as the LP, that amplify or harness the positive effects of PNI.

NLP, health and research issues

To understand the development of the LP and some of the reasons for the paucity of evidence in NLP, a brief review of the history of NLP and its relationship to health is valuable. The initial modelling of Perls by Bandler and the collaboration of Grinder and other early contributors in the '70s resulted in the development of NLP as a new approach to psychotherapy which was more focused, often more rapid and less traumatic (Bandler, Grinder, Satir, & Bateson, 2005). Naturally, the initial practitioners, many of whom were trained therapists, worked with clients with a range of mental health issues including anxiety and depression.

The ability of NLP to model and learn from those who had recovered from mental health issues was a valuable starting point for understanding the process of change. Taking that model of recovery and change and identifying how those with continuing mental health issues differed from it, was for many ground-breaking. This recognition that a range of mental health issues could be understood as the result of certain thinking patterns and strategies that were tangible and changeable was freeing for many patients and practitioners (Andreas & Andreas, 1989). This approach contrasted strongly with the pre-existing models of psychodynamic therapy (Izenberg, 2015) and its reactionary offspring, the human-centred approach (HCA, Rogers, 2004). Whilst NLP was brief, strategic, and solution orientated, psychodynamic therapy's focus was on interpreting and understanding factors in the past, unconscious drives, and long-term therapy to assist change. NLP had more in common with HCA's recognition of the individuality of each patient and its less past-orientated and collaborative nature, but differed from HCA's loose relationship with 'techniques or strategies' and timeframes, which were often more open-ended in terms of outcome or duration.

As a result of the initial successes of NLP in providing solutions for those with mental health issues, NLP modelling projects began to be applied to other areas, such as spelling, accurate shooting, healthy eating, sales, and health issues of a more physical nature. Some of these advances in modelling health were the result of people finding ways to work through personal challenges (Andreas & Andreas, 1989; Dilts, Hallbom, & Smith, 2012). Others, such as observed changes in allergic reactions after transformational experiences were the unexpected benefits of interventions (Dilts & DeLozier, 2000).

Research issues in health

Early anecdotes of success with NLP resulted in research interest, and some published papers, but initial research into NLP had several issues to contend with. It has been argued that the early developers of NLP, like many of their peers in the early 1970s west coast culture, wanted a change from the existing establishment and its structures (Grinder & Pucelik, 2013) and this, unfortunately, included the prevalent research model. The earliest research (Sharpley, 1984) has been criticised for methodological flaws and a poor understanding of what was being studied and confused conclusions, setting up misunderstandings that would be repeated and foundational for subsequent papers (Wake, Gray, & Bourke, 2013). These factors resulted in a sparse evidence base for NLP of questionable quality, a situation that continued until a resurgence of research interest in NLP within the last decade.

For those teaching NLP for personal or professional development, this lack of evidence is less of an issue than for those working using NLP for health. This is highlighted by Sturt et al., (2012) who notes that £800,000 was spent on NLP-related training for NHS employees by National Health Service (NHS) trusts and strategic authorities between 2006–9. This suggests NLP is valued for training NHS staff, however, the NHS has not generally adopted or accepted it for use with its patients. This mismatch derives from how evidence is evaluated in healthcare environments. Anecdotal evidence of change, which may drive peoples' participation in NLP training courses, carry little weight in supporting claims of the potential efficacy of an intervention. Instead, a robust evidence base, including Randomised Control Trials (RCT), is required for adoption of any new interventions. There is also evidence of caution about interventions that have been created outside of the health care system. Caution is also applied to approaches that are paid for directly by the patients in countries like the UK with state-funded healthcare provision. This can be seen in this quote from Prof. Dorothy Bishop about an RCT involving the LP (Crawley et al., 2018), "The gains for patients in this study do seem solid, however, I am still rather uneasy because while the patient allocation and statistical analysis of the trial appear to be done to a high standard, *the intervention that was assessed is commercial*" (Science Media Centre, 2017).

There is no logical or evidential basis for this caution, and it involves a circular argument. Interventions without a good quality evidence base cannot be provided by state-funded healthcare. They can only, therefore, be accessed by self-funding by private individual. They are labelled 'commercial' meaning that any research evidence on commercial interventions can be dismissed.

The Register of Lightning Process practitioners, the LP's professional body, has recognised the importance of research in gaining acceptance of a new approach in healthcare. It has a small research team and has liaised and collaborated with researchers over the years to help foster a wider understanding of the LP's, and NLP's, approach to health and to develop an evidence base, aspects of which are presented and discussed in the rest of this chapter.

Description and origins of the approach

The LP was developed in the late 1990s by Dr Phil Parker as the result of a qualitative inquiry answering the research question 'why do some people respond well to treatment and others, with the same issues, seem to gain no change?'. From an NLP perspective, this can be seen as comparatively modelling change and stuckness. The rationale for this inquiry was that being able to better understand how these factors operate could provide important insights into how to assist individuals in managing change.

The findings of this project, published in two books (Parker, 2011, 2012), identified some patterns that differed between the two groups, particularly around a sense or lack of agency and empowerment with regards to finding solutions to their issues. Additionally, it was found that two specific language patterns were identified in speech patterns of participants with regard to the stuckness group. First was the use of negatively phrased language to describe their issues and likely futures. Second, described as 'passive language' (Parker, 2011), was a range of language structures, including specific verb use and nominalisations, that reinforced their sense of a lack of agency and disempowerment.

This led to the creation of the LP programme to help people to first switch over from the disempowering patterns observed, and second to help them apply a set of PNI tools to develop conscious influence on physiological processes.

Details of the approach

The LP begins with a three-hour interactive home-study audio programme that covers PNI research. It also provides an opportunity for exploration of held beliefs, conceptualisations, agency and language used about illness, health and recovery. This is followed by a face-to-face coaching session with their LP practitioner to support the audio content. Next are the 3 training seminars (4 hours each) with their LP practitioner, which are delivered face to face or online with 1–8 attendees.

The course content was developed from concepts from: NLP, Positive Psychology, health education theory, mindfulness, osteopathy and coaching and has two phases i. teaching core concepts and ii. adopting practical tools (Parker et al., 2018).

In phase i, participants engage with the relevant theory and research to understand the mechanisms of how PNI can be used to influence physiology (Locher et al., 2017). Attention is paid to how language can affect neural pathways (Parker et al., 2018; Richter et al., 2014) and the role that patient activation and empowerment (Hibbard & Greene, 2013; Parker, 2011), chronic stress and response expectancy can have on physiology (Kirsch, 2018; Selye, 1978).

In phase ii a set of steps are taught so participants can:

a. detect disempowering language, negative expectancies and changes in physiology (Grossman, Niemann, Schmidt, & Walach, 2004),
b. pause them by employing an interruptive 'stop' process (Aldao, Nolen-Hoeksema, & Schweizer, 2010; Wise, 2002),
c. employ a set of self-coaching interventions.

This final step includes developing self-compassion (Neff, Kirkpatrick, & Rude, 2007) and a series of Socratic questions designed to identify immediate goals and desired physiological states (to replace those identified in step a) (this can be seen as a brief version of NLP's well-formed outcomes process). The final step is to access and savour memories (NLP's state accessing processes) that recall previous experiences of those goals and states (Bryant, Smart, & King, 2005) in order to encourage improved physiology (Speer & Delgado, 2017). The use of body movements and voice tone and speed, (Davis, Senghas, Brandt, & Ochsner, 2010; Hamann, 2001) congruent with those memories, as emphasised by Ericksonian and NLP approaches, is employed to increase the strength of that recall.

In step i.a) the use of the constructed verb, dû (Parker, 2011), specific to the LP, is taught. It means 'to be unconsciously and unintentionally involved in a process' such as- '*I am worried*' becomes '*I am dûing worried*'. This is shorthand for '*I am involved in the process of producing worry, albeit it at an unconscious and unintentional level. This unconscious and unintentional involvement also identifies that I have some say in this process and some power to influence what happens next*'. It, therefore, provides a practical way for attendees to adopt several cognitive shifts.

First, it reframes trait or identity statements as automatic *behaviours,* providing a sense of distance between the individual and something they thought was intrinsic to them. Second, it recasts (denominalizes) the concept of illness as a mutable *process* rather than a single static un-influenceable event. Third, it encourages a sense that the current illness/issue experience has a temporal dimension (i.e., it is currently occurring but is not necessarily permanent, and therefore holds out the possibility it will change). Fourth it provides a shift from a perceived lack of agency (passive) to one of empowerment (active), (similar to elements of the NLP cause and effect metamodel pattern), especially with respect to health (Parker, 2011).

The utilisation of an unfamiliar verb is hypothesised to cause an alteration in neural processing, as suggested by Norm theory (Kahneman & Miller, 1986), activating system 2 processing, and its ability to take a more considered perspective on events (Kahneman, 2011). Additionally, its specific use, rather than the more familiar '*do*', highlights the unconscious and unintentional, and therefore blame-free nature, of the individual's involvement in the issue (Parker, 2011). Clarity about this point is of particular importance, especially when working with health. It is essential to underline that the identification of the existence of those patterns is not the same as implying that someone is at fault or to blame for these patterns or their consequences. This important point equally applies to the earlier description of NLP as a process for identifying patterns and strategies (modelling) that are running or maintaining an issue at an unconscious level.

A review of its evidence base

A systematic review of the evidence base for the LP (Parker, Aston, & de Rijk, 2020) collated the key studies on the LP to date. This section presents an overview of that review, along with other subsequent studies and programmes developed from the LP that were not included in that paper.

Systematic review

This important step in developing the evidence base for the LP was undertaken to assess the quality and present a descriptive narrative of the published evidence on the intervention (Parker et al., 2020). The authors searched five electronic reference databases (PsycINFO, PubMed, CINAHL, Embase, ERIC) along with manual searches in Google Scholar and Google for studies of the LP in clinical populations that had been published in peer-reviewed journals or in grey literature. Reviews, editorial articles, and studies/surveys with unreported methodology were excluded from the search parameters. The decision to include grey literature and google search engines was made to ensure capture of the majority of published research on the LP. 568 records were found and once inclusion criteria were applied 14 studies remained (four qualitative studies and case reports, six quantitative surveys and four quantitative non-survey studies). The included studies were then assessed for quality using criteria suggested by Long and Godfrey (2004) and NIH study quality assessment tools (2014), and although all passed that assessment there were limitations identified in some studies. These results and location, sample size and demographics of the studies are reported in Table 8.1. A narrative synthesis was employed to present the results from studies using such differing methodologies (Ahn & Kang, 2018; Popay et al., 2006). To clarify reasons for some variance and contradictions present in the results a commentary on the quality and issues of each study has been included.

Qualitative studies

Four qualitative studies were included in the review.

One recruited patients (N = 22, 95% female) with self-reported CFS/ME (Sandaunet & Salamonsen, 2012) who reported significant improvement (n = 13), no response (n = 6), adverse response (n = 3), 10–26 months after the LP-course. The study found those reporting a positive response to the LP felt that they had improved understanding of their illness, trust in their trainer and had continued positive physical effect of the LP after the seminar, factors that were not reported by the other respondents. There are some issues with this study, particularly the self-reported diagnosis of the participants and the extensive gap between LP course and study participation.

In 2011 The Norwegian National Research in Complementary and Alternative Medicine (NAFKAM) institute created a protocol to release a warning notice if three negative reports for an alternative treatment from patients with the same condition were received (NAFKAM, 2011). As a result, they reported on three patients with self-reported CFS/ME who described how they experienced 'unfavourable outcomes' 12 months after LP, which they all related to the seminar (Fønnebø, Drageset, & Salamonsen, 2012). There are issues with this report. It represents a sample of three people's reported experience and doesn't represent other positive cases reported to NAFKAM (as can be seen in the Sandaunet & Salamonsen study which was recruited from the NAFKAM database) and therefore has

Table 8.1 Overview of studies

Author/Year	*Title*	*Country*	*Peer reviewed/ controlled (PR/C)*	*Method*	*N*	*Age group*	*Quality*
Finch, 2010	LP Snapshot Survey of clients' experiences	INTL	x	Survey	1297	Not reported	Fair
ME association, 2010	Managing my M.E	UK	x	Survey	4217	All	Fair
Sussex & Kent ME/CFS Society, 2010	ME/CFS Patients Survey	UK	x	Survey	457	Not reported	Fair
Fønnebø et al., 2012	Worst Cases Reported to the NAFKAM International Registry of exceptional Courses of disease	Norway	x	Case report	5	Not reported	Fair
Reme, Archer & Chalder, 2012.	Experiences of young people who have undergone the Lightning Process to treat chronic fatigue syndrome/myalgic encephalomyelitis - a qualitative study.	UK	PR	Qualitative	9	Adolescent	Good
Sandaunet & Salamonsen, 2012	CFE-/ME-pasienters ulike erfaringer med Lightning Process.	Norway	PR	Qualitative	22	Adult	Good
Bringsli et al., 2013	The Norwegian ME Association national survey	Norway	x	Survey	1096	All	Fair
Finch, 2013	Outcome measures study	UK	x	Quantitative	205	All	Good

(*Continued*)

Table 8.1 (Continued)

Author/Year	*Title*	*Country*	*Peer reviewed/ controlled (PR/C)*	*Method*	*N*	*Age group*	*Quality*
Crawley et al., 2013	The feasibility and acceptability of conducting a trial of specialist medical care and the Lightning Process in children with chronic fatigue syndrome: feasibility randomized controlled trial (SMILE study)	UK	PR	Qualitative	56	Adolescent	Good
Finch, 2014	Lightning Process & Multiple Sclerosis: Proof of Concept Study	UK	x	Proof of Concept	11	Adult	Fair
Hagelsteen & Moen Reiten, 2015	Evaluation of a treatment strategy	Norway	x	Quantitative	12	Adolescent	Good
Aktiv Prosess., 2016	Chronic fatigue syndrome and experience with the Lightning Process	Norway	PR	Survey	196	All	Fair
Kristoffersen et al., 2016	Use of complementary and alternative medicine in patients with health complaints attributed to former dental amalgam fillings	Norway	PR	Survey	324	Not reported	Good
Crawley et al., 2018	Clinical and cost-effectiveness of the Lightning Process in addition to specialist medical care for paediatric chronic fatigue syndrome: randomised controlled trial	UK	PR/C	Randomised Controlled Trial	100	Adolescent	Good

limited generalisability to larger populations. It also wrongly reports the LP being instructed '*to ignore what they sensed as their bodies symptoms*' (Fønnebø et al., 2012, p. 30). This erroneous statement is repeated in later studies on the LP, mirroring the repetitions in later NLP studies of errors in early NLP research. Additionally, there is uncertainty as to the causal link between LP course and the reports of unfavourable outcomes due to the extensive temporal gap between the LP course attendance, and the reports, and the natural history of severe fluctuation in symptoms identified in this illness.

A qualitative study (Reme, Archer, & Chalder, 2012) evaluated the experiences of young people (female = 89%, age range 14–26), who had attended the LP for CFS/ME. Of the nine adolescents, seven reported being satisfied and were much or very much better, and two reported a lack of satisfaction and absence of improvement. It identified that the presentation of the theoretical rationale for the LP and the practical exercises were considered helpful. Concerns expressed by those who noticed no benefits focused on their perception of secrecy surrounding the LP and their interpretation of the need to apply the taught tools to aid recovery as being blamed for lack of change. The study raises important issues. Despite the majority experiencing much improvement, in two cases the communication of the complex issues of influence and not bearing guilt or blame, mentioned earlier and discussed further later, had not been effectively delivered.

As a result, the LP registering body responded to these findings with a practitioner audit and CPD programme to ensure the points raised were communicated even more effectively throughout the practitionership. There are issues with this study, including the small sample preventing generalisation, recruitment from a single ME charity, increasing the potential for selection bias of those with negative experiences, reliance on self-reported experiences, and the use of Oxford criteria (Sharpe et al., 1991) which some consider inadequate for diagnosis due to its lack of inclusion of Post Exertional Malaise. The description of the LP that appears in the text of this study repeats earlier errors (Fønnebø et al., 2012, p. 30), wrongly describing the approach having an 'extreme position taken by the Lightning Process in denying the limitations of the illness'(Reme et al., 2012, p. 509).

A 2013 feasibility trial (N = 56, female = 76.4%, mean age = 14.8 years (SD = 1.6), age range 12–18) included a qualitative section that evaluated "participants' beliefs, expectations, preferences and experiences of the interventions" (Crawley et al., 2013, p. 4). It noted the potential for confusion that new instructions regarding the speed of change that differed from those used in other versions of the LP were potential sources of confusion. Importantly, no serious adverse events related to their involvement in the study were reported. The study benefited from the inclusion of participants' reports during and shortly after, rather than months after the intervention, and from effective communication between the researchers and the LP practitioners involved in the study about details of the intervention.

Quantitative surveys

Six quantitative studies were included in the review.

A survey (Finch, 2010) evaluated experiences of the LP on the third day of the seminar (*N* = 1297, female = 78.5%. Reported presenting issues: ME/CFS 84%, low self-esteem 57%, anxiety 56%, guilt 43%, depression 34%,). Table 8.2 presents the results for the question 'Did you get the changes you wanted?'. A further question asked how appropriate, or not, the training was for their needs, and 98.8% reported that it was. Although this survey does not report on more long-term responses, it benefits from its non-selective recruitment, requesting responses from all participants who had taken the LP within the timeframe, and gives a reliable overview of the delivery of the LP representing seminars run by 34 different LP practitioners.

Three surveys were undertaken by ME charities. A UK ME charity undertook a survey (*N* = 4,217, female = 78%, age range 11–66), asking about their experiences of managing ME (ME Association, 2010). A Likert scale was used to rate perceptions of 25 different approaches, including Cognitive Behavioural Therapy (CBT) (*n* = 997), Graded Exercise Therapy (GET) (*n* = 906) and the LP (the third least used of the 25 approaches, *n* = 101). Results showed that of the 25 approaches, LP received the highest percentage of participants who rated themselves as '*greatly improved*'. However, this was not the case for all participants (see Table 8.3). A similar study was undertaken by the Norwegian ME Association (Bringsli, Gilje, & Wold, 2013). It surveyed members and visitors to its website (*N* = 1096, 85% female, age range 11–80+). A summary of the reported effects of 18 interventions is presented in Table 8.4. A further study by the Sussex & Kent ME/CFS Society and Brighton & Sussex Medical School (2010) evaluated the experiences of those with CFS (*n* surveys sent = 900, returned = 457, female 77%, mild CFS 29%, moderate 54%, severe 16%, very severe 1%). 16 treatments were rated as 'very helpful', 'reasonably helpful' or 'not at all helpful'. The LP received the highest percentage of all approaches in the 'very helpful' category (results are summarised in Table 8.5). These studies benefit from having reasonably large samples. However, there are issues, noted in the studies, of the potential for selection bias, with those who have recovered from the condition being less likely to be represented.

A study evaluated the 'use of complementary and alternative medicine in those with health complaints attributed to former dental amalgam fillings' (Kristoffersen et al., 2016) via data collected from the Norwegian Dental Patient Association (NDPA) (*N* = 324, female = 71.6%). Responses to the LP (*n* = 16) were: six reporting good effect, seven reporting no change, no reports of worsening, and three non-responders. The results from this small sample are useful in identifying the lack of reported adverse events.

The Journal of the Norwegian Medical Association reported on a survey evaluation of participants (*N* = 196, age-range 10–76) attending the LP in

Table 8.2 Did you get the changes you wanted? Score your answer out of 10 (0 = definitely no, 10 = definitely yes)

Score	*0*	*1*	*2*	*3*	*4*	*5*	*6*	*7*	*8*	*9*	*10*
No. of respondents	0	1	0	11	10	32	39	94	188	223	683
% of 1281 respondents	0%	0.1%	0%	0.9%	0.8%	2.5%	3.0%	7.3%	14.7%	17.4%	53.3%
No. of those with CFS/ME	0	1	0	9	7	26	27	77	145	187	601
% of 1080 respondents	0%	0.1%	0%	0.8%	0.65%	2.4%	2.5%	7.1%	13.4%	17.3%	55.65%

Table 8.3 Results of Sussex & Kent ME/CFS Society Survey, 2010

Category	*Intervention*		
	LP	*CBT*	*GET*
Very helpful	44%	24%	12%
Reasonably helpful	36%	50%	51%
Not at all helpful	20%	26%	37%

Table 8.4 Norwegian ME Association Survey, 2013

Category	*Intervention*		
	LP (n = 166)	*CBT (n = 368)*	*GET (n = 328)*
Greatly Improved	8%	2%	1%
Improved	13%	13%	13%
No Change	30%	63%	20%
Worse	22%	14%	41%
Much Worse	27%	8%	25%

Table 8.5 Results of ME Association Survey, 2010

Category	*Intervention*		
	LP(n = 101)	*CBT(n = 997)*	*GET(n = 906)*
Greatly Improved	25.7%	2.8%	3.4%
Improved	18.8%	23.1%	18.7%
No Change	34.7%	54.6%	24.4%
Worse	7.9%	11.6%	23.4%
Much Worse	12.9%	7.9%	33.1%

2008 (Aktiv Prosess, 2016). Data was collected by phone interviews using a structured questionnaire. Increased activity levels, school and work attendance increased (from 17% to 60%), while time in bed/sofa reduced (from 15 hours to 10 hours per day) and better life quality was reported by the majority of participants. Compared to baseline, the improvement lasted more than a year after the LP with no reports of serious adverse effects. This study employed useful measures for evaluating change but is limited by having the second smallest sample of the included surveys.

Quantitative Studies (non-survey)

An outcome measures, cross-sectional study of LP participants (N = 205, female = 80%, mean age = 37.4 years (SD = 15.6), age range 9–73) with CFS/ME (64.4%), anxiety/depression disorders (17.1%), Multiple Sclerosis

(2.9%) and Fibromyalgia (2.9%) was undertaken (Finch, 2013). RAND SF-36 was used to assess health change, physical functioning, role limitations due to physical health, role limitations due to emotional problems, energy/fatigue, emotional well-being, social functioning, pain and general health. Repeated measures ANOVA using Time of Testing (three levels; pre-test, six weeks, three months) identified a significant difference in all sub-scales of RAND SF-36 (Ware & Sherbourne, 1992) ($p < .0001$) indicating that the LP is associated with positive change on all dimensions of health tested by RAND SF-36. This significant improvement persisted in all scales, with the exception of the emotion-related measures, at six weeks and three months ($p < .0001$). This study contributes to the evidence base by using a well-validated measure and providing data for a longer period after the intervention than previous studies reported this far.

A proof of concepts study arranged by the Multiple Sclerosis Research Council (MSRC) evaluated if MS symptoms could be improved by the LP (Finch, 2014). Functional Assessment of MS scale (FAMS) (Yorke & Cohen, 2015), RAND SF36, (Ware & Sherbourne, 1992) and Fatigue Severity Scale (FSS) (Krupp, Alvarez, LaRocca, & Scheinberg, 1988) questionnaires were completed by 11 participants (female = 7) at four time intervals (pre- and six weeks, three and six months post- LP seminar). Attrition resulted in seven remaining in the study at six months. Improvements in all sub-scales of the RAND SF-36 at all data collection points were found, with general health, energy/fatigue levels, role limitations due to emotional problems and emotional well-being showing the greatest change. The limitations and benefits of this study are well reported by the MSRC, who concluded that despite the small scale and high attrition rates, the study's results showed that the LP provides measurable benefits to those with MS (Parker, 2012).

A treatment evaluation of 12 adolescents (14–18 years) with chronic headaches (female = 7) was undertaken in Norway (Hagelsteen & Moen Reiten, 2015). Analysis of pain levels, measured via the Visual Analogue Scale (Price, McGrath, Rafii, & Buckingham, 1983), found pain was significantly reduced for nine of the participants at three months and this change was maintained at 12 months. Quality of life also had improved for the majority, who were more active and more able to spend time with friends and there was a significant increase in school attendance. Despite being a small study, it adds to the evidence base by reporting on pain and following up the effects of the intervention over a 12 month period.

An RCT (Crawley et al., 2018), the Specialist Medical Intervention and Lightning Evaluation (SMILE) ($N = 100$, mean age = 14, 76% female) was run by the UK's NHS and University of Bristol. It compared Specialist Medical Care (SMC) ($n = 49$) to SMC plus LP ($n = 51$) for 12–18-year-olds with mild/moderate CFS/ME. SMC incorporated several approaches including CBT for anxiety and low mood, activity and sleep management and GET.

Analysis found those receiving SMC plus LP had significantly improved physical functioning at six months compared to those receiving SMC (with an adjusted difference in means 12.5 [95% CI 4.5, 20.5], $p = 0.003$), and at 12 months this had increased (15.1, 95% CI 5.8, 24.4, $p = .002$). Compared to those in the SMC arm, participants in the SMC plus LP had less fatigue (adjusted difference in means −4.7 [95% CI −7.9 to −1.6], $p=0.003$) and had a greater reduction of anxiety symptoms measured by both the Hospital Anxiety and Depression Scale (HADS) (Snaith & Zigmond, 1986) (−3.3, [95% CI −5.6, −1.0], $p = .005$) and the Spence Children's Anxiety Scale (SCAS) (Spence, 1998) (−8.7, [95% CI −16.9, −0.5], $p = .039$) at six months, and that continued at 12 months. Depression was reduced in participants in the SMC plus LP arm compared to those in the SMC arm at 12 months (adjusted difference in means in HADS depression score -1.7 [95% CI −3·3, −0·2] $p = .030$). A reduction in pain scores was found in participants receiving SMC plus LP compared with those receiving SMC at both six and 12 months, but confidence intervals were wide and unreported. School attendance improved for those in the SMC plus LP arm at 12 months compared to those receiving SMC (adjusted difference in means 0.9 days of school per week [95% CI 0.2, 1.6] $p = .018$). It found evidence that suggested combining SMC with LP was more cost-effective than delivering SMC on its own. Nine participants reported a worsening of symptoms at six months (eight in SMC arm, one in SMC + LP arm). Of these nine, five had deterioration of ≤10 on the SF-36 physical function subscale (range 0–100). This is considered to be less than the minimal clinically important difference. It is of note that none of the participants in the SMILE trial had any serious adverse events attributable to receiving either SMC or SCM plus LP. This study provides important weight to the evidence base utilising the robust methodology of an RCT, providing data over a 12 month period, identifying benefits from the addition of the LP to SMC, and the absence of serious adverse events from the intervention.

Additional studies

Since the completion of the systematic review, three new papers have been produced. Two concern the Rediscovery Process (TRP) an adaption of the LP for substance use and a third paper that was not included in the systematic review as it did not involve a clinical population, reviewed the disease process of CFS/ME and the LP approach (Parker, Banbury, & Chandler, 2020; Parker, Banbury, & de Rijk, 2021; Parker et al., 2018).

Substance use

A preliminary randomised wait-list controlled and cohort study (Parker, Banbury, & Chandler, 2020) evaluated outcomes in those misusing alcohol ($n = 72$). Alcohol use, flourishing, impulsivity and recovery capital were analysed pre-, 1- and 3-month post-intervention comparing TRP to treatment as usual (TAU). Data was collected on alcohol usage (days and amounts) and of recovery capital (psychological and physical health, quality of life (QOL), days at work or college and housing issues) were collected using the TOP form (Marsden et al., 2008). Data on flourishing were collected using the Flourishing Scale (Diener et al., 2010) and data on impulsivity was measured using the impulsivity section of the Low Self-Control Measure (LSC) (Grasmick, Tittle, Bursik, & Arneklev, 1993). The study found TRP significantly decreased alcohol use and impulsivity and increased flourishing and some elements of recovery capital, compared to TAU. The changes were maintained at 1- and 3-months post-intervention, compared to pre-intervention. The study on alcohol use, although limited by attrition levels common in this field, increases the evidence for the applicability and efficacy of the LP concepts across a range of health issues.

A qualitative study (n = 15) (Parker et al., 2020) used thematic analysis to evaluate how the TRP approach was adopted and valued by participants and how it compared to other approaches. It also considered how aware participants were of any changes achieved through the intervention. It identified two main themes (1) control and (2) flourishing. All participants reported positive experiences of the intervention, with only one reporting no change in alcohol use. Differences between this approach and others were also noted. This small-scale study is useful as a counterpoint to earlier qualitative studies as it identifies positive experiences of the intervention and none of the more negative reports or issues found in those by Reme et al. (2012) and Sandaunet & Salamonsen (2012).

The LP protocol paper (Parker, 2020) detailed the mechanics of the approach, referencing each step and concept of the intervention from evidence bases familiar to those experienced in psychology, positive psychology, PNI and educational theory. The review paper also described the LP's approach and its relevance to the CFS/ME disease mechanisms (Parker et al., 2018). It highlighted that the approach, although grounded in psychology, does not approach the illness as a psychological one, but as a physical illness that can be helped by applying the concepts identified in PNI research to change physiological function.

Discussion of findings

Developing quality of the evidence and resistance

These studies provide a timeline of the research, starting with the earliest studies published in 2010, with subsequent studies improving in quality with time, culminating in a well-conducted RCT. The limitations present in the early studies, with the recognised potential for bias in recruitment and issues with the use of small scale qualitative or survey methodology (Bringsli et al., 2013; Fønnebø et al., 2012; ME Association, 2010; Reme et al., 2012; Sandaunet & Salamonsen, 2012), might account for some the variability reported in the outcomes not found in the later quantitative studies. These later higher-quality studies provide more robust evidence – for example the absence of severe adverse events reported in the RCT (n =100) (Crawley et al., 2018) compared to self-reports, attributed to the intervention 6-12 months after it, of worsening of symptoms (n =3) (Fønnebø et al., 2012).

The systematic review concluded that it 'identified an emerging body of evidence supporting the efficacy of the LP for many participants with fatigue, physical function, pain, anxiety and depression' (Parker et al., 2020, p. 6). The significant outcomes seen in the RCT (Crawley et al., 2018) were also found in the RCT into substance use (Parker, Banbury, & Chandler, 2020). However, echoing some of the issues faced by NLP, the ME/CFS community and aligned charities seem inclined to be negative towards any non-pharmacological approach, including the LP. Despite the LP being the approach considered to be 'greatly improved' (25.7%) in their survey (2010), the ME association focused on those feeling much worse (12.9%) see Table 8.3. The same charity actively attempted to prevent the RCT research (ME Association, 2017) and the Action for ME charity commented on the findings, 'We are extremely surprised to see that the Lightning Process... offers improvement for some young people with M.E.' (Action for ME, 2017), with no evidence to support their presumption of a different expected outcome or for interpreting the findings reported as 'significant' as 'improvement for some'. Others attempted, unsuccessfully, to discredit the RCT (Brown, 2019) but clarifications in a second edition of the paper addressed all the criticisms raised. It is hoped the systematic review, the additional research and the detailed explanation of the LP approach and the PNI research that supports it will allow for a more informed and evidenced-based discussion of the benefits for some of the approach.

Contribution to PNI

As can be seen from the discussion on PNI research there is a great deal of interest in the field and extensive evidence for its potential applications in health. Many of the studies rely on the placebo effect and utilise a variety of interactions to create the effect. These include verbal suggestion (this cream will help), conditioning (pairing strong-tasting drinks with drugs), developing an expectation of change through previous experience, trust in the practitioner, social learning (seeing others improving through taking the drug) or explanations of how the substance will work. This work has been recommended for adoption into medical training and consultations (Hansen & Zech, 2019), but there are fewer programmes that use the PNI as their main therapeutic mechanism. The LP's use of these PNI concepts as the grounding for its techniques, therefore, contributes appreciably to the clinical applications of the field. As an NLP derived approach this helps place NLP within the evidence base of the increasingly valued field of PNI.

Suggestions for future research

These studies suggest the LP, and therefore NLP, may provide solutions to illnesses like ME/CFS with currently poor outcomes, however, more research is needed. LP is helped by its clear methodology and standardised delivery structure so that the intervention can be easily replicated. These are issues that NLP needs to address to achieve similar research goals. The LP research requires larger more diverse populations to help identify who would most benefit and, by comparing the LP to a single intervention, evaluate if the results of the RCT can be replicated on a larger scale. Finally identifying the biochemical and neurological changes, hypothesised by LP and NLP, using biochemical and functional imaging investigations, would assist in understanding the proposed mechanisms of action of these intriguing approaches.

References

Action for ME. (2017). SMILE Trial results published: Action for M.E. comment. *Action for ME.* https://www.actionforme.org.uk/news/smile-trial-results-published-action-for-me-comment/

Ahn, E., & Kang, H. (2018). Introduction to systematic review and meta-analysis. *Korean Journal of Anesthesiology*, 71(2), 103–112. doi:10.4097/kjae.2018.71.2.103

Aktiv Prosess. (2016). *Deltakerevaluering-uten-diagnoser.pdf.* https://www.livelandmark.no/wp-content/uploads/2011/11/Deltakerevaluering-uten diagnoser.pdf

Aldao, A., Nolen-Hoeksema, S., & Schweizer, S. (2010). Emotion-regulation strategies across psychopathology: A meta-analytic review. *Clinical Psychology Review*, 30(2), 217–237. doi:10.1016/j.cpr.2009.11.004

Andreas, C., & Andreas, S. (1989). *Heart of the mind.* Boulder, CO: Real People Press.

Bandler, R., Grinder, J., Satir, V., & Bateson, G. (2005). *The structure of magic, Vol. 1:A book about language and therapy* (1st edition). Palo Alto, CA: Science and Behavior Books.

Benedetti, F., Colloca, L., Torre, E., Lanotte, M., Melcarne, A., Pesare, M., Bergamasco, B., & Lopiano, L. (2004). Placebo-responsive Parkinson patients show decreased activity in single neurons of subthalamic nucleus. *Nature Neuroscience*, 7(6), 587–588. doi:10.1038/nn1250

Bringsli, G. J., Gilje, A., & Wold, B. K. G. (2013). *ME-syke i Norge – Fortsatt bortgjemt?* Norges ME–forenIng. http://www.me-foreningen.info/wp-content/uploads/2016/09/ME-Nat-Norwegian-Survey-Abr-Eng-Ver.pdf

Brown, N. (2019). Editor's note on correction to Crawley *et al. (2018). Archives of Disease in Childhood,* 104(10), 155–164. doi:10.1136/archdischild-2017-313375 ednote

Bryant, F. B., Smart, C. M., & King, S. P. (2005). Using the past to enhance the present: Boosting happiness through positive reminiscence. *Journal of Happiness Studies*, 6(3), 227–260. doi:10.1007/s10902-005-3889

Crawley, E., Gaunt, D., Garfield, K., Hollingworth, W., Sterne, J., Beasant, L., Collin, S. M., Mills, N., & Montgomery, A. A. (2018). Clinical and cost-effectiveness of the Lightning Process in addition to specialist medical care for paediatric chronic fatigue syndrome: Randomised controlled trial. *Archives of Disease in Childhood*, 103, 155–164. doi:10.1136/archdischild-2017-31337

Crawley, E., Mills, N., Beasant, L., Johnson, D., Collin, S., Deans, Z., White, K., & Montgomery, A. (2013). The feasibility and acceptability of conducting a trial of specialist medical care and the Lightning Process in children with chronic fatigue syndrome: Feasibility randomized controlled trial (SMILE study). *Trials*, 14(1), 415. doi:10.1186/1745-6215-14-415

Davis, J. I., Senghas, A., Brandt, F., & Ochsner, K. N. (2010). The effects of BOTOX injections on emotional experience. *Emotion*, 10(3), 433. doi:10.1037/a0018690

Diener, E., Wirtz, D., Tov, W., Kim-Prieto, C., Choi, D., Oishi, S., & Biwas-Diener, R. (2010). New measures of well-being: Flourishing and positive and negative feelings. *Social Indicators Research*, 39, 247–266. doi:10.1007/s11205-009-9493-y

Dilts, R., & DeLozier, J. (2000). *Allergy Process*. http://nlpuniversitypress.com/html/AaAj22.html

Dilts, R., Hallbom, T., & Smith, S. (2012). *Beliefs: Pathways to health and well-being* (2nd edition). Crown House Publishing.

Eck, J., Richter, M., Straube, T., Miltner, W. H., & Weiss, T. (2011). Affective brain regions are activated during the processing of pain-related words in migraine patients. *Pain*, 152(5), 1104–1113. doi:10.1016/j.pain.2011.01.026

Finch, F. (2014). *MS proof of concept study*. doi.org/10.13140/RG.2.2.26462.79686

Finch, F. (2013). *Outcomes measures study*. doi.org/10.13140/RG.2.2.29818.24002

Finch, F. (2010). *LP* snapshot survey for clients. doi.org/10.13140/RG.2.2.231 07.35366

Fønnebø, V., Drageset, B. J., & Salamonsen, A. (2012). Worst cases reported to the NAFKAM International Registry of Exceptional Courses of Disease. *Global Advances in Health and Medicine*, 1(1), 30. doi:10.7453/gahmj.2012.1.1.008

Goebel, M. U., Meykadeh, N., Kou, W., Schedlowski, M., & Hengge, U. R. (2008). Behavioral conditioning of antihistamine effects in patients with allergic rhinitis. *Psychotherapy and Psychosomatics*, 77(4), 227–234. doi:10.1159/000126074

Goebel, M. U., Trebst, A. E., Steiner, J., Xie, Y. F., Exton, M. S., Frede, S., Canbay, A. E., Michel, M. C., Heemann, U., & Schedlowski, M. (2002). Behavioral conditioning of immunosuppression is possible in humans. *The FASEB Journal*, 16(14), 1869–1873. doi:10.1096/fj.02-0389com

Grasmick, H. G., Tittle, C. R., Bursik, R. J., & Arneklev, B. J. (1993). Testing the core empirical implications of Gottfredson and Hirschi's general theory of crime. *Journal of Research in Crime and Delinquency*, 30(1), 5–29. doi:10.1177/002242 7893030001002

Grinder, J., & Pucelik, F. (2013). *Origins of Neuro Linguistic Programming*. Bancyfelin: Crown House Publishing.

Grossman, P., Niemann, L., Schmidt, S., & Walach, H. (2004). Mindfulness-based stress reduction and health benefits: A meta-analysis. *Journal of Psychosomatic Research*, 57(1), 35–43. doi:10.1016/S0022-3999(03)00573-7

Hagelsteen, J. H., & Moen Reiten, I. M. (2015). Evaluation of a treatment strategy. *Dagens Medicin*. http://www.dagensmedisin.no/artikler/2015/10/12/evaluering-av-en-behandlingsstrategi/

Hamann, S. (2001). Cognitive and neural mechanisms of emotional memory. *Trends in Cognitive Sciences*, 5(9), 394–400. doi:10.1016/S1364-6613(00)01707-1

Hansen, E., & Zech, N. (2019). Nocebo effects and negative suggestions in daily clinical practice – forms, impact and approaches to avoid them. *Frontiers in Pharmacology*, 10. doi:10.3389/fphar.2019.00077

Hibbard, J. H., & Greene, J. (2013). What the evidence shows about patient activation: Better health outcomes and care experiences; fewer data on costs. *Health Affairs*, 32(2), 207–214. doi:10.1377/hlthaff.2012.1061

Izenberg, G. N. (2015). *The existentialist critique of Freud: The crisis of autonomy*. Princeton University Press.

Kahneman, D. (2011). *Thinking, Fast and Slow*. Penguin.

Kahneman, D., & Miller, D. (1986). Norm theory: Comparing reality to its alternatives. *Psychological Review*, 93(2), 136–153. doi:10.1037/0033-295X.93.2.136

Kaptchuk, T. J., Friedlander, E., Kelley, J. M., Sanchez, M. N., Kokkotou, E., Singer, J. P., Kowalczykowski, M., Miller, F. G., Kirsch, I., & Lembo, A. J. (2010). Placebos without Deception: A Randomized Controlled Trial in Irritable Bowel Syndrome. *PLoS ONE*, 5(12), e15591. doi:10.1371/journal.pone.0015591

Kirchhof, J., Petrakova, L., Brinkhoff, A., Benson, S., Schmidt, J., Unteroberdörster, M., Wilde, B., Kaptchuk, T. J., Witzke, O., & Schedlowski, M. (2018). Learned immunosuppressive placebo responses in renal transplant patients. *Proceedings of the National Academy of Sciences*, 115(16), 4223–4227. doi:10.1073/pnas.1720548115

Kirsch, I. (2018). Response expectancy and the placebo effect. In *International Review of Neurobiology* (Vol. 138, pp. 81–93). Elsevier. 10.1016/bs.irn.2018.01.003

Kristoffersen, A. E., Musial, F., Hamre, H. J., Björkman, L., Stub, T., Salamonsen, A., & Alræk, T. (2016). Use of complementary and alternative medicine in patients with health complaints attributed to former dental amalgam fillings. *BMC Complementary and Alternative Medicine*, 16, 22. doi:10.1186/s12906-016-0996-1

Krupp, L. B., Alvarez, L. A., LaRocca, N. G., & Scheinberg, L. C. (1988). Fatigue in multiple sclerosis. *Archives of Neurology*, 45(4), 435–437. doi:10.1001/archneur.1988.00520280085020

Locher, C., Frey Nascimento, A., Kirsch, I., Kossowsky, J., Meyer, A., & Gaab, J. (2017). Is the rationale more important than deception? A randomized controlled trial of open-label placebo analgesia. *PAIN*, 158(12), 2320–2328. doi:10.1097/j.pain.0000000000001012

Long, A. F., & Godfrey, M. (2004). An evaluation tool to assess the quality of qualitative research studies. *International Journal of Social Research Methodology*, 7(2), 181–196. doi:10.1080/1364557032000045302

Marsden, J., Farrell, M., Bradbury, C., Dale-Perera, A., Eastwood, B., Roxburgh, M., & Taylor, S. (2008). Development of the treatment outcomes profile. *Addiction*, 103(9), 1450–1460. doi:10.1111/j.1360-0443.2008.02284.x

Mathôt, S., Grainger, J., & Strijkers. (2017). Pupillary responses to words that convey a sense of brightness or darkness. *Psychological Science*, 2017, 956797617702699. doi:10.1177/0956797617702699

ME Association. (2010). *Managing my M.E.* ME Association. http://www.meassociation.org.uk/wp-content/uploads/2010/09/2010-survey-report-lo-res10.pdf

ME Association. (2017). *Lightning Process and SMILE trial*. https://meassociation.org.uk/2017/09/me-association-statement-lightning-process-and-smile-trial-in-young-people-with-mecfs-19-september-2017/

Meeuwis, S. H., van Middendorp, H., van Laarhoven, A. I. M., Veldhuijzen, D. S., Lavrijsen, A. P. M., & Evers, A. W. M. (2019). Effects of open- and closed-label nocebo and placebo suggestions on itch and itch expectations. *Frontiers in Psychiatry*, 10, 436. doi:10.3389/fpsyt.2019.00436

NAFKAM. (2011). *Nafkam warning note*. https://uit.no/Content/279128/RESF,%20varsel%20LP%2023122011.pdf

National Heart Lung and Blood Institute. (2014). *Study Quality Assessment Tools -*. https://www.nhlbi.nih.gov/health-topics/study-quality-assessment-tools

Neff, K. D., Kirkpatrick, K. L., & Rude, S. S. (2007). Self-compassion and adaptive psychological functioning. *Journal of Research in Personality*, 41(1), 139–154. doi:10.1016/j.jrp.2006.03.004

Nickel, B., Barratt, A., Copp, T., Moynihan, R., & McCaffery, K. (2017). Words do matter: A systematic review on how different terminology for the same condition influences management preferences. *BMJ Open*, 7(7), e014129. doi:10.1136/bmjopen-2016-014129

Parker, P. (2011). *Dû: Unlock your full potential with a word*. Nipton Publishing.

Parker, P. (2012). *An introduction to the Lightning Process®: The first steps to getting well*. Hay House.

Parker, P. (2013). Get *the* lif*e* you lo*ve*, now*:* H*o*w to use *t*he Li*ghtning Process® toolkit for happiness and fulfilment*. Hay House.

Parker, P. (2020). *LP Protocol 2020*. 10.13140/RG.2.2.22761.72801

Parker, P., Aston, J., & de Rijk, L. (2020). A Systematic Review of the Evidence Base for the Lightning Process. *EXPLORE*, 1–30. https://doi.org/10.1016/j.explore.2020.07.014

Parker, P., Aston, J., & Finch, F. (2018). Understanding the Lightning Process approach to CFS/ME; a review of the disease process and the approach. *Journal of Experiential Psychotherapy*, 21(2), 8. https://jep.ro/images/pdf/cuprins_reviste/82_art_2.pdf

Parker, P., Banbury, S., & Chandler, C. (2020). Efficacy of the rediscovery process on alcohol use, impulsivity and flourishing: A preliminary randomised controlled study and preliminary cohort study. *EJAPP*, 4(13). https://www.nationalwellbeingservice.org/volumes/volume-4-2020/volume-4-article-13/

Parker, P., Banbury, S., & de Rijk, L. (2021). Self-control or flourishing? A thematic analysis of experiences of alcohol users of The Rediscovery Process. *International Journal of Mental Health and Addiction*. https://doi.org/10.1007/s11469-021-00520-3

Popay, J., Roberts, H., Sowden, A., Petticrew, M., Arai, L., Rodgers, M., Britten, N., Roen, K., & Duffy, S. (2006). Guidance on the conduct of narrative synthesis in systematic reviews. *A Product from the ESRC Methods Programme Version*, 1, b92.

Price, D. D., McGrath, P. A., Rafii, A., & Buckingham, B. (1983). The validation of visual analogue scales as ratio scale measures for chronic and experimental pain. *Pain*, 17(1), 45–56. doi:10.1016/0304-3959(83)90126-4

Reme, S. E., Archer, N., & Chalder, T. (2012). Experiences of young people who have undergone the Lightning Process to treat chronic fatigue syndrome/myalgic encephalomyelitis—A qualitative study. *British Journal of Health Psychology*, 18(3), 508–525. doi:10.1111/j.2044-8287.2012.02093.x

Richter, M., Eck, J., Straube, T., Miltner, W.H.R., & Weiss, T. (2010). Do words hurt? Brain activation during the processing of pain-related words. *PAIN*, 148(2), 198–20510.1016/j.pain.2009.08.009.

Richter, M., Schroeter, C., Puensch, T., Straube, T., Hecht, H., Ritter, A., Miltner, W. H., & Weiss, T. (2014). Pain-related and negative semantic priming enhances perceived pain intensity. *Pain Research and Management*, 19(2), 69–74. doi:10.1155/2014/425321

Rogers, C. R. (2004). *On becoming a person a therapist's view of psychotherapy.* Edinburgh: Constable.

Sharpe, M. C., Archard, L. C., Banatvala, J. E., Borysiewicz, L. K., Clare, A. W., David, A., Edwards, R. H., Hawton, K. E., Lambert, H. P., & Lane, R. J. (1991). A report--chronic fatigue syndrome: Guidelines for research. *Journal of the Royal Society of Medicine*, 84(2), 118–121.

Sharpley, C. (1984) Predicate matching in NLP: A review of research on the preferred representational system. *Journal of Counseling Psychology*, 31(2): 238–248.

Snaith, R. P., & Zigmond, A. S. (1986). The hospital anxiety and depression scale. *British Medical Journal (Clinical Research Ed.)*, 292(6516), 344. doi:10.1136/bmj.292.6516.344

Sandaunet, A.-G., & Salamonsen, A. (2012). CFE-/ME-pasienters ulike erfaringer med Lightning Process. *Sykepleien Forskning*, 7(3), 262–268. doi:10.4220/sykepleienfReme.2012.0132

Science Media Centre. (2017, September 20). *Expert reaction to controversial treatment for CFS/ME.* http://www.sciencemediacentre.org/expert-reaction-to-controversial-treatment-for-cfsme/

Selye, H. (1978). *The stress of life* (Rev. ed). McGraw-Hill.

Speer, M. E., & Delgado, M. R. (2017). Reminiscing about positive memories buffers acute stress responses. *Nature Human Behaviour*, 1(5), s41562-017-0093–017. doi:10.1038/s41562-017-0093

Spence, S. H. (1998). A measure of anxiety symptoms among children. *Behaviour Research and Therapy*, 36(5), 545–566. doi:10.1016/S0005-7967(98)00034-5

Sturt, J., Ali, S., Robertson, W., Metcalfe, D., Grove, A., Bourne, C., & Bridle, C. (2012). Neurolinguistic programming: a systematic review of the effects on health outcomes. *British Journal of General Practice*, Nov, 62(604):e757–e764. doi:10.3399/bjgp12X658287. PMID: 23211179; PMCID: PMC3481516.

Sussex & Kent ME/CFS Society. (2010). *Pacing Helps ME 2010*. Sussex & Kent ME/CFS Society. http://measussex.org.uk/pacing-helps-me-2010/

Wake, L., Gray, R. M., & Bourke, F. S. (Eds.). (2013). *The clinical effectiveness of neurolinguistic programming: A critical appraisal.* Routledge.

Ware, J. E., & Sherbourne, C. D. (1992). The MOS 36-item short-form health survey (SF-36). I. Conceptual framework and item selection. *Medical Care*, 30(6), 473–483. doi:10.1097/00005650-199206000-00002

Wise, J. H. (2002). The S.T.O.P. Sign Technique. *The Family Journal*, 10(4), 433–436. doi:10.1177/106648002236764

Yorke, A. M., & Cohen, E. T. (2015). Functional assessment of multiple sclerosis. *Journal of Physiotherapy*, 61(4), 226. doi:10.1016/j.jphys.2015.05.021

9 Applying the mental space psychology paradigm in eating disorders in women

Jacqueline Heemskerk-Scholten

This chapter explores how the mental space of women with weight and binge-eating problems is structured. The chapter explores how and where they perceive their self-image, their overweight, and the food they cannot avoid and considers the appropriate NLP interventions to remedy this.

Twelve women with long-term overweight complaints were coached for a period of five months with 1 session monthly. By keeping the focus on the spatial representation of the complaints, the contours of a possible working protocol rapidly began to take shape. The results hold out the prospect of a more effective approach.

A mental-space approach to compulsive eating behaviour and overweight

This chapter explores how NLP therapy can be used to change the spatial representation of food and body fat surplus in women who complain of being overweight from binge eating and at the same time guide them towards balanced eating patterns.

Background

Beginning when the author joined the board of the Society for Mental Space Psychology (SOMSP) and continuing with her involvement as a therapist in the MSP – Depression research project (see Chapter 6) (Derks, 2016; Beenhakker, 2016; Beenhakker & Manea, 2017), the author started to investigate how overweight women, with Binge Eating Disorder, experience this problem in their mental space and what forms of treatment are effective for this condition.

This case series pilot study, starting in November 2017, was aimed at women who had been trying for years, if not their whole adult life, to lose weight by means of diets and sports. These women were not able to motivate themselves to adhere to a diet or exercise. As a result, slimming succeeded only temporarily. As a consequence they have faced much disappointment,

DOI: 10.4324/9781003198864-9

frustration and the yo-yo effect (Wallner et al., 2004). Despite many attempts their problem with food persisted. Over the past 25 years the author has regularly treated overweight women with Binge Eating Disorder in her psychotherapy practice using a combination of Mental Space Psychology and NLP techniques and appeared successful. This research project aims to make this experience available for other professionals.

Binge Eating Disorders (BED) is broadly similar to bulimia nervosa. There is one major difference. Clients with bulimia try to get rid of the food after the binge. Clients with binge disorder do not. This increases their weight, which makes the binge disorder visible. BED is a recently proposed eating disorder diagnosis that first appeared in the appendix of DSM-IV (Birgegård, Clinton, & Norring, 2013), now in the DSM5 (American Psychiatric Association); 307.51 (F50.81). During a binge, the clients feel that they have completely lost control over their eating behaviour. They stuff themselves in a short time with a large amount of food (often snacks, chocolates, and other fatty foods) and can't stop. These clients derive little pleasure from the binge, they don't even particularly taste the food. Afterwards, they feel weak and guilty.

Women whose dieting and slimming succeed with ease don't seek counselling, as they solve the problem on their own, or with the help of a dietician. In those who fail to do so, the issues may have a higher level of complexity. The author recognised that for the latter clients there is always another problem underlying the problem of BED and overweight (Brewerton, 1999; Payton, 2012; Fitzsimmons-Craft et al., 2014).

In the footsteps of Bandler (1985), Derks (2016) has prioritized the role of spatial organization in all thought and experience. This paradigm is now called Mental Space Psychology. This idea largely inspired this pilot study. Based on this idea, the hypothesis in this study is, that the locations (distance, level, size, and direction) of where people perceive food in their mental space determines the amount of (unconscious) motivation to eat it.

The initial aim of the study was to investigate the spatial representation of food and also how they experience their overweight in their mental space: two striking observations had already been made in clients with binge eating and overweight problems. In these clients, the author observed that attempts to change their eating behaviour, by just moving the images of food, worked only partially. Hence, the author wished to probe the clients' lack of success and searched for underlying problems using NLP questioning methods followed by NLP interventions. This approach led to a brief treatment method.

Furthermore, the author wanted to investigate which NLP techniques were most effective in dealing with any underlying issues, and subsequently whether the images of food and overweight remained in their new sites once and for all, (at least within the observation period). Measures included reductions in body weight and changes in eating habits.

Design of the pilot study

Participants

Participants were recruited by convenience sampling through advertisements in regional media or on Facebook. An appeal was made to overweight women who would be willing to participate in a study around binge-eating and overweight. After receiving 20 calls, 12 participants were selected for this study. Inclusion criteria were: female, pre-menopausal, age range 16–55. Exclusion criteria: obesity due to a medical condition (e.g., hypothyroidism, insulin resistance, polycystic ovary syndrome, Cushing's syndrome), postmenopausal, on a current diet, on medication, current therapy for eating disorder.

The 12 overweight participants varied in age between 17 and 52 years (median 31, mean 34). The participants were numbered in order of their acceptance into the study. All participants had tried different diets, with and without professional help. None had succeeded in losing weight. Others had gained even more weight than they had lost after finishing the diet, the so-called yo-yo effect (Wallner et al., 2004). The motivation to lose weight in other ways, such as by exercise was generally insufficient. So the treatment offered to them was presented as an alternative way to whatever they had tried before. The participants were invited to visit the private practice. The sessions took between 60 and 120 minutes. No fees were charged. They were asked to read and then sign a contract (informed consent) that included information on what was expected from them in time and commitment and what service they could expect from the author as well as the importance of this research. In the course of the study, 2 out of 12 participants dropped out for personal reasons after their first consultation. Data is included as an intent to treat.

Pseudo control group

In parallel with the overweight and binge eating participants, the author assembled a comparison group of 6 normal-weight women. These women were convenience sampled from the acquaintances of the author. None of the control group had any affinity with NLP or Mental Space Psychology.

Diagnostic phase

The first session opened with an inventory of the participants' history with overweight. Also, as well as in the following sessions, the location of problem foods, overweight and their self-image were pinpointed in subjective space (Bandler, 1985; Derks, 2016). This was done by first having the participant concentrate on herself, and next ask her to think about a specific food item. Then followed the question where the image of this food item appeared in the space around her. The distance, direction, and height of the images were subjectively measured by having the participants first point out the locations with their hands. Then, the distance, direction, and height from the position and level of the eyes were estimated by the author in centimetres, and the direction in clock hours – where straight in front is 12 o'clock. Where the images appeared was sketched on paper. In this way, breakfast, lunch and dinner, as well as more specific "sweets", "salty snacks", and "junk food", and diversity of drinks were mapped. This created a clear representation of where the participant had unconsciously stored the most consumed (problem) food items in her mental space. The image of overweight was examined by first letting the participants focus on themselves and next by asking them what they thought was their excess weight. Here, the author uses the words/names the participants themselves gave to their overweight, such as: fat, kgs, weight, overweight. After that they were asked to look at the image of this excess and indicate with their hands where this image appeared. The position of the overweight image (its sub-modalities) was also sketched on paper. This drawing included the distance, the colour, the width, the height, and where it was in relation to the body of the participant. The quality of the self-image was explored, as this is believed to be of great influence in eating disorders (Derks, 2005; Massimo, Bellini, Donini, & Santomassimo, 2008; Runfola, Thornton, Pisetsky, Bulik, & Birgegård, 2014).

Interventions

Right after the mapping of the food items in mental space, spatial interventions were applied, in the sense of shifting the images of the problem foods further away, downwards and out of the visual centre. Any signs of resistance were noted. The latter helped to find the underlying causes of the binge eating and overweight. Based on what the resistance revealed, a variety of NLP and related interventions were used.

- Reframing (Bandler & Grinder,1982).
- Six-Step Reframing (Bandler & Grinder, 1982).
- Working with Submodalities (Bandler, 1985).
- Reimprinting (Dilts, 1997).
- Double Dissociation (Bandler & Grinder, 1979).
- Silent Abreaction (Watkins, 1980).
- Social Panorama, transferring resources to parents/ancestors (Derks, 2002, 2005).
- New Behaviour Generator (Bandler & Grinder, 1979).
- Compulsion Blowout (Bandler, 1999: in Andreas & Andreas, 1989).
- Progressive relaxation (Jacobson (1938).
- Mindfulness exercise, in eating consciously and slowly (Kabat-Zinn, 1991).

All results were recorded and in the next session, similar spatial explorations were carried out, and related to the remaining tendencies to over-eat.

By using the previously mentioned NLP interventions, these remaining tendencies were dealt with. Besides the reported behavioural changes, the maintained shifts to a greater distance of the represented problem food were regarded as the main indicators of therapeutic effect.

Results of the pilot study

Binges

At the start, all 12 overweight participants had regular eating binges, ranging from 4 times per week to several times per day. When they returned a month after the first consultation (or in a follow-up check with 2 dropouts), 7 out of 12 reported no binges, 3 reported fewer binges and 2 remained unchanged.

Weight

At intake, the lightest participant weighed 79 kg (174 lb) and the heaviest one 134 kg (295 lb) (median 98 kg, mean 99.33). Over the five months of the pilot study the mean weight of the participants dropped nearly 7 kg to 92.40 kg (corrected for dropouts; the weight loss ranged from 2 kg to 15 kg with a median of 4). Only one participant had gained (1 kg). In comparison, the 6 normal weight (pseudo control) participants had a median age of 46.5 years (range: 33 to 58). Their median weight was 67.5 kg (mean 67.1; range: 59 kg to 76 kg). These women had only one exploration session.

General findings from spatial diagnostics

The central focus in this pilot study was on the spatial representation of problem foods. During the first consultation the mental spatial locations of the unhealthy food items that the participants craved for and binged on, in general, appeared within arms reach (Wildes & Marcus, 2013). Usually they see the problematic food items close to themselves, in the centre of their visual field and just below eye level. The direction in which the problem food appeared in their visual field was indicated in clock hours, where 12 o'clock represents straight in front of their eyes. The locations of a variety of food items were investigated. Here we present these as they appeared before treatment, in the 3 main categories:

1. Sweets, including cake, pastry, and chocolate.
   Distance: range 5 cm to 55 cm; median 27.5 cm; mean 27.9 cm
   Elevation in relation to eye level: range down −35 cm up to +10 cm; median −2.5 cm; mean −6.7 cm under eye level.
   Direction in clock hour: range (left) 9 to (right) 13 o'clock; median 12:00; mean 11:50.

2. Salty snacks including potato chips.
   Distance: range 10 cm to 80 cm; median 50 cm; mean 49.6 cm
   Elevation in relation to eye level: range down −60 cm up to +20 cm; median −7.5 cm; mean −16.3 cm under eye level
   Direction in clock hour: range (left) 8 to (right) 13:30 o'clock; median 12:00; mean 11:28.
3. Junk food like fried potato, burgers, pizza.
   Distance: range 30 cm to 80 cm; median 50 cm; mean 49.6 cm
   Elevation in relation to eye level: range down −60 cm up to +30 cm; median −10 cm; mean −10 cm under eye level.
   Direction in clock hour: range (left) 10 to (right) 13 o'clock; median 12:00; mean 11:53.

Other attractive food is usually situated from about 100 cm up to 150 cm directly or obliquely before themselves and between 0 cm and −60 cm below their own eye level. Disliked food is located further away, at a distance from about 100 cm up to 1800 cm. and/or behind them. They are often seen at more than +50 cm above their eye level. (Figure 9.1)

The spatial diagnostics with slender women

As already mentioned, for the purpose of comparison, the author studied the spatial representation of food in six women without any eating problems. These women did not represent unhealthy fattening food as being within reach in their mental space. When they discussed fattening foods, they spoke about "occasional sweets, biscuits", etc. They also represented these as one single item at the time and not in a large amount: like a couple of nuts or a small piece of cake. For example, participant #25 has potato

Figure 9.1 The spatial diagnostics with slender women.

chips at a distance of 100 centimetres but eats these about once every two weeks and sees them as just a small portion (a teacup full). In fact, these normal-weight women seemed to give food little or no extra thought. If experimented with, it appeared that the food they had nearby in their mental space could be easily shifted away without any resistance whatsoever.

Five of six members of the pseudo-control group had a positive self-image (are happy with themselves) in the context of family, acquaintances and work (Derks, 2005). In the context of strangers, three of them had a positive self-image, the other two had self-images that were slightly lower than eye level (−20 cm and −50 cm).

There was one control participant who in all explored contexts had a self image that was lower than her own eye level (−40 cm). That image was also described as being negative. Her explanation was that she had received the diagnosis of personality disorder (NOS) in the past.

The spatial representation of overweight

The 12 participants in this pilot study are for the most part focused on losing the excess weight. The question is, where in their mental space do they experience their overweight?

Nine out of twelve participants indicated that they saw their overweight as a girdle of fat around them, ranging from a girdle around the abdomen to a full-body image reaching from the shoulders to the ankles. The girdle could be seen as fitting tightly, but also with a small space between it and the body. The subjectively experienced thickness of such a girdle varied from 10 to 60 cm.

The girdles were coloured and included dark grey, brown, yellow, skin colour, and were sometimes translucent.

There were two participants, the numbers 10 and 11 who did not see their overweight as a girdle of fat around the body. Number 10 saw it as a heap of grease, at three metres distance on the floor in front of her, while number 11 saw it as two large bags of fat. Thus, overweight can also be seen dissociated from the body. In such cases, the participant did not perceive it as belonging to her. At the second consultation, client number 11 no longer saw the bags of fat, the perception had changed to a half girdle of fat on her belly. Participant number 12 saw the overweight as a shadow of herself at 2 metres distance.

The perception of the self-image

All participants had a self-image with a negative content evaluation (ugly, appalling). This surfaced when they felt aversion when focussing on who they are, which then made their self image taller and closer (Derks, 2005; Massimo et al., 2008; Runfola et al., 2014). At the start of the treatment these self-images were situated lower than their eye level and they saw themselves smaller than they see other people. This was explored within the contexts of family, their circle of friends, their work situation, and when among strangers.

Treatment: interventions and their effects

Spatial interventions with food

The therapist helped to clarify the mental locations of (problem) foods: by having the participant make them visually concrete in sketches and by physically indicating their locations in mental space with their hands.

When participants tried to move the food around in their mental space, to out of reach or out of sight positions, they all discovered that this cannot be done just like that: "stronger objecting forces" appear to be working from the inside; forces that put the food back to the foreground. And what did not succeed in their imagination also appeared difficult in the participants' reality. Not thinking about unhealthy food, or not buying it proved almost impossible, the desire for it remained, because images of the unhealthy food were unconsciously so emphatically present (Latner et al., 2006).

The effect of the exploration of the food panorama

Because, during this work, the participant starts to understand how she unconsciously keeps (problem) food within sight and reach in her mental space, it becomes evident to her that this makes it difficult to forget about it. This insight helps the participant to understand her own patterns. This is helpful, but usually insufficient for a change in behaviour. But being aware of the situation *does* help to have less guilt, disappointment or anger towards themselves.

The experience of not being able to simply move the food in mental space by one's own willpower ensures that the participant begins to focus on her underlying problems. Why do they experience the food so near at hand and why can't it be moved to a greater distance?

Spatial interventions with the overweight

The representation of fat as appearing in mental space, cannot just be intentionally removed, nor can it be moved or changed by the therapists' suggestions. When the attempt is made, it encounters resistance: it jumps back, the participant feels fear rising, or she completely loses contact with the fat girdle.

The effect of exploring the overweight in mental space

The representation of the overweight, which is seen in 9 out of 12, as a kind of girdle of fat around the participant, is at first seen as something completely negative. The participant is disgusted, angry or does not want to accept it. It gives her a bad or sad feeling. When felt at home, this may cause an eating binge, so that she is caught up in a negative spiral. Usually this is a fully unconscious process, but now the participant has become aware of it because the overweight is made visible in mental space. The participant had always tried to dissociate that part of themselves. This was especially true for the three participants who saw the overweight at a distance, for example, as a pile or a bag or a shadow of fat. These participants were even more negative about themselves and found it even harder than the rest to see the positive intention behind their overweight.

By default, the participants wanted to get rid of the overweight. But attempts to scale it down in size or shift this girdle of fat to another position in their imagination lead to meagre results: the girdle 'wants to stay'. It doesn't seem possible to make the girdle smaller, to move it further away, to give it a different colour, let alone eliminate it.

This, too, is very confrontational. The participant now understands that losing weight with diets won't succeed, and that there is more going on. She understands that her overweight and the overeating of unhealthy food is the result of an underlying problem and that it is this underlying problem that needs to be solved.

Now it is up to the participant to make a choice: do they commit to the presented perspective of working at the underlying issue or do they rather maintain their (ineffective) superficial approach to weight control?

Participants no. 7 and no. 10, who dropped out due to personal circumstances, had already shown (unconsciously), during the initial consultation that they were not prepared to look into the underlying problem.

Understanding the effectiveness of some NLP interventions in eating disorders

Exploring the positive intention of compulsive eating

Through advanced questioning techniques (Bandler & Grinder, 1982) insight can be gained in the positive intention of compulsive eating behaviour and of having and keeping overweight. By positive intention (PI) we mean the unconscious useful purpose. This helps considerably to grasp the underlying problem.

The commonest positive intentions of compulsive eating, are that the food helps to:

- suppress emotions,
- get a physically good feeling,
- get an emotionally good feeling,
- reward or encourage the person,
- get a sense of emotional control

Paradoxically, the positive feeling people get by compulsive (out of control) eating consists of a sense of (apparent) emotional control. Binge eating suppresses the dysphoric emotions like sadness, anger, fear and those evoked by a sense of being disapproved of or rejected by others. In addition, the food can also give an emotionally satisfying feeling. For example, the need for support, appreciation or love is replaced by tasty food. And also, the large amount of food causes a blood sugar peak, which causes a brief feeling of physical satisfaction (Herbozo, Schaefer, & Thompson, 2015).

The disturbing feelings raised by compulsive eating tend to reflect the opposite of emotional control; the participant may have a strong feeling of the loss of control. They lose control over their body (that is craving for food) and their behaviour (the binge); they have to give in to the urge to eat and cannot stop this process.

When the binge and the sugar peak are over, the participant usually feels guilty, disappointed in, or angry at themselves; but that too, distracts them from the underlying cause. The binges and the subsequent emotions usually cause an even more negative self-image than the participant often have already.

That is why the compulsive eating and being overweight to the point of being obese are in the minds of the participants as the crux of their problems. All of their conscious attention goes to this behaviour and condition respectively, which makes the chances of identifying and solving the underlying problems very slim. They are entering into an (almost) unwinnable fight with themselves.

The commonest positive intention of overweight (of having the girdle of fat)

- Denying and/or suppressing a negative self-image.
- A form of protection: usually protection against disapproval and rejection.
- Hiding, avoiding or denying an (old) problem.
- Denying and/or suppressing (trauma related) emotions.

Using overweight for protection, suppression, or denial, signals ineffective coping with earlier problem situations, where awkward emotions such as anger, sadness or pain, played a major role. The participant is usually no longer aware of these old problematic situations.

By discovering this link with the deeper issue, the participants are confronted with the problem underlying their binges and overweight. Most participants experienced it as a revelation and now understands their compulsive eating behaviour and why her excessive weight never comes off.

The usefulness of reframing

Now that the participant understands that the overweight girdle has a positive intention, a more positive name for it can be found. This is a standard part of the classical NLP technique Six Step Reframing (Bandler & Grinder, 1982).

Along with that comes the acceptance of the overweight as a part of themselves. In most participants, the formerly negatively rated overweight part, is now called the "protecting part" but also the "appreciating part" and the "awareness part" or something similar. In this way, the participants had immediately given themselves a better self-image, because the negative part of themselves has now changed into something positive. They may react happily and enthusiastically, often with amazement and relief. One participant remarked that she had accepted the changed overweight part as belonging to herself.

The effect of Six Step Reframing

After Six Step Reframing, most participants notice a "spontaneous" changed mental representation of food and overweight. It also becomes easier to change the subjective locations of food items by means of direct (sub-modality) suggestions. Then the images of problem foods can often be (partially) shifted away. With nine out of ten participants the girdle "spontaneously" got either less spacious or changed colour.

When the previously rejected overweight part becomes accepted, this in itself gives a significant shift in attitude:

- Self-acceptance is a healing force in all psychological change.
- The participants begin to realize that they themselves can change something, a positive way of experiencing control.
- The fight against the kgs and the food has changed into a process of awakening to oneself.
- They tend to become motivated to learn to better cope with the underlying issues and with (emotionally) awkward situations.

These elements are often at the heart of the underlying problem. Often they do not even feel their emotions because they have always suppressed them with food. If the participant knows how to cope with their problems in a better way, this will give them confidence, and as a consequence a better self-image. Then they no longer need the binges, and the excess weight, and they will begin to slowly lose weight.

Many therapists (and dieticians) have discovered that it usually doesn't help to simply tell the participant how they can (should) change their behaviour, because, indeed, they normally already know that themselves. The problem is that an old, unconscious pattern continues the emotional charge. This is stronger than the power of reason and therefore the participant continue to overeat and (unconsciously) does not want to let go of their overweight.

The value of Six-Step Reframing in changing behaviour

As the participant now understands that there is a Positive Intention, it may be focused upon, and the participant can look for new fulfillment of that intent.

So instead of eating, they can become aware, for example, of their awkward emotions. Consequently, they can begin to recognize and acknowledge them, and, as a result, deal with them in an effective manner. At this point the therapist may help the participant to find coping styles based on examples provided by other's behaviours who are more successful (new behaviour generator).

Clients in therapy may sometimes become aware of the fact that the problem-causing part still responds in a childish way, even though she herself is mature now. To find an appropriate coping strategy, the therapist may ask: Do you know someone who might react in a mature way to that awkward situation and who can also deal with the difficult emotions? (New Behavior Generator, Bandler & Grinder, 1979).

Together with the creative part, activated in Six-Step Reframing, therapist and participant can conceive better behaviours and propose them to the former overweight part, the protecting part, or otherwise renamed problem part. If, after finding alternative behaviours, there are no inner objections, the participant will be able to try the new behaviour in the following weeks (Bandler & Grinder, 1979). If there are still objections, an intervention other than Six-Step Reframing can be sought, to help find the right resources (capabilities). But sometimes there is already a strong resistance before Six-Step Reframing can be started, and therefore a different intervention must be used first (such as Reimprinting, Dilts, 1997).

As part of a test for ecology (the search for inner objections to change at the end of Six Step Reframing) one can monitor the locations of originally problematic foods in mental space as signs of progress; like whether the (former) overweight girdle has changed place and shape, and whether the original problematic personality part is now willing to bypass the issues of being overweight as a (surrogate) solution for the underlying issue?

The next consultation starts with checking the spatial representations of food and overweight as well as how the eating behaviour has changed. The personality part that was holding on to the excess weight is also tested to determine if it can now let go of it.

Evaluating the treatment effects

Behavioural changes reported as resulting from the treatment in this pilot study

At the start of the 2nd consultation (thus after the first session), seven (out of the 10) participants, who later completed all 5 consultations, reported they no longer had any binges, three others had fewer binges (Table 9.1). Seven of these participants had lost some weight after the first session, two had stayed the same, and one gained weight (1 kg). The latter participant (No. 1) still craved binges. However, she provided a strong case for the effectiveness of this five sessions therapy program. With her we had to break off the

Table 9.1 Overall overview of the results of the survey listed according to individual participant

Participant No. Age/ Height, Binges	*1st consultation*	*1st consultation*	*1st consultation*	*2nd consultation*	*2nd consultation*	*2nd consultation*	*5th consultation*	*5th consultation*	*5th consultation*	*5th consultation*
	Weight	*Image food*	*Image overweight*	*Image food*	*Image overweight*	*Binges*	*Image food*	*Image overweight*	*Weight and binges*	*Behaviour change*
Participant 1 20/ 1.66 yes	114.5	Dist. 20–80	Belt around 50 cm thick	As first consul-tation	As first consul-tation	yes	Everything is behind her	1 cm, at 60 cm distance	111 kg No	Positive self-image Better eating pattern
Participant 2 31/ 1.74 yes	104	Dist. 20–80 cm	Belt around 25 cm thick	Distance between 2 and 5 m.	Thinner 8 cm thick	No			98 kg; After the 2nd time stopped (opera-tion) No	
Participant 3 38/ 1.66 yes	83	Distance 20–80 cm	Belt around 10 cm thick	10 metres behind her	Thin and supple 2/ 3 cm thick	No		Robust, trans-parent 2 cm	79 kg, 1 size smaller. No	More peace Eating healthier Sport
Participant 4 45/ 1.67 yes	93	Distance 20–80 cm	Belt around 10 cm thick	Distance between 3 and 5 m.	Slimmer and 5 cm thick	Less	Everything is behind her	Belt is gone, internal little angel	89 kg No	More exercise, healthier food
Participant 5 31/ 1.70 yes	103	Distance 20–80 cm	Belt around 17 cm thick	Everything behind her out of reach	Is now wall 1.50 m. high at 45 cm distance	No	Everything is behind her at 6 to 7 m.	Wall is 30 cm high, 8 cm narrow, distance 1 m.	88 kg No	Positive self-image Sport

Participant 6 28/ 1.72 yes	114	Distance 20–80 cm	Belt around 30 cm thick	Diagonally behind her	Thin 1 cm and also as a dancing doll	Less	Everything is behind her or/ and far away 50 to 100 m	Belt is now small layer on belly. Puppet is clearer and stronger	112 kg, no Doesn't think about eating anymore	Positive self-image Can express feelings More exercise Other job, cheerful
Participant 7 44/ 1.73 yes	134	Distance 20–80 cm	Belt around 10 cm thick	Stopped, pers. circum-stances Called		Yes				
Participant 8 43/ 1.70 Yes	81.5	Distance 20–80 cm	Belt around 10 cm. thick	Stopped, moved house Called		No				
Participant 9 27/ 1.67 yes	81	Distance 20–80 cm	Belt around 20 cm. thick	Everything from 2 m. distance	As in the first consul-tation	No	everything from 3.5 m.	Belt 5 cm. thick	78 kg No	More exercise More confi-dent, can express emotions better

(*Continued*)

Table 9.1 (Continued)

Participant No. Age/ Height, Binges	*1st consultation* *Weight*	*1st consultation* *Image food*	*1st consultation* *Image overweight*	*2nd consultation* *Image food*	*2nd consultation* *Image overweight*	*2nd consultation* *Binges*	*5th consultation* *Image food*	*5th consultation* *Image overweight*	*5th consultation* *Weight and binges*	*5th consultation* *Behaviour change*
Participant 10 24/ 1.67 yes	84.5	Distance 20–80 cm	Big heap of fat of 30 cm at 3 m distance	Fatteners from 3 m. distance	Small heap 20 cm at 4 m.	Less, no sweet stuff anymore			78; after the 2nd time stopped (job too busy)	Sport Awaren-ess of emotions
Participant 11 52/ 1.71 Yes, every day	120	Distance 5–60 cm	2 large bags of fat on the ground at 10 cm and 50 cm	Food is gone, some-times it comes back but she puts it away again	Bags are gone, now half a rubber ring on belly 20 cm thick	No	Only 3 normal meals at 1 m	No more fat to be seen She sees herself slim	115 kg No	Much more peace Conscio-us of own emotions

Participant 12 27/ 1.73 yes	79	Distance 60–120 cm At eye level in front of her	As a shadow of herself at 2 m distance	Food is farther away and moved to the side. It can now be moved easily	Shadow has changed into a photo from a period when there were problems.	No	No problem food anymore in picture, only healthy products, but not in front of her	No longer sees overweight	76 No	Can be more herself. Positive self-image. Better dealing with emotions. Calmer

coaching during the first session, just after completing the mental spatial diagnosis, because her husband came to pick her up and couldn't wait any longer. This left no time for the behaviour-changing interventions. This was rectified in the 2nd consultation and then when she returned for the 3rd session her binge eating had also stopped.

All ten participants who completed the 5 sessions reported the loss of appetite for unhealthy food. Nine (out of 10) of these women also reported application of the alternative behaviour they had creatively conceived during Six-Step Reframing. Five (out of 10) of the participants who completed 5 sessions said they were now motivated to do more physical exercise. Apart from these self-reports no other evidence was collected.

Changes in the food panoramas

Since the main hypothesis in this study is the prediction that, the stable location in mental space of food governs someone's level of motivation to eat it, changes in the food panoramas of the participants were considered to be critical. By the second session, a stabilized improved food panorama was already observed for participants 2, 3, 9, 10, 11, and 12. Participant 1 and 6 reached that in the 3rd session and participants 4 and 5 in the 4th session. Below we have enlisted the same 3 categories of problem foods and their spatial locations, as they were provided above from session one in the section: *general findings from spatial diagnosis.* The comparison between these lists shows the therapeutic results as visible in mental space.

Test results of the stabilized locations of the 3 main problem food categories:

1. Sweets, including cake, pastry and chocolate.
   Distance: range 150 cm to 1200 cm; median 375 cm; mean 450 cm.
   Elevation in relation to eye level: range down −100 cm up to +50 cm; median −40 cm; mean −28 cm below eye level.
   Direction in clock hour: range all hours except 12:00 and 11:00 o'clock; median 08:30; mean 08:00.
2. Salty snacks including potato chips.
   Distance: range 150 cm to 2000 cm; median 450 cm; mean 571 cm
   Elevation in relation to eye level: range down −100 cm up to +50 cm; median −50 cm; mean −41 cm.
   Direction in clock hour: range all clock hours direction; median 07:30; mean 08:23.
3. Junk food like fried potato, burgers, pizza.
   Distance: range 150 cm to 2000 cm; median 350 cm; mean 554 cm.
   Elevation in relation to eye level: range down −100 cm up to +20 cm; median −25 cm; mean −33 cm below eye level.
   Direction in clock hour: range all clock directions except 11:00 and 12:00; median 10:00; mean 09:36.

The overall conclusion from these numbers is, that all categories of problem foods had moved much further away, had gone down in level with respect to eye level; and the straight in front position (12:00) was no longer occupied by these images, they had moved to the sides and to the back.

For nine (out of 10) participants present at the second consultation (who returned after the first session), the problem food had largely stayed where it had been moved to during the first session. However, with participant No. 1, with whom no intervention was done at the first consultation, the image had not changed. Two of the participants noted after the first session that chocolate was still nearby, but just out of reach. One participant had the problem food much further away but still straight in front of herself at eye level. Another participant noticed that the problem food had returned to be near at hand after a birthday and that she, however, had shifted it back to the desired location established during the first session. Only chips were still close by. But it was no longer a big family-size bag. Participant 11 noticed that the problematic food items incidentally came into view, but that she now could easily shift it back to a safer distance.

Of the remaining 10 participants, who completed the program, eight noted in the second consultation, that their images of them overweight had changed, while for two of them these images remained unchanged.

Remarks about the third and fourth consultations

During the third and fourth sessions in addition to spatial monitoring and treatment with classical NLP interventions, in depth enquiries were made with all remaining ten participants. Two participants stopped in-person treatments after the 2nd consultation, No. 2 had to undergo surgery (unrelated to her overweight) and No. 10 could not keep to her commitments due to unrelated training and work. Nevertheless, these two continued for two more sessions by phone.

Behavioural change and weight loss at the fifth consultation

At arrival at the final, fifth session, nine of the ten remaining participants had experienced no further binges. The eight participants who were at all five appointments were losing weight without dieting. They all paid attention to what they ate: less and healthier food. If they ate something unhealthy, then this was only a small amount. Eight participants said that they exercised more. These self-reports were not checked.

Change in the image of overweight

The images of the overweight girdles changed dramatically from the first consultation. They became thinner and changed colour and shape:

including, a dancing doll, a tiny protective wall, and a little internal angel. All ten participants found to have positive feelings with respect to their overweight, and eight (out of 10) participants could now be tested (Derks, 2005) to have positive self-images.

Follow-up after several months

In May 2018, one month after their last session participants 1, 2, 3, 4, 5, 6, and 9 reported on the phone that they still had not had any binges and were slowly losing weight without dieting. In September 2018, five months after their last session these 7 participants again reported on the phone that they had had no binges, had lost some more weight and were now at a weight that they were satisfied with. There was no one-month follow-up available on participants number 11 and 12 since they did not have their last appointment until September 2018. However, in February 2019, participant number 11 reported that she had not had any binges and had lost more weight. Participant number 12 has not had any binges and was satisfied with her weight.

Follow up notes on drop-out participants

Participant No. 2, who had to stop because of an operation, reported during the phone appointment (instead of the third consultation) that she no longer had binges and had also lost weight. At the last phone appointment, she had reported no binges. Participant No. 7, who stopped after the first consultation because of personal circumstances, still had binges and had not lost weight.

Participant No. 8, who could not attend anymore because of moving. This participant no longer had binges but had also not lost weight. Participant No. 10 stopped after the second appointment because she was unable to meet her appointments. This participant, who, instead of an overweight girdle, had a pile of fat at 300 cm distance, reported that more consciousness had developed during the first consultation, but, in the authors opinion, she had not yet reached the core problem. She still suppressed her emotions and did not dare or want to look at what caused them. At the second appointment she said she only wanted to lose some of her weight. And even then, only her belly fat was allowed to vanish, the rest of the fat (especially breasts and buttocks) had to remain, because that is what she liked.

This exception provides immediate insight into the limiting beliefs that can make this therapeutic work even more complex (Dingemans, Spinhoven, & van Furth, 2006). As stated, this participant had not come back after the second appointment. She had started working out and had lost weight (based on her report via a phone call) but during a later call (after eight weeks), she said that she occasionally had binges again and had put on half a kg.

General conclusions

Clients who show up in private psychotherapy practice because of eating disorders, do not expect the therapist to explore their food panoramas. They may be used to the setting of goals, the exploration of traumas, the scrutiny of their beliefs and to receive behavioural directions, or, of course talk about their diet. Since many compulsions have as their positive intention (psychological benefit), the hiding of other issues, clients may also try to keep the focus of the therapist on their weight issue and their eating patterns, and away from their core problems. The mental spatial approach provides an alternative opening that automatically brings the confrontation with the underlying problems with it, however in a gentle manner. Since these issues are hidden behind their compulsive behaviour, for the reason that they were not yet able to cope with them, they need a supportive and skilled therapist to guide them to learn how to do that. Thus, although the strategy of this mental spatial approach appears simple at first, it takes an experienced and skilful NLP-er to make it work.

One can state in general that the participants in this pilot study had changed their food panoramas in the direction of those of the six slim women whose spatial representation of food was surveyed as a pseudo-control. For all eight women, who finished the entire 5 session treatment program, the fattening food had moved away and often out of sight. Healthy products appeared to have come closer. This all was supporting the hypothesis at the root of this study: that the location where food is unconsciously imagined dictates the motivation to eat it.

The study shows something about the conditions that need to be fulfilled to make this approach work well.

1. The therapist must be capable of applying a vast range of NLP-techniques.
2. The therapist must be willing and able to assume the relevance of the locations of food in mental space as a major determinant of eating behaviour.
3. The therapist must be able to motivate the client for an unusual approach.
4. The client needs to be open to try out an alternative approach, even out of despair, an approach that may not appear so relevant at the start.
5. The client needs to possess a sufficient level of creativity, focus and intelligence to follow the steps of techniques like Six Step Reframing.
6. The client must be eager enough to change their focus from the binge/weight issue to put effort in the survey of deeper issues.

7. The client needs to believe that it is possible to resolve an eating disorder by working on underlying issues. And that losing weight will automatically follow suit, when the "real" problems are solved.
8. The social panorama work with negative self-images has probably contributed more to the effects than was visible in the used study design.

When the above conditions are fulfilled, which was the case for at least 8 out of 12 participants in this study, the mental spatial approach to binge eating disorder and overweight seems to be an efficient tool. The author hopes to inspire researchers to repeat a similar clinical trial on a larger scale and with better methodological controls.

Eating disorders, like Bulimia Nervosa and Anorexia Nervosa, have always been part of the work of many NLP practitioners. However, the submodalities of the food were not always in the centre of their attention, neither were the submodalities of the overweight. This pilot study and the clinical experience it evolved from, show that especially the location of the representation of problem food and problem weight offers an extra direct access to the underlying problems, that by themselves can be treated with tools that NLP already provides for many years.

References

Andreas, C., & Andreas, S. (1989). *Heart of the mind.* Boulder, CO: Real People Press.

Bandler, R. (1999). *Introduction to DHE.* Chicago (Audio).

Bandler, R. (1985). *Using your brain for a change.* Moab, UT: Real People Press.

Bandler, R., & Grinder, J. (1982). *Reframing: Neuro-linguistic programming and the transformation of meaning.* Moab, UT: Real People Press.

Bandler, R., & Grinder, J. (1979). *Frogs into princes.* Moab, UT: Real People Press.

Beenhakker, C. (2016). Black Matter; Depressie en mentale ruimte. Een experimentele pilotstudie naar de psychologische methodiek Depression in Awareness Space als behandelmethode voor depressie in een therapeutische context. *Eindscriptie.* HBO Bachelor Toegepaste Psychologie.

Beenhakker, C. & Manea, A. I. (2017). Dark matter: Mental space and depression – a pilot investigation of an experimental psychotherapeutic method based on mental space psychology to reduce the distress of moderate depression. *Journal of Experiential Psychotherapy*, 20, 21– 26.

Birgegård, A., Clinton, D. & Norring, C. (2013). *Diagnostic Issues of Binge Eating in Eating Disorders.* Published online 26 February 2013 in Wiley Online Library (wileyonlinelibrary.com) doi:10.1002/erv.2227

Brewerton T.D. (1999). *Binge eating disorder diagnosis and treatment. Options eating disorders program,* Charleston, South Carolina, USA: Department of Psychiatry and Behavioural Sciences, Medical University of South Carolina. 11(5), 351–361. CNS Drugs 1999 May; 1172-7047/99/0005-0351/$05.50/0 © Adis International Limited.

Derks, L.A.C. (2016). *Clinical experiments: what cognitive psychotherapies – like CBT, NLP and Ericksonian hypnotherapy – reveal about the workings of the mind. A theoretical analysis over 35 years of clinical experimentation.* Dissertation. Nicaragua: Universidad Central de Nicaragua.

Derks, L.A.C. (2005). *Social Panoramas; Changing the unconscious landscape with NLP and psychotherapy.* Camarthen, Wales: Crown House Publishing.

Derks, L.A.C. (2002). S*ociale Denkpatronen: NLP en het veranderen van onbewust sociaal gedrag.* Servire, Utrecht, Netheralnds.

Dilts, R., (1997) The Process of Reimprinting, *Anchor Point*, July & August 1997. Salt Lake City, UT.

Dingemans, A. E., Spinhoven Ph. & van Furth, E.F. (2006). Maladaptive core beliefs and eating disorder symptoms. *Eating Behaviors*, 7(2006), 258–265, Science Direct.

Fitzsimmons-Craft, E. E., Ciao, A. C., Accurso, E.C., Pisetsky, E.M., Peterson, C.B., Byrne, C.B. & Le Grange, D., (2014). Subjective and Objective Binge Eating in Relation to Eating Disorder Symptomatology, Depressive Symptoms, and Self-Esteem Among Treatment-Seeking Adolescents with Bulimia Nervosa. *NIH Public Access European Eating Disorders Review*, available in PMC 2014 july 08: Published in final edited form as: Eur Eat Disord Rev. 2014 July; 22(4), 230–236. doi:10.1002/erv.2297.

Herbozo, S., Schaefer, L.M., & Thompson, J.K. (2015). A comparison of eating disorder psychopathology, appearance satisfaction, and self-esteem in overweight and obese women with and without binge eating. *Eating Behaviors*, 17, April 2015, 86–88.

Jacobson, E. (1938). *Progressive relaxation.* Chicago: University of Chicago Press

Kabat-Zinn, J. (1991). *Full catastrophe living*. Dell Publishing. ISBN 0385303122.

Latner J.D., Thomas Hildebrandt T., Juliet K. Rosewall J.K., Chisholm A.M., & Hayashi K. (2006). Loss of control over eating reflects eating disturbances and general psychopathology. Received 23 July 2006; received in revised form 2 December 2006; accepted 6 December 2006. *Behaviour Research and Therapy*, 45(2007), 2203–2211 www.elsevier.com/locate/brat

Massimo, C., Bellini M., Donini L., & Santomassimo C., (2008). Binge Eating Disorder and Body Uneasiness. *Psychological Topics*, 17(2008), 2, 287–312, Original Scientific Article – UDC – 616.89-088.441.42 613.25

Payton, E., (2012). *Bodies under Siege: Women, Eating Disorders, and Self-Injurious Behavior*. Senior Project submitted to The Division of Social Studies of Bard College by Emily Margaret Payton Annandale-on-Hudson, New York May 2012. Bard Digital Commons.

Runfola C. D., Thornton L. M., Pisetsky E. M., Bulik C. M. & Birgegård A. (2014). Self-image and suicide in a Swedish national eating disorders clinical register. Available online at www.sciencedirect.com. *ScienceDirect Comprehensive Psychiatry*, 55(2014), 439–449.

Wallner, S.J., Luschniggg, N., Schnedll, W. J., Lahousen, T., Sudi, K., Crailsheim, K., Möller, R., Tafeit, E., & Horejsi R., (2004). Body fat distribution of overweight females with a history of weight cycling. *International Journal of Obesity and Related Metabolic Disorders*, 2004 Sept: 28(9), 1143–1148. doi:10.1038/sj.ijo.0802736.

Watkins, H. H., (1980). The silent abreaction. *International Journal of Clinical and Experimental Hypnosis*, 28(2), 1980.
Wildes J. E., Marcus M. D., (2013). Alternative methods of classifying eating disorders: models incorporating comorbid psychopathology and associated features. *Clinical Psychology Review* 2013; Apr; 33(3), 383–394.

10 Indirect evidence update

Dr Richard Gray

Many of the fundamental ideas of NLP have appeared and been validated in the work of classical, cognitive, and behavioral psychologists. Hall, Tosey & Mathison (Hall, 2010; Tosey & Mathison, 2009), and others have documented these historical connections (de Rijk, Derks, & Hollander, 2019). As noted in the previous volume (Wake, Gray, & Bourke, 2013), many of NLP's basic tenets and observations have found significant support in the literature of Experimental Psychology. Here we will seek to update some of that scientific evidence.

We will present supportive evidence from psychologists, linguists, and social scientists for:

1. NLP's theoretical base, focusing especially upon the presuppositions and the structure of subjective experience (VAKOG, submodalities, and TOTE).
2. NLP's empirically testable claims regarding eye accessing cues, physical mirroring, etc.
3. We will not revisit preferred representational systems as these have been disavowed by the early developers (Grinder & Pucelik, 2013).

After summarizing the findings of the original work (Wake et al., 2013), the chapter will focus on peer-reviewed experimental research since 2010, developed using a search of Science Direct, ProQuest, PsycINFO, and NCBI. The searches will focus upon:

- the presuppositions
- the sensory basis of subjective experience
- the evidence for submodalities as they may be defined in cognitive and experimental research.

We will include similar searches for NLP's testable claims including eye accessing cues, physical mirroring, etc.

While this chapter focuses heavily on neuroscientific evidence (the "Neuro-part"), we note, for the record, that neither the author nor NLP,

DOI: 10.4324/9781003198864-10

more generally, take any position on the nature or source of consciousness. Behavior and neurology are highly correlated and for NLP, these associations need to be specified.

The state of indirect Research in 2013

In 2013, Gray et al. (Gray, Wake, Andreas, & Bolstad, 2013) summarized the then current indirect research for NLP. They began by pointing out that much of the past research had been devoted to the largely non-existent preferred representational system (PRS), and that most of those studies had other serious flaws. Continuing, they observed that NLP's focus on multiple sensory systems and its analysis of behavior on that basis had caused significant difficulty for researchers in getting research accepted by peer-reviewed publications and obtaining research grants. We can assure you that that difficulty has continued.

Moving on to the neurological basis of NLP, they noted that since NLP's inception in the mid-1970s Neuroscience had developed significant means for observing brain states. By 2010, new instruments and methods including fMRI, MEG, MRI, PET, and CAT scans were regularly being used to examine correlations between behavior and brain areas. Insights from these studies were applied to modalities and submodalities, sensory representations, synesthesias, and other elements of NLP.

Reviewing the research on modalities and sub-modalities, they pointed out that these dimensions of experience had been observed by Galton, James, and Luria (Wake, 2010) in the late 19th Century, and they appeared in the 20th Century's Marshmallow experiment (Moore, Mischel, & Zeiss, 1976). They discussed the auditory digital modality in some detail followed by eye accessing cues (EACs), the spelling strategy, and various features of time organization. The continuing need for experimental validation of the eye accessing cues was emphasized. Their coverage of sub-modalities and synesthesia was fairly extensive. They also reviewed early observations on spatial priming (the submodality of distance; Chartrand & Bargh, 1999; Williams & Bargh, 2008) and other materials that equated distance with safety. Research reflecting the neurological basis of synesthesia across sensory systems was also reviewed (Sparks, 1999). One striking example was a study reported by Bell, Meredith, Van Opstal, & Munoz (2005) such that changes in the submodality structure of one sensory system are quickly reflected by similar changes across systems. Continued discussions of submodalities included their use in applications including the Brooklyn Program (Gray 2008/2012), the visual kinesthetic dissociation protocol (Gray & Liotta, 2012), and the swish protocol (Andreas, 2008). Further discussions covered imagery and metaphor, their history in NLP, and their validation in the scientific literature.

There was an extensive discussion of the TOTE algorithm (Miller, Galanter, & Pribram, 1960). The TOTE was explained and illustrated with examples of strategies for a dog barking at an intruder and creating a depressed state. A section on state-dependent memory followed with discussions of the neurologically distinct, and dissociable patterns of neural activation for various states. This was described in terms of reported research on multiple personality disorder (Adler, 1999), repression, OCD (Baxter et al., 1987) and PTSD (Diamond, Campbell, Park, Halonen, & Zoladz, 2007). They continued with a discussion of how expectation affects physiological response and that states, frames, and contexts exist meta to sub-modalities. This included a brief discussion of Hall's (1996) concept of meta-states and the historical development of the concept in the field of NLP preceding Hall.

A section on rapport and mirror neurons covered the then new research establishing a physiological basis for rapport in physical mirroring. This was followed by a review of the then current and extensive supportive research on rapport and predicate matching. In a separate section on syntax, they reviewed the history of the concept as it appears in linguistics. Continuing, they covered well-formedness conditions, and examples of syntactic regularities in linguistics, outcomes, behavioral change, and the structuring of reconsolidation in PTSD. They opined that syntactic structures are fundamental to understanding human behavior.

The current state of indirect research in NLP

One of the problems that has followed the field since its inception is its failure to standardize the model. Presented as a series of approximations that are allegedly not subject to scientific evaluation, NLP has consistently resisted formalization. However, in order to achieve even a modicum of scientific respectability, NLP must present a clear, empirically testable model. Here, using the basics as outlined by Dilts, Grinder, Bandler, & DeLozier (1980) with the addition of submodalities (Bandler, 1985; Bandler & MacDonald, 1987; Andreas & Andreas, 1987) we will provide (inter alia) a summary of the basic elements of NLP, and their evidence from sources outside of the NLP realm.

In order to adequately assess the indirect evidence for NLP and its claims, we need to spend a little time defining the field, what can be researched, what should be researched, and what has been researched. As noted in Chapter 2, NLP is the realm of psychology that investigates the structure of subjective experience (Dilts et al., 1980). Here we understand that realm to be consistent with what biologists and psychologists have termed phenomenal consciousness and the realm of qualia (Capra & Luisi, 2017; Jerath, Crawford & Barnes, 2015; Mashour, Roelfsema, Changeux, & Dehaene, 2020; Tononi, Boly, Massimini, & Koch, 2016). This is the physiological level that supports reflexive consciousness and the emergent experience of reality. It is that realm of behavior, which, although normally unconscious, may be brought into awareness during NLP strategy elicitation, and to which NLP turns its attention. Insofar as NLP describes a set of theoretical assumptions, they appear and may be stated as testable propositions in NLP's structural elements, the sensory systems (VAKOG) and the images that they structure, the submodalities, presuppositions, synesthesia, syntax, and the TOTE Model.

Our list of structural and other elements relies in part upon the survey of de Rijk et al. (2019) who conducted a Delphi Poll to discover a consensus model of NLP among a group of Senior NLP trainers, developers, and thinkers (The NLP Leadership Summit). Each of the elements, strategies, and interventions that we discuss was endorsed by a majority (generally more than 80%) of respondents.

For the remainder of the chapter, we will discuss NLP as consisting of three levels of information and organization (Bradbury, 2011):

1. the field of NLP that includes NLP proper, its foundational elements – sensory modalities and submodalities, presuppositions, synesthesia, syntax, and the TOTE.
2. the process of NLP modeling and its tools – strategies, rapport, calibration, and testing.
3. the techniques that have emerged from NLP as consistent, reusable models. Each represents a distinct level of investigation.

The field of NLP

The field of NLP, its foundational elements – sensory modalities and submodalities, presuppositions, syntax, and the TOTE algorithm

NLP's theoretical principles are generally non-controversial and may be found, often with full sourcing, in the works of their exemplars and inspirations (e.g., Ashby, Bateson, Erickson, Perls, Satir). They are also extensively reported, despite some varying attributions, by Dilts & DeLozier (2000), Dilts et al. (1980), Grinder & Pucelik (2013), Hall (2010), Tosey & Mathison (2009), and Wake (2008, 2010). Importantly, they have formed an implicit base for NLP thinking almost since the inception of the field. They are the structural elements and the syntactical rules that effectively describe behavior (Dilts et al., 1980). On this basis, independent of the protestations of many members of the NLP community, the following may be considered as the elements of a theoretical base for NLP.

1. All behavior is organized by internal representations ('images") of sensory elements corresponding to the five senses: vision, audition, kinesthesis, olfaction, and gustation (VAKOG) and their combinations.
2. Sensory images in all senses are subject to submodality distinctions that include, inter alia, foreground-background, intensity, complexity, contrast; frequency, and source movement.

3. Behavior is defined as all sensory representations, including movement, experienced and expressed internally or externally for which evidence is available from a subject or from an observer of that subject.
4. Structural elements may be ordered and nested to create complex systems with emergent properties giving rise to behavior, whether internal as perceptions, beliefs, and cognitions, or as overt action that were not predictable from their constituent parts.
5. All behavior is organized in terms of subjective maps based upon personal capacity and experience.
6. Those maps contribute to unique, subjective representations of persons, objects, percepts, memories, abstractions, and other contents of consciousness, and determine a highly individualized structural syntax of behavior.
7. That syntax is ordered in terms of the TOTE algorithm as originally propounded by Miller et al. (1960) in *Plans and the Structure of Behaviour*.
8. Syntactical relations are crucial determinants of behavior and may be expressed as well-formedness criteria at multiple levels of integration.
9. Novelty, news of difference, is a crucial driver of new learning.
10. Effective behavioral change must focus upon this subjective structure, not the content of any cognition.

A set of presuppositions has also arisen that serve as a conceptual foundation upon which NLP praxis depends (Andreas & Faulkner, 1994; Bostic St Clair & Grinder, 2002; Dilts et al., 1980; Dilts & DeLozier, 2000; Gray, 2008/2012; IASH & DeLozier, 2006; Linden & Perutz, 1998; O'Connor & Seymour, 1990; Tosey & Mathison, 2009). Most of these elements are scattered throughout the early NLP books. Tosey & Mathison (2009) call them "*the axioms or beliefs upon which the practice of NLP is predicated*" (p. 97).

Presuppositions that are foundational to NLP practice

At the heart of NLP is a group of presuppositions that emphasizes its radical humanistic perspective and its optimistic focus on human flexibility (Andreas & Faulkner, 1994; Dilts & DeLozier, 2000; Tosey & Mathison, 2009). The following seven presuppositions underscore the humanistic roots of NLP:

- People are, for the most part, not broken. They are more often stuck.
- People already have all the internal resources they need. Humans have an almost unlimited capacity for combining and recombining the data of their own experience into new possibilities.
- If one person can do something, anyone can learn to do it. If we know the subjective structure of the task and break it down into small enough chunks, any skill can be mastered.
- People always make the best choices available to them. NLP expands awareness of choices and converts seemingly external constraints into options for choice and action.

- The person with the most options can most often control the situation. Pathology often reflects a lack of flexibility.
- Underlying every behavior is a positive intention. People do things for reasons that we may not intuitively appreciate from the outside.
- There is no such thing as failure, only feedback. That is, any apparent failure is a source of valuable information for course correction in the next effort.

These axioms (Tosey & Mathison, 2009) are contextualized by a second set of presuppositions that establish the cognitive frame under which that first set of presuppositions function.

- The mind and body are parts of the same system.
- Experience has a structure. It is not about *what* you do or perceive (content); it is how you experience it (structure).
- The map is not the territory. For example, the internal representations of a telephone pole are probably quite different for a Freudian psychoanalyst and an electrician.
- The meaning of your communication is the response you get. People always reflect their own understanding of what you said, and it may not be what you intended.
- You cannot *not* communicate.

The evidence

The foundational elements of the Field of NLP

The Root Structural Elements of NLP's Behavioral Analysis: Modalities and Submodalities.

All behavior is organized by internal representations ('images') of sensory elements corresponding to the five senses: vision, audition, kinesthesis, olfaction, and gustation (VAKOG) and their combinations.

To evaluate some of the major tenets of the field of NLP, in terms of their support in the literature of neuroscience, we began by using a group of authors from a list of theoretical approaches to consciousness reviewed by Northoff & Lamme (2020). Assuming that these authors used informative and authoritative exemplars from each perspective, we reviewed at least one of the referenced papers for the perspectives noted. We have indicated their agreement or lack thereof with a few (fairly random) NLP tenets throughout the text. We note that these studies are cited not because they agree conceptually but because each adduces evidence for the specific phenomenon for which they are cited (Brown, Lau, & LeDoux, 2019; Engel & Singer, 2001; Fingelkurts, Fingelkurts, & Neves, 2010; Graziano & Kastner, 2011;

Lamme, 2006, 2010; Mashour, Roelfsema, Changeux, & Dehaene, 2020; Naccache, 2018; Northoff & Huang, 2017; Park & Tallon-Baudry, 2014; Tononi, Boly, Massimini, & Koch, 2016). Several other studies which we have found relevant are also included (Alcaro, Carta & Panksepp, 2017; Edelman, 2003, 2005; Jerath, Crawford, & Barnes, 2015; Pessoa, 2017).

We examined each of the noted articles for the presence or absence of the following concepts from NLP. To assess their appreciation of the role of phenomenal non-reflexive consciousness – the level of NLP's formal elements, we looked for how and whether they construed the concepts of phenomenal consciousness. We looked for the word *qualia* and its definition in each article. We looked to see whether the articles posited a subjective 3-Dimensional organization of subjective space. To assess their embrace of General Systems principles, we looked for the use of the terms meta-stable and emergence, invocation of systems principles (implicitly or explicitly). NLP depends upon the integration of sensory systems across modalities, so we looked for the authors to discuss the integration of information from the 5 sensory systems. We observe below that the brain responds to salience markers (submodalities) in a bottom-up manner for new or external objects, and in a top-down manner for subjective percepts. If this was reflected in the papers, we indicated its presence. Prediction error and novelty are essential for new learning, and the elements of novelty and 'news of difference' (Bandler & Grinder 1979; DeLozier & Grinder, 1995), have been emphasized by NLP. We noted whether the authors referenced prediction error or novelty. The existence of mental maps is a central tenet of NLP and pathology is often a reflection of conflicts between personal maps and the 'real world'. We assessed whether subjective maps and such conflicts were discussed. NLP is an embodied perspective; we noted whether the authors held this point of view. Flexibility is a crucial criterion for outcomes in NLP and we checked the articles for this evolutionary perspective. We also sought to determine whether the perspective identified intentionality, the idea that motivation and action are only had with regard to objects, persons, and other percepts. We also looked for an affirmation of consciousness as a process or a stream of experience. Finally, we assessed whether the perspective reflected the statement from Dilts et al. (1980) that the task of change work is the transformation of external problems into internal possibilities. We caution the reader that the elements reported by these and other independent investigators were not explicitly targeting their appearance in NLP. Results from Experimental Psychology and Cognitive Neuroscience, however, support them as general principles.

NLP begins its behavioral analysis with descriptions of the subjective aspects of personal experience. These are internal images representing the percept, thought, or memory in any, or all of the five senses (VAKOG). The sensory data for those internal images appear in idiosyncratic orderings for any event, independent of whether the source is external (the taste of a cookie dipped in tea) or internal (the memory of that tea-soaked cookie; Bandler &

Grinder, 1975; Dilts et al., 1980; Dilts & DeLozier, 2000; Grinder & Bandler, 1976). This perspective is supported by modern researchers who describe consciousness as inseparable from neural processing and it includes contributions from all available senses (Alcaro et al., 2017; Edelman, 2003, 2005; Engel & Singer, 2001; Feinberg, & Mallatt, 2020; Fingelkurts et al., 2010; Graziano & Kastner, 2011; Jerath & Beveridge, 2019; Jerath, Beveridge, & Jensen, 2019; Jerath, Crawford, Barnes, 2015; Lamme, 2006, 2010; Mashour et al., 2020; Northoff & Huang, 2017; Park & Tallon-Baudry, 2014; Pessoa, 2017; Redies, Grebenkina, Mohseni, Kaduhm, & Dobel, 2020; Tononi et al., 2016).

NLP-based behavioral analysis – strategy analysis – rejects cartesian dualism. It does not posit an image apart from its neural representation, nor a discarnate homunculus to view the image. This is supported by most modern researchers (Fingelkurts et al., 2010; Polák & Marvan, 2018).

NLP's subjective experience appears to be interchangeable with the concept of phenomenal consciousness (Alcaro et al., 2017; Brown et al., 2019; Edelman, 2003, 2005; Feinberg, & Mallatt, 2020; Jerath et al., 2015; Mashour et al., 2020; Tononi et al., 2016), and, for some authors, the concept of qualia space (Jerath et al., 2015; Mashour et al., 2020; Tononi et al., 2016). This is a level of experience without reflexivity. It is held in common with most mammals.

This level of phenomenal consciousness is the level of the NLP sensory modalities and submodalities. They, for the most part, remain below the level of reflexive consciousness (their product; Alcaro et al., 2017; Edelman, 2003, 2005; James, 1950/1890) until attention is directed towards them as in NLP strategy analysis.

The proposition that multisensory representations of target stimuli are essential for consciousness is commonplace and non-controversial (Alcaro et al., 2017; Edelman, 2003, 2005; Engel & Singer, 2001; Feinberg, & Mallatt, 2020; Fingelkurts, Fingelkurts, & Neves 2010; Graziano & Kastner, 2011; Jerath, et al., 2015; Kiefer & Barsalou, 2013; Kringelbach, 2005; Lamme, 2006; Mashour et al., 2020; Northoff & Huang, 2017; Park & Tallon-Baudry, 2014; Pessoa, 2017; Redies et al., 2020; Tononi et al., 2016). We also note that recent evidence supports the NLP position that the kinesthetic sense merges emotion, proprioception, motor action, and feelings in a combined sensory-motor modality and that there is both sensory overlap and multimodal processing for all sensory systems, supporting NLP synesthesias (Kiefer & Barsalou, 2013; Kuhnke, Kiefer & Hartwigsen, 2021).

Submodalities

Sensory images in all senses are subject to submodality distinctions that include, inter alia, foreground-background, intensity, complexity, contrast; frequency, and source movement.

Submodalities are the fine-grained structural elements of perception that code for valence, meaning (position in 3-D space), and salience (importance). Salience is expressed in the following dimensions with examples for each of the major sensory systems (visual, auditory, and kinesthetic): intensity (brightness, volume, pressure), complexity (hue, timbre, texture), contrast (granularity, frequency contrast, textural disparity); foreground-background (all modalities), frequency (color, pitch, felt distinctions of type: emotions, temperature, hedonic impact), etc.

Submodality distinctions in NLP were first reported by Bandler (1985), Gordon (1978), Andreas & Andreas (1987), and MacDonald (Bandler & MacDonald, 1987). Although these distinctions are most directly derived from the discipline of NLP (Andreas & Andreas, 1987; Bandler, 1985; Bandler & MacDonald, 1987), they have all been described as individual stimulus qualities in the peer-reviewed literature (Gray et al., 2013; NLPWIKI, 2014). Those studies have confirmed the behavioral relationship between submodalities – by whatever name – and emotional impact. References to their experimental evaluation are reviewed in the NLPWIKI database (2014).

Recent research indicates that most of the stimulus qualities that NLP has labeled submodalities are represented, for all senses, in the superior colliculus by a series of saliency maps that code sensory information for importance. Visual saliency maps sort (minimally) for color, edge, edge overlap, brightness, and movement (Itti, Koch, & Niebur, 1998; Kalinli & Narayanan, 2007; Kaya & Elhilali, 2012; Knudsen, 2018; Perrault, Stein, & Rowland, 2011; Veale, Hafed, & Yoshida, 2017; Vetter, Smith, & Muckli, 2014; White et al., 2017). The importance of various stimuli is mediated in a bottom-up manner by external stimulus qualities (typically for new or unexpected stimuli) and in a top-down manner determined by expectations and subjective motivational states (hunger, thirst, sexual deprivation, present-time outcomes, and personal preferences; Alcaro et al., 2017; Itti et al., 1998; Mashour et al., 2020; Zhou & Desimone, 2011). Other submodality features including the position in three-dimensional space have correlated in a three-dimensional perceptual schema. These maps are thought to have evolved to enable organisms to navigate in 3-dimensional space (Derks, 2018; Edelman, 2003, 2005; Fingelkurts et al., 2010; Graziano & Kastner, 2011; Jerath et al., 2015; Mashour et al., 2020; Northoff & Huang, 2017; Park & Tallon-Baudry, 2014; Park, Miller, Nili, Ranganath, & Boorman, 2020).

NLP has observed that percepts, whether internal or external may be observed to have a specific locus in 3-Dimensional space centered around an individual's then current locus of identity (Bandler, 1999; Derks, 2011, 2018; Fingelkurts et al., 2010). These spatial distinctions code for content, valence, personal relevance, temporal distance, and more complex elements of meaning including trustworthiness and value (Connirae Andreas, Personal communication, August 2020; Derks, 2018).

Derks (2011, 2018) has described a set of spatial distinctions that enlarge upon both the standard NLP perspective, and Bandler's descriptions in the

Design Human Engineering (DHE) materials (Bandler, 1999). Significantly, this submodality of place seems to have a reciprocal relationship between itself and the other submodalities. That is, a change in an image's location in subjective 3-D space affects some or all of the submodalities in a given subjective representation. Just so, changes in submodality structure, both individually and in aggregate, affect the image's location in 3-D space. Context and ecology (Bateson, 1972; Bostic St Clair & Grinder, 2002; DeLozier & Grinder, 1995; Tosey & Mathison, 2009) determine which organization takes precedence.

We note here, that one of the tell-tale signs of client success with the RTM Protocol (Chapter 3), is the movement of the trauma content-image from a space directly in front of the client (where it appears as an emergent threat), to a space consistent with older, less relevant past memories (behind the client).

Although NLP takes no stance as to the ontological validity of mystical or spiritual experiences, their internal dimensions have been successfully mapped by several NLP developers (Andreas, 2018; Andreas & Andreas, 1994; Gray, 2008/2012). Of special note here is the work of Andreas, who, in *Coming to Wholeness* (2018), teaches a model of what has been called spiritual experience in terms of the *location* of ego constructs in 3-Dimensional space.

> *Structural elements may be ordered and nested to create complex systems with emergent properties giving rise to behavior, whether internal as perceptions, beliefs, and cognitions, or as overt action.*

Some of the root concepts in NLP arise out of the cybernetic approaches of Ashby (1956) and Bateson (1972; Bandler & Grinder, 1975, 1979; Dilts et al., 1980; Tosey & Mathison, 2009). Arising at about the same time, but in a much more cumbersome mathematical form, was the field of General Systems Theory as originally promulgated by Bertalanffy (1968; Capra & Luisi, 2017; Gray et al., 1982). While NLP, in general, relates to its cybernetic roots, we believe that its dynamic nature is better captured by the pulsating rhythms of GST, which incorporates the insights of cybernetics (Capra & Luisi, 2017). This position is also supported by Dilts & DeLozier (2000) and was the subject of *The Art of Systems Thinking: Essential Skills for Creativity and Problem Solving* by O'Connor & McDermott (1997).

General systems and syntax

There is considerable evidence that neurological systems evolve according to the principles of General Systems Theory (GST) (Buzsáki, 2010; Damasio, 1989; Dresp-Langley, 2020; Gray, 2006; Gray, Fidler, & Battista, 1982; Sun et al., 2011). The idea appears throughout the literature of consciousness and neurophysiology more generally (Alcaro et al., 2017; Buzsáki, 2010; Edelman, 2003, 2005; Feinberg, & Mallatt, 2020; Fingelkurts et al., 2010;

Dresp-Langley, 2020; Gray et al., 1982; Graziano & Kastner, 2011; Jerath et al., 2015; Lamme, 2006; Mashour et al., 2020; Northoff & Huang, 2017; Park et al., 2020; Park & Tallon-Baudry, 2014; Pessoa, 2017; Redies et al., 2020; Tononi et al., 2016).

According to GST, more complex behaviors are the emergent properties of the interaction of simpler behavioral systems such that the whole is not predictable from the sum of its parts (Dresp-Langley, 2020; Feinberg & Mallatt, 2020; Gray et al. 1982). In any complex system the telic element or behavior defines the functional relations between the parts that it integrates. Each subordinate part remains a whole, functional element that retains its internal integrity including its specific outcomes and behaviors. Assembly into larger systems repurposes those outcomes and behaviors in service of the larger whole. Pessoa (2017) describes such emergents as "momentary circuits"

Fishman, Rotgers & Franks (1988, pp. 308–309), as reported by Gray (2001), provide the following explanation of emergence:

Emergent properties are ubiquitous in nature. The classical example of emergent properties concerns the individual properties of hydrogen and oxygen as atoms versus the unique properties that emerge when hydrogen and oxygen unite and become the molecular system called water. The unique properties of water expressed as a liquid at room temperature cannot be predicted by studying the behavior of hydrogen and oxygen independently (i.e., un-united) as separate gases at room temperature.... the properties that are unique to water can only be revealed (i.e., discovered) when the *particular components are allowed to interact as a unique, integrated system* (Fishman, Rotgers, & Franks; 1988, p. 308–309).

Importantly, general systems principles predict that the elements of a complex system tend to self-organize into larger and more complex systemic elements on a higher logical and functional level. There is an abundant and growing literature linking GST to biology and consciousness on multiple levels. (Buzsáki, 2010; Capra & Luisi, 2017; Damasio, 1989; Dresp-Langley, 2020; Feinberg & Mallatt, 2020; Gray, 2006; Gray et al., 1982; Pessoa, 2017; Sun et al., 2011). Self-organization occurs in physical systems as dissipative structures (Prigogine & Stengers, 2017). Neurons assemble in neural words and larger assemblies (Buzsáki, 2010; Feinberg & Mallatt, 2020; Sun et al., 2011; Sukenik et al., 2021). Neural assemblies combine to form, through their interaction, localized areas of specialized function in the brain and these interact to produce moods, feelings, dispositions, thoughts, actions, personalities, and other denizens of subjectivity, none of which is predictable from their constituent parts.

The interplay of the diverse elements of phenomenal consciousness with their varied intakes and outputs gives rise to the possibility of orderly structural relations between those elements–syntax. Each element of the system can only operate with the others in a certain specifiable number of ways. Syntax gives rise to well-formedness conditions as the expression of the intrinsic relations of production among the constituent elements at the relevant level of organization. Context determines the character of the system as one or another element arises as the emergent property that defines the system and the relevant syntax at that time (Capra & Luisi, 2017; Gray, Fidler, Battista, 1982; Pessoa, 2017; Sun et al., 2011).

Chomsky (1957) famously declared that the genius of language was that a limited number of elements with specific properties could combine in an almost infinite manner to produce language. Phonemes combine to build morphemes, morphemes combine to build words, and words to build sentences, paragraphs, and yet more complex elements of verbal communication. Moreover, these developments are constrained at each level by cultural linguistic norms. This allows for the development of an unbelievable variety of languages. Workable forms, the most efficient, were said to be well-formed.

For NLP, Dilts & DeLozier (2000) describe how a limited number of elements, combine in predictable ways to produce an almost infinite variety of percepts and actions (Dilts et al., 1980). The resulting behaviors (including all behavior: language, actions, and percepts) may be said to be well-formed when they enhance the individual's capacity to achieve both proximal and distal outcomes, to survive and thrive. Here, we note that well formedness conditions are expressions of syntax.

> *All behavior is organized in terms of subjective maps based upon personal capacity and experience.*

NLP's Map-territory distinction is non-controversial and is supported by researchers from Cognitive Behavior Therapy (Clark, 1999; Ottaviani & Beck, 1987; Wells & Hackmann, 1993) as well as from cognitive neuroscience more generally (Alcaro et al., 2017; Jerath et al., 2015; Kringelbach, 2005; Lamme, 2006; Mashour et al., 2020; Park & Tallon-Baudry, 2014; Tononi et al., 2016). Other researchers support the existence of highly personal maps and observe that conflicts between subjective maps and the world "out there" are significant sources of psychopathology (Alcaro et al., 2017; Jerath et al., 2015; Kringelbach, 2005; Lamme, 2006; Mashour et al., 2020; Park & Tallon-Baudry, 2014; Tononi et al., 2016)

> *Those maps contribute to unique, subjective representations of persons, objects, percepts, memories, abstractions, and other contents of consciousness, and determine a highly individualized structural syntax of behavior. That syntax is ordered in terms of the TOTE algorithm as originally propounded by Miller, Galanter, & Pribram (1960) in Plans and the Structure of behavior.*

Maps order the world in terms of beliefs, understandings, recipe knowledge – what we are taught independent of experience, e.g., church doctrine (Schutz, 1967), one-off experiences involving specific kinds of people places and things, and pathological rigidities. They are created and maintained also by the voluntary association groups to which we belong and which may justify criminal activities by redefining them as acceptable (Cressey, 1960; Gray, 2001; Merton, 1938; Zoja, 1990). They are modified by the effects of addictive behaviors so that those behaviors and the contexts that support them are more highly valued than previously preferred non-addictive behaviors and contexts (Bechara, 2005; Bechara, et al, 2019; Bickel et al, 2019; Bickel et al, 2014).

The TOTE Operator was adopted from Miller, Galanter, and Pribram's, *Plans and the Structure of Behavior* (1960) and is an essential element of any NLP-based strategy. TOTE is an acronym standing for Test, Operate, Test, Exit (T.O.T.E.). Briefly, the TOTE is a program that instructs the organism to: "Do this, until this result is achieved". TOTEs may be nested so that many smaller sub-routines combine to create a larger behavioral entity (Dilts et al., 1980). Nested behavioral TOTE elements are commonplace on the level of neurology (Buzsáki, 2010) and the algorithm has been extensively evaluated in the literature of cognitive neuroscience (See e.g., Kopp, 2012; Kragel, Reddan, Labar, & Wager, 2019; Walsh & Phillips, 2010).

Novelty, news of difference, is a crucial driver of new learning.

In recent years, the importance of novelty, prediction error, and news of difference, has become an essential part of understanding neurological functioning (Kaplan & Oudeyer, 2007; Kroes & Fernández, 2012; Daw et al., 2011). There is a great deal of agreement that one of the major functions of memory is prediction, that is, memory allows the organism to recognize familiar contexts, people, places, and things and to respond appropriately (Buckner, 2010; Mullally & Maguire, 2014; Nadel, Hupbach, Gomez, & Newman-Smith, 2012; Williams & Bargh, 2008).

We suggest that the speed of NLP interventions relies in part on the introduction of novelty into personal experience as, in general, the presence of a prediction error suggests that there is something to be learned (Sevenster, Beckers, & Kindt, 2012). In light of NLP's emphasis on novelty, and the speed of some of its effects, there may be a reason to appeal to the literature of reconsolidation across interventions (Almeida-Correa & Amaral, 2014; Fernandez, Boccia, & Pedreira 2016; Kindt & van Emmerik, 2016; Kindt, Soeter, & Vervliet 2009; Lee, 2009; Pedreira et al., 2004).

In 2013, we reviewed the basic syntax of reconsolidation.

1. There is a pre-existing memory structure.
2. That memory is briefly evoked in order to activate it on a physiological level.
3. After a brief pause, new information is added that conflicts with the expectations generated by the memory. This is a prediction error.
4. Insofar as the new information is relevant to the original memory

context, the new elements are incorporated into the structure of the memory.
5. After a period of dreaming sleep, the memory becomes permanent.

These kinds of prediction errors, the addition of new information that reframes or otherwise changes the meaning of the original memory, are ubiquitous in NLP. They are central to the efficacy of RTM (see Chapter 3). They appear in pattern interruptions generally (Bandler & Grinder, 1979; Grinder & Bandler, 1981). They can be found in the way Bandler (nd) structures interrupted loops in his trainings to guarantee the full attention of his participants. It appears in Farrelly and Brandsma's (1981) and Kemp's (2015) Provocative Therapy where the integration of the absurd and unexpected is raised to a high art. It appears in the movie theater setting and the restructuring of traumatic memories in the V/K-D (Andreas & Andreas, 1989, Bandler, 1985; see also Chapter 6) and in the RTM Protocol for PTSD (see Chapter 3).

Throughout NLP, the emphasis on speed (Bandler, n.d.; 1999; Bandler & Grinder, 1979), and the retention of the client's map (the relevant memory structure), with the ADDITION of new, relevant information, as in the introduction of relevant resource states, sets the stage for reconsolidative effects. According to Nader, who published the first study to establish reconsolidation as a standard memory process (Nader, Schafe, & Le Doux, 2000, Nader, 2003), speed and immediate behavioral change are hallmarks of reconsolidative memory function (Karim Nader personal communication, 2019). There is reason to believe that NLP, rightly done, takes advantage of reconsolidation as a general, if unintended, consequence of its structure. We suggest that NLP would profit by making this mechanism explicit.

> *Effective behavioral change must focus upon this subjective structure, not the content of any cognition.*

Cognitive Behavioral Therapy has made an extensive search for effective trans-diagnostic solutions to problems like anxiety disorders (Clark & Taylor, 2009; Farchione et al., 2012; Gros, 2014; Newby, McKinnon, Kuyken, Gilbody, & Dalgleish, 2015). Because most of the diagnoses to which they appeal (DSM and ICD-based) are made at an external, descriptive level (see Chapter 6; Allsopp, Read, Corcoran, & Kinderman, 2019; Bakker, 2019; Feczko et al., 2019); because they seek to apply cognitive interventions to problems that lie at the phenomenal level (subjective, and largely non-verbal patterns of sensory images) that are not generally accessible to cognitive modalities, those efforts provide mediocre results (Ost, 2008; Visser, Lau-Zhu, Henson, & Holmes, 2018). NLP remedies this by focusing on the phenomenal level of experience, applying interventions appropriate to the structure of subjective experience, not its content.

The NLP presuppositions

The NLP presuppositions structure a perspective on people and their behaviors allowing for an objective, positive, non-judgmental attitude of curiosity about persons and what they do. The presuppositions add what amounts to axiomatic principles (Tosey & Mathison, 2009) about the structure of behavior and the relationship between communicators. Some have the status of perspective, while others are based on scientific observation. Judith DeLozier (IASH & DeLozier, 2006) has opined that the presuppositions alone may be sufficient to define an effective approach to people and behavior.

> *More specifically, we can make the following observations and report some of the research associated with NLP's presuppositions.*

People are, for the most part, not broken. NLP assumes that every person who is otherwise physically whole can learn to change and adapt as needed. Limitations not imposed by physiology (which can often be overcome), are more often imposed by conflicts between internal maps and external "reality" (see below). Dilts Grinder Bandler & DeLozier (1980, p. 7) note that "... one of the major historical trends in the evolution of models of behavior is the transformation or utilization of experiences once regarded as environmental variables into decision variables."

People already have all the internal resources they need. Humans have an almost unlimited capacity for combining and recombining the data of their own experience into new possibilities (viz. syntax, above; Buckner, 2010; Mullally & Maguire, 2014; Nadel et al., 2012; Williams & Bargh, 2008). Insofar as all behavior is generated based upon the formal elements already described, humans are only limited by what they can imagine. Evidence from the mirror neuron system indicates that seeing or hearing another person enacting a familiar behavior is enough to activate the subconscious replication of that behavior (Gallese, Keysers, & Rizzolatti, 2004; Kiefer & Barsalou, 2013; Kilner, Friston, & Frith, 2007; Koul et al., 2018; Lyons, Santos, & Keil, 2006; Mazurek, & Schieber, 2019; Perry et al., 2018; Ramsey, Kaplan, & Cross, 2021; Rizzolatti, Cattaneo, Fabbri-Destro, & Rozzi, 2014; Rizzolatti, & Fogassi, 2014; Salo, Ferrari, & Fox, 2019).

NLP has emphasized the utility of "acting as if" (Bandler & Grinder, 1975, 1979; Dilts et al., 1980; Grinder & Bandler, 1976). There is solid neuroscientific evidence to suggest that facial and postural imitation is capable of awakening corresponding emotions (Blanke, 2012; Bohns, & Wiltermuth, 2012; Carney, Cuddy, & Yap, 2010; Hung & Labroo, 2011; Kiefer & Barsalou, 2013; Mazurek, & Schieber, 2019; Niedenthal et al., 2005; Peelen & Downing, 2007; Riskind & Gotay, 1982; Rizzolatti & Sinigaglia, 2010; Salo, Ferrari, & Fox, 2019). This is a special case of observational learning, allowing persons who have not had an experience to learn it from watching others, whether or not acquisition of the behavior is intended (Bandler & MacDonald, 1987; Bandura, Ross, & Ross 1961, 1963; Carcea, & Froemke, 2019).

If one person can do something, anyone can learn to do it. If we know the subjective structure of the task and break it down into small enough chunks, any skill can be mastered. This is the essence of NLP as a modeling discipline. It will be discussed in another section on modeling, below.

Any behavior can be modeled and taught if it is broken down into small enough pieces. Those smaller pieces are behavioral chunks which, when sequenced and brought together in the service of a specific outcome, coalesce into the telic behavior – the emergent property of that specific system. The emergent property is in general not deducible from the simple sum of the parts, but they may be analyzed in retrospect from the perspective of the telic behavior. Although behavior can be analyzed to the level of molecular action, the most practical level for analysis is the level at which behavior can be meaningfully observed or described. For NLP, this is the phenomenal level, the level of subjective experience.

The map is not the territory. This is one of the key ideas from Alfred Korzybski (1994): we do not interact with the world but with our perception of the world. This indicates that the contexts we perceive are distorted in terms of experience so that they may or may not correspond to present time "objective" reality. It is found in the work of Varela Thompson & Rosch (1991) and others (Brown et al., 2019; Capra & Luisi, 2017; Engel, & Singer, 2001; Lamme, 2006; Northoff, & Huang, 2017; Pessoa, 2017; Tononi, et al., 2016); in the observation that up to 90% of neural activity is endogenous, feeding back upon itself in multiple, multisensory, re-entrant circuits. Moreover, because meaning occurs in the interface between memory – as embodied consciousness – and perception, perception is always distorted by previous experience (Buzsáki, 2010; Damasio, 1989; Glenberg, 1997; Kiefer & Barsalou, 2013; Niedenthal et al., 2005; Niedenthal et al., 2009). Crucially for NLP, it appears in the work of Chomsky in the transforms – deletions, distortions and generalizations – that occur in the process of perceiving and communicating (Bandler & Grinder,1975, 1979; Chomsky, 1965; DeLozier & Grinder, 1995; Dilts et al., 1980) and is generally supported in the literature (Alcaro et al., 2017; Jerath et al., 2015; Mashour et al. 2020; Tononi et al., 2016; Park & Tallon-Baudry, 2014).

People operate in regard of a context. This idea is reflected In Dilts' Neurological levels (1995) in which the lowest level of behavior is environmentally determined. Environmental determinism and higher logical levels (in Dilts' system) represent various kinds of subjective contexts. *The same general idea is reflected in* Bateson's (1972) level 0 learning and Kolodny, Edelman & Lotem's (2015) environmentally bound learning. It reflects the behaviorist idea that context is an important part of any behavior (Bouton & Moody, 2004; Pavlov, 1927; Rescorla, 1988; Skinner, 1957; Watson & Raynor, 1920). Context also reflects the concept that behavior is situated (Kiefer & Barsalou, 2013; Niedenthal, Barsalou, Winkielman, Krauth-Gruber, & Ric, 2005; Niedenthal, Winkielman, Mondillon, & Vermeulen, 2009) or shaped by environmental affordances—opportunities to respond (Gibson, 1977). The assessment of contextual variables and the appropriate setting for responses is comprehended in the NLP concept of ecology (Bandler & Grinder, 1979; Bateson, 1972; Bostic St Clair & Grinder, 2002; Delozier & Grinder, 1995; Tosey & Mathison, 2009)

Internal contexts drive or maintain behavior, independent of external "realities." In NLP these are often described as states, stuck states, and resource states that maintain particular perspectives, maps, and attitudes (Bandler & Grinder, 1975, 1979; Grinder & Bandler, 1976, Dilts et al., 1980). In general, they give rise to familiar phenomena including state dependent memory effects, priming effects, expectancy sets, and internally generated distortions of thought and action, both adaptive and maladaptive (Bargh, Chen, & Burrows, 1996; Duncan & Barrett, 2007; Dutton & Aron, 1974; Gendolla & Brinkmann, 2005; Gillihan, Kessler & Farah, 2007; Holland, & Kensinger, 2010; Lewis, Critchley, Smith, & Dolan, 2005; Ramel, Goldin, Eyler, Brown, Gotlib, & McQuaid, 2007; Selcuk, Zayas, Günaydin, Hazan, & Kross, 2012; van Wingen, van Eijndhoven, Cremers, Tendolkar, Verkes, Buitelaar, & Fernández, 2010).

Bickel (Bechara et al., 2019; Bickel et al., 2019; Bickel et al., 2014) has described a pathology of reinforcement so that the immediacy and intensity of certain experiences (drugs, sex, chocolate) actively decrease the reward value (incentive salience; Balleine & Killcross, 2006; Berridge, & Robinson, 1998; McClure, Daw, & Montague, 2003) of other stimuli. This is also true for religious and spiritual experiences, deeply felt emotional commitments – falling in love, and other experiences that can outframe and render irrelevant other less valued behaviors (Gray 2008/2012, 2014; Prochaska, 1994). The principle is practically applied in Andreas' *Wholeness Work* (Andreas 2018), Andreas and Andreas' work in *Core Transformations* (1994), and Gray's Brooklyn Program (Gray, 2001,2002, 2008/2012). In each, overwhelmingly positive experiences are accessed using NLP patterns. Those experiences, often identified by the participants as spiritual, outframe and devalue negative behaviors.

Behaviors may depend upon internal contexts that are no longer objectively relevant. Events only have meaning in regard to the perspective of the perceiver (Mannheim, 1998). Mood-dependent memory phenomena make environmental features more or less salient. Social norms dictate what is worthy or unworthy of attention. These elements actively modify meanings through internal feedback within the brain-body system (Brown et al., 2019; Capra & Luisi, 2017; Engel, & Singer, 2001; Lamme, 2006; Northoff, & Huang, 2017; Pessoa, 2017; Tononi, et al., 2016; Varela, Thompson, & Rosch 1991).

People always make the best choices available to them. NLP has always emphasized the expansion of options as may be best for the individual

(Bandler & Grinder, 1975, 1979; Dilts et al., 1980; Grinder & Bandler, 1976). Options, however, are often limited by the constraints of personal maps as when a representational system becomes so dominant that a person cannot perceive other options (Bandler & Grinder, 1975, 1979; Grinder & Bandler, 1976); when cultural (religious, tribal, political, and family) definitions constrain choice and perceptual capacity; or when constraints imposed by social and geographical factors (poverty, location, access to opportunity) skew the attention or limit its scope. When trauma, fear, depression, addiction, and other problems, skew the attention, the focus turns to the most salient element and the world is interpreted in those terms (See Chapter 4, Diagnosis and the discussion in Chapter 6 for spatial cues; Bechara et al., 2019; Bickel et al., 2019; Bickel et al., 2014).

The person with the most options can most often control the situation. This presupposition was first stated by Ashby (1956) as a principle of population genetics so that the organism with the most options (for food, shelter, and mating) in a given environment is the one most likely to survive and reproduce. Here, it is applied to the ability to perceive and utilize the affordances provided in any psychological context, internal or external.

Fredriskson (2001), in her broaden-and-build-theory posits that repeated experiences of mild or moderate positive emotions increase the number of perceived options for the individual. A later study (Fredriskson & Joiner, 2018) reviewed the results of the broaden-and-build theory and found that repeated positive experiences increased the ability to perceive new options, and that those new options gave rise to more positive feelings. Subsequently, those positive feelings led to more positive experiences after more than a month.

Kolodny, Edelman, & Lotem (2015) hypothesized that creativity, as behavioral flexibility, involves the use of generalization and analogy among already known behaviors. They also indicate that novel behaviors are not environmentally constrained (situations in which similar organisms respond alike) as in ethological releasers (instinct) and classical conditioning (see also Bateson, 1972; Tosey & Mathison, 2009). Behavioral inflexibility is widely associated with psychopathology (Alcaro et al., 2017; Jerath et al., 2015; Mashour et al., 2020; Tononi et al., 2016; Park, & Tallon-Baudry, 2014).

Underlying every behavior is a positive intention. People do things for reasons that we may not intuitively appreciate from the outside. People operate in regard of anticipated positive outcomes (Andreas & Andreas, 1994; Dilts & DeLozier, 2000; Dilts et al., 1980). Positive intent may be satisfied, most superficially, by an external outcome – earning money. It may be satisfied by need satisfaction-the hungry man seeks food. It may be satisfied by a change of state – escape from a fearful or painful condition (Alcaro et al., 2017; Skinner, 1957). Outcomes may range from executing the next step in a chain of neural elements (Buzsáki, 2010; Damasio, 1989; Feil et al., 2010; Miller et al., 1960) on the micro level, to consummatory behaviors with self-actualizing implications on the macro level (Andreas, 2018;

Andreas & Andreas, 1994; Gray, 2008/2012; Maslow, 1971). Kolodny Edelman & Lotem (2015) suggest that a positive behavior is one that provides, on average, a selective advantage.

Andreas & Andreas (1994) have found that outcomes have self-similar dimensions of feeling that reach down to context-free oceanic depths. This accords with the depth dimension of archetypal experience documented by Alcaro, Carta and Panksepp (2017).

There is no such thing as failure, only feedback. That is, any apparent failure is a source of valuable information for course correction in the next effort. This presupposition reframes failure as information. It reflects the optimism of NLP's Humanistic roots (Hall, 2010) encouraging participants to learn from their mistakes. When we consider the importance of internal contexts, how we feel about our behaviors is important (Hall, 1996) positive affect expands options (Fredriskson & Joiner, 2018). Increased options lead to more creative responses. Schmidhuber (2010) emphasizes the need for exploration and surprise in behavior.

NLP is an embodied psychology. Abstractions are derived from the capabilities of action and movement delimited by physiology, environment, and culture (Glenberg, 1997; Kiefer & Barsalou, 2013; Niedenthal et al., 2005; Niedenthal et al., 2009). Early on, NLP included the observation that indications that abstract words (Nominalizations) could not be fully understood until they were reconverted into action words: verbs (Bandler & Grinder, 1975). In defining patterns and strategies, NLP does not differentiate between perception and action. Kinesthetic elements include motion and its perception with the notation that it may be either internal or external (Dilts et al., 1980). It is further identified as an embodied psychology by its focus on physical matching, acting 'as if' and its acknowledgment that role playing provides actual experience of having a trait and its consequences (Andreas & Andreas, 1987, Bandler & Grinder, 1975).

NLP as a modeling discipline

At the heart of NLP and making use of its formal elements, is the process of modeling. Modeling is the distinctive research method of NLP; it lies at the heart of its practice. It consists of discovering the maps, schemas, patterns, or strategies that underlie specific behaviors in individuals, and where appropriate, for groups of individuals. Once discovered, those patterns are tested to determine whether they will reproduce the ability or problem. It is validated empirically when the resulting models allow the modeler, or someone using the model to replicate the behavior or modify the behavior effectively (Bandler & Grinder, 1975, 1979; Bostic St Clair & Grinder, 2002; Bradbury, 2011; Dilts, 1995, 1998; Dilts et al., 1980; Gordon & Dawes, 2005).

Modeling is the core activity of NLP. It is supported by several presuppositions including the idea that all humans possess the same general set of capacities and resources and in the absence of any debilitating defect, can learn to do anything that another human being can do. This does not discount differences in capacity but only affirms that behaviors are patterned and that those patterns can be analyzed and learned. Further, NLP holds that people suffering psychological problems are not, for the most part, neurologically defective. Non-biological problems arise as expressions of inappropriate or distorted maps that do not match the external territory. In this case, the modeler seeks out the structure of the problem behavior or belief to provide more options for change. NLP instructs the clinician to focus on how the client has limited their choices and to help provide new possibilities of action and belief (Ashby, 1956; Grinder & Bandler, 1976).

Chunking

Chunking was one of the crucial ideas that flowed from the cognitive revolution. Miller (1956), advised that short-term memory has a limited capacity consisting about 7 individual elements, or chunks. The chunk is the operational unit of the TOTE algorithm, larger chunks may be broken down into smaller elements (component systems) and smaller components nested in larger. The successful completion of a TOTE operation may signal the system to move to a superordinate level of function – the emergent property of the previous operations. Chunks may be composed of smaller elements, or larger systems of integrated elements. A budding guitarist learns to play chords, and then assembles the chords in order to play a song, a group of such songs is assembled into a set list, and the set lists form a performance repertoire. We can also think of chunks in terms of places (the method of loci, Yates, 1966), families, tribes, ethnicities. Racism is in some cases a reflection of chunking by racial characteristics. Once these chunks have been properly assessed and are of a manageable size, any behavior can be modeled and transferred to another individual by learning and assembling its component parts. Chunks correspond to functional modules, subsystems in the language of GST. They are also units under the control of a specific TOTE such that a specific behavioral outcome defines the transition from one process to another. Each may have a separate organization and their complimentary interactions reveals the syntax relevant to that chunk in its association with others.

Yamaguchi, Randle, Wilson, & Logan (2017) report that the development of skilled performance depends upon the ability to break larger motor and semantic elements into smaller components for ease of learning. For ease of recall, smaller elements may assemble together, creating the larger systems that emerge from their interactions. Bera, Shukla, & Bapi (2021), have shown that motor responses are learned in a chunk-wise fashion independent of whether the cuing stimulus is internal or external. This accords with work from the mirror neuron system showing that goal-targeted behavior is organized by the assembly of specific motor chunks with particular syntactical relations (Kilner, Friston, & Frith, 2007; Rizzolatti & Sinigaglia, 2010). It also matches the role of the ventral striatum in the assembly of motor actions (Feil et al., 2010; Koul et al., 2018; Salo et al., 2019; Yin, & Knowlton, 2006). In general, we suggest that well-formed chunks correspond to independent behavioral subsystems that may be assembled into larger systems.

In a previous section it was noted that NLP is ordered hierarchically and in accord with systems principles. The lowest level of the hierarchy of behavioral elements, for the purposes of modeling, are the sensory elements (often referred to as the VAKOG) and their sequencing into larger units called patterns or strategies. Patterns or strategies describe discrete behaviors. More complex behaviors are analyzed into a sequence of patterns or strategies that combine to create complex behavior as the emergent property of the system. Because, by definition, the emergent property of a complex system is different from the sum of its parts, modeling is a top-down process. That is, it begins with the final product, analyzes that into its component behaviors and those into sequences of sensory experience and submodality distortions.

Because the modeler has no direct access to the client's inner subjective experience he must rely on responses to questions, personal observation, and empirical testing of the models. Central to the process is the concept that communication is redundant and occurs across multiple channels (Bateson, 1972). By matching these channels to the subject's description of the process, the modeler is provided with multiple descriptions of the process that can either confirm or lead them to modify their understanding of the process.

An alternative view of modeling is presented by Bostic St Clair & Grinder (2002). These authors argue that only living models are legitimate, and that before any strategy analysis is possible, the behavior must be reproduced unconsciously in the modeler. One question they ask in defense of the first proposition, is whether anyone has learned to act like Disney, or Tesla, or Mozart after following Dilts' (1995) models (Grinder & Pucelik, 2013)?

The question fails to recognize that although we can learn those patterns, the resources that we bring, or do not bring to bear on the skills will determine whether we can fully replicate the behavior of the model. DeLozier & Grinder (1995) usefully point out that modeling a pilot without their years of practice will not impart the skills necessary to fly an airplane. While most persons will not learn to write masterpieces using Dilts' analysis of the Mozart Strategy (1995), they may learn to organize the musical skills and experiences *that they have* in new, creative ways.

Although modeling lies at the heart of NLP (Dilts, 1998; Dilts et al., 1980), there appear to be few discussions of the practice in the peer-reviewed literature. Searches of NCBI and PsycInfo for NLP AND modeling AND Bandler for dates after 2013, found no relevant studies.

The process of modeling makes use of several tools which are derived from the process itself. These include calibration, eye accessing cues, the Meta-Model and the T.O.T.E. heuristic.

Calibration is the skill of observing and responding to minimal cues in physiology and language manifested by the model while accessing the behavior. Every human response has some effect on general physiology. These effects may include changes in skin tone, breathing rate, pupil dilation, pulse, muscle tension, micro expressions, and subtle movements, among others. Insofar as NLP makes a claim to being an empirical discipline, this claim is based in part upon the skill of calibration. A skilled practitioner is expected to have developed sufficient sensory acuity to be able to observe subtle changes in physiology as the client moves from state to state. In the process of modeling, calibration allows the modeler to confirm the client's reports of state changes through his own observation of physiology.

A related model is the NLP eye accessing cues (EACs). The eye accessing cues are understood to reflect the sequencing of sensory systems as a percept or idea moves into consciousness (Bandler & Grinder, 1975). Evidence for the eye accessing cues was reviewed in the previous volume (Wake et al., 2013). There is broad agreement from the literature of cognitive neuroscience that persons looking upward are likely accessing visual information and those looking to the side are accessing auditory information. The downward gaze of auditory digital (down and to the left), and kinesthetic (down and to the right) access have little support from the journal literature (Carlei & Kerzel, 2020). Nevertheless, Carlei & Kerzel suggest that the upper visual field may be more closely associated with the dorsal "what" network and the lower visual field with the ventral "where" network – aligned with movement and feeling more generally. These authors have confirmed that looking up and to the left enhances verbal performance.

Beyond behavioral evaluations of the EACs, there exists a body of peer-reviewed literature that is generally supportive. Micic, Ehrlichman & Chen (2010) studied eye movements (saccades and fixations), not related to external visual stimuli-- non-visual gaze patterns (NVGPs). This is the realm of the EACs. They report that NVGPs reflect the episodic retrieval of auditory and visual information in visual imagery, fantasy, daydreaming, mental multiplication, and other long-term memory-related tasks. Saccades are followed by brief fixations during long-term memory retrieval (Ehrlichman, Micic, Sousa, & Zhu, 2007). These findings suggest that EACs are likely associated with trans-derivational search, the search for information in long-term memory, independent of sensory system, as reported by Bandler & Grinder (1975, 1979).

Beattie & Barnard (1979), investigated NVGPs during phone conversations and found that participants, in a visually neutral setting (facing a blank white wall) were most likely to make NVGPs when starting to speak or at phrase boundaries. This is supported by Laeng & Teodorescu (2002), and Ferreira, Apel, & Henderson (2008) who showed that NVGPs occur at empty visual locations during the recall of both visual and linguistic information. This suggests that there are places in conversations and their surroundings where experimenters testing the validity of the NLP EACs should focus their investigations. They should avoid visual distractors and focus their efforts on LTM access (transderivational search), and pauses in conversation.

Pomper & Chait (2017) indicate that visual gaze, independent of the attended modality, reflects the direction of an already attended stimulus. They also indicate that there is evidence of auditory and visual integration at the level of the midbrain. This confirms earlier research by Richardson, Dale, & Spivey (2007) who indicate that saccades shift the eyes to new information sources in the visual environment.

Braga, Fu, Seemungal, Wise, & Leech (2016), in an experimental context without visual cueing, found that eye movements tracked sound and activated elements of the dorsal frontoparietal attentional network. Their observations are consistent with others that indicate that NVGPs increase while accessing long-term memories (Ehrlichman et al. 2007; Ehrlichman & Micic, 2012). There appears to be a general agreement that eye movements follow attention and rarely direct it. With this information we can say with some assurance that EACs reflect the anticipated stimulus source: "This is where I will experience X," or orienting: "This is where I think X came from" (Leigh & Kennard, 2004). Braga Fu Seemungal Wise & Leech (2016) also note that the response to endogenous and exogenous, as well as to auditory and visual stimuli produced patterns of gaze orientation that differed across persons. This may relate to some of the difficulty NLP has had in validating the EACs, they are inconsistently represented across persons.

The Meta-Model is an element of NLP practice that has its roots in Chomskian Linguistics (Bandler & Grinder, 1975; Lewis & Pucelik, 1990; O'Connor & Seymour, 1990; Tosey & Mathison, 2009). It is paralleled in the lists of irrational language patterns in CBT and REBT (Ellis, 2017; Grohol, 2019). It is non-controversial. In the context of modeling, the Meta-model allows the therapist to recognize deletions, distortions, and generalizations in the language of the model and to thereby obtain more specific information about the behavior being modeled. The Meta-Model was reviewed in Wake, Gray, & Bourke (2013) and is more fully reviewed here, in Chapter 3, Diagnosis, above.

Evaluating NLP as a modeling discipline

Like the Field of NLP, with the single exception of the eye accessing cues, none of the assertions of NLP are unique or controversial. Strategies are very similar to cognitive schemas, with the exception that the submodality distortions are understood to be the key to the affective elements so often ignored by cognitive models. Behavioral modeling has been a commonplace in sports, music, dance, and art for centuries; NLP provides it with a systematic structure and well-defined tools.

NLP as a stream of technologies that have arisen out of the field

On its most superficial level, NLP is known as a stream of technologies for modeling, therapy, coaching and personal development. Over the years it has provided techniques for the treatment of grief (Andreas & Andreas, 1989), phobias, (Einspruch & Forman, 1988; Ferguson, 1987; Hale, 1986; Kammer & Lanver, 1997; Liberman, 1984), Trauma (Gray & Liotta, 2012; Hossack & Bentall, 1996; Koziey & McLeod, 1987; Muss, 1991, 2002; Utuza, Joseph & Muss, 2011), Anxiety and Depression (Bigley et al., 2010; Field, 1990; Kirenskaya et al., 2011; Konefal & Duncan, 1998; Konefal, Duncan & Reese, 1992) and others. On a generative level it has been used for sports coaching, enhancing spelling performance (Ampuero Lopez, 2017; Malloy, 1995; Nahari & Hind, 2016), and developing altered states of consciousness (Andreas, 2018; Andreas & Andreas, 1989; Andreas & Andreas, 1994; Bandler, 1985; Gray, 2008/2012, 2014). We have reviewed several such techniques extensively in previous chapters.

All of these might be tested using standard research methods, but none of them would stand as a test of NLP, only of the individual techniques themselves. Even here the researcher must be careful that they have respected the inclusion and exclusion criteria specified by the authors of the technique and that the target problem or symptom is operationalized in accordance with the author's description.

Where are we now?

In the materials above, we have attempted to detail how NLP can and should be studied, and here we report, to our own chagrin, that NLP has not been studied with systematic rigor. Where it has been studied, the research has varied significantly from the above program and many researchers have defined NLP and its principles as they have seen fit. As a result, they have left a stream of bad research in the psychological literature that purports to study NLP, but for the most part does nothing of the sort (see Sharpley, 1984, 1987; Heap, 1988; Witkowski, 2010).

Some of the research that supports NLP is often focused on techniques and consists of case studies and field reports which do not map onto the current model of objective validation for therapeutic application. However, there is a growing body of support for variants of the fast phobia cure (whether as the V/K-D protocol, the Rewind technique or Reconsolidation of Traumatic Memories). That corpus includes a solid body of evidence including the extensive work on RTM (reviewed in Chapter three above); Arroll and colleagues' (2017) experimental evaluation of the V/K-D protocol in the treatment of acrophobia; and the work of Adams and Allan documenting the use of David Muss' (1991, 2002) rewind technique (Adams & Allan, 2018, 2019; Adams et al., 2020). We also note that there is a large and still growing body of supportive research for the lightning Process (Chapter 8, this volume.).

There have been two randomized, waitlist- controlled studies of the Core Transformation pattern (Braganza & Piedmont, 2015; Braganza, Piedmont, Fox, Fialkowski, & Gray, 2019). Both studies reported significant decreases in anxiety and depression and increases with measures of a spirituality construct and positive affect.

There have been several systematic reviews and Meta-analyses that review the support for NLP as a clinical intervention style. These studies meet the external criteria for high quality research, however, the variables that they define and the conclusions that they reach are weakened by their breadth (Genser-Medlitsch, M., & Schütz, P., 1997, 2004; Konefal, Duncan, & Reese, 1992; Konefal & Duncan1998; Stipancic, Reiner, Schütz, & Dond 2010).

Many of the above-mentioned areas for evaluation have strong support from research outside of the bounds of NLP (Wake, Gray & Bourke, 2013), but despite their apparent utility, they are not tests of NLP. While deserving of a place in our literature reviews and otherwise providing strong support for what NLP does, they are no substitute for the development and testing of hypotheses driven by the above observations.

Summary and Conclusions

Here, in an update to our 2013 offering, we have presented indirect evidence for NLP framed in terms of what must and what may be legitimately investigated with regard to the field. That review focused upon three logical levels of NLP and its products. These included the structural and theoretical elements of NLP, its efficacy as a modeling process, and support for the applications generated based upon the modeling process. Throughout, we have noted that only the theoretical elements and the practice of modeling represent legitimate targets for the evaluation of NLP. Supportive practices like rapport, calibration, and eye accessing cues, as well as techniques and interventions based on NLP (V/K-D, RTM, Spelling, Core Transformation) are the products of NLP. Their evaluations are not evaluations of NLP.

Beginning with support for the structural/theoretical elements of NLP including sensory modalities and submodalities, presuppositions, syntax, and the TOTE algorithm, each was reviewed with regard to support from major theories of consciousness and searches of the literature, more generally. We found strong support for the presence of integrated sensory streams that structure and define consciousness at the phenomenal level—the level of subjective experience. Submodalities found strong and continuing behavioral support with neurological evidence for their definition at the anatomical level focused most distinctively in the midbrain. Syntax was described in terms of the properties of systems and their interactions according to GST. We found that each syntactical element has distinctive inputs and outputs that determine its relationship to other members of that system. The function of each is limited by its interactions with its neighbor, giving rise to well-formedness conditions. The TOTE algorithm was discussed and found to be essential at every level of integration and with wide support throughout the literature. The presuppositions were discussed with an acknowledgment of their humanistic and pragmatic foundations.

Turning to Modeling, we were unable to find peer-reviewed articles specifically addressing the practice in NLP. In the course of our research, though, we found support for the sequencing of sensory elements in strategies including cognitive schemas, mirror neurons, and the analysis of behavior more generally. The evidence for rapport and calibration was briefly reviewed. We also reviewed the literature of the eye accessing cues, noting that although there appears to be a solid neurological base for the observations, they are variable and are supported for the most part by studies of visual and auditory cues. We did not address left right distinctions as there appears to be little agreement and little progress in terms of the constructed/remembered dichotomy in NLP.

At last, we took a brief look at some of the products of NLP which have enjoyed growing support from a series of randomized controlled trials.

Having considered the independent research that supports NLP concepts we can say that in general, the theoretical elements of NLP, as defined here, are non-controversial and appear throughout the field of psychology. We believe that major psychological theories have acknowledged the level of subjective experience, qualia space, and phenomenal consciousness, which NLP targets, but seem to approach it with tools appropriate to a verbal, not an experiential level. When correctly targeted at the experiential level, as in prolonged exposure, the applications tend to be theory bound, and are applied without an appreciation for meaning at the subjective level.

References

Adams, S., & Allan, S. (2018). Muss' rewind treatment for trauma: Description and multi-site pilot study. *Journal for Mental Health*, 27(5), 468–474. doi:10.1080/09638237.2018.1487539

Adams, S., & Allan, S. (2019). The effectiveness of Human Givens Rewind treatment for trauma. *Mental Health Review Journal*, 24(3), 228–242. doi:10.1108/MHRJ-10-2018-0033

Adams, S., Allan, S., Andrews, W., Guy, K., Timmins, J., & Barr, E. (2020). Four practice-based preliminary studies on Human Givens Rewind treatment for posttraumatic stress in Great Britain. *F1000Research*, 9, 1252. doi:10.12688/f1000research.25779.1

Adler, R. (1999, December 18). Crowded minds. *New Scientist*. https://www.newscientist.com/article/mg16422174-800-crowded-minds/.

Alcaro, A., Carta, S., & Panksepp, J. (2017). The affective core of the self: A neuro archetypical perspective on the foundations of human (and animal) subjectivity. *Frontiers in psychology*, 8. doi:10.3389/fpsyg.2017.01424

Allsopp, K., Read, J., Corcoran, R., & Kinderman, P. (2019). Heterogeneity in psychiatric diagnostic classification. *Psychiatry Research*, 279, 15–22. doi:10.1016/j.psychres.2019.07.005

Almeida-Correa, S., & Amaral, O. B. (2014). Memory labilization in reconsolidation and extinction--evidence for a common plasticity system? *Journal of Physiology*, Paris. 2014 Sep-Dec;108(4–6), 292–306. PubMed PMID: 25173958. Epub 2014/09/01. eng.

Ampuero Lopez, E. (2017). The impact of the NLP spelling strategy in the early years of bilingual education La influencia de la estrategia de ortografía de la PNL en los primeros años de la enseñanza bilingüe, *Educación y Futuro*, 37 (2017), 93–125. ISSN: 1576-5199

Andreas, C. (2018). *Coming to wholeness: How to awaken and live with ease*. Boulder, CO: Real People Press.

Andreas, C., & Andreas, S. (1989). *Heart of the mind*. Boulder, CO: Real People Press.

Andreas, C., & Andreas, T. (1994). *Core transformations: Reaching the wellspring within*. Real People Press.

Andreas, S. (2008). How to ruin the Swish Pattern: "Let me count the ways" by Steve Andreas' NLP Blog. *Steve Andreas' NLP Blog*. https://realpeoplepress.com/blog/how-to-ruin-the-swish-pattern-let-me-count-the-ways

Andreas, S., & Andreas, C. (1987). *Change your mind—and keep the change*. Boulder, CO: Real People Press.

Andreas, S., & Faulkner, C. (1994). *NLP: The new technology of achievement*. New York: Harper Collins.

Ashby, W. R. (1956). *An introduction to cybernetics*. Oxford, England: John Wiley and Sons.

Bakker, G. (2019). A new conception and subsequent taxonomy of clinical psychological problems. *BMC Psychology*, 7(1). doi:10.1186/s40359-019-0318-8

Balleine, B. W., & Killcross, S. (2006). Parallel incentive processing: An integrated view of amygdala function. *Trends in Neuroscience*, 29(5), 272–279. doi:10.1016/j.tins.2006.03.002

Bandler, R. (nd). The genius of Richard Bandler. Boulder, CO: NLP Comprehensive (Audio).

Bandler, R. (1999). *Introduction to DHE*. Chicago (Audio).

Bandler, R. (1985). *Using your brain for a change*. Moab, UT: Real People Press

Bandler, R., & Grinder, J. (1979). *Frogs into princes*. Moab, UT: Real People Press.

Bandler, R., & Grinder, J. (1975). *The structure of magic*. Palo Alto, CA: Science and BehaviorBooks.

Bandler, R., & MacDonald, W. (1987). *An insider's guide to submodalities*. Moab, UT: Real People Press.

Bandura, A., Ross, D., & Ross, S. (1961). Transmission of aggression through imitation of aggressive models. *The Journal of Abnormal and Social Psychology*, 63(3), 575–582.

Bargh, J., Chen, M. & Burrows, L. (1996). Automaticity of social behavior: Direct effects of trait construct and stereotype activation on action. *Journal of Personality and Social Psychology*, 71(2), 230–244.

Bateson, G. (1972). *Steps to an ecology of mind: Collected essays in anthropology, psychiatry, evolution and epistemology*. University Of Chicago Press.

Baxter, L. R., Jr, et al. (1987). Local cerebral glucose metabolic rates in obsessive-compulsive disorder: A comparison with rates in unipolar depression and in normal controls. *Archives of General Psychiatry*, 44(3), 211–218.

Beattie, G. W., & Barnard, P. J. (1979). The temporal structure of natural telephone conversations (directory enquiry calls). *Linguistics – An Interdisciplinary Journal of the Language Sciences*, 17(3–4), 213–230. doi:10.1515/ling.1979.17.3-4.213

Bechara, A. (2005). Decision making, impulse control and loss of willpower to resist drugs: A neurocognitive perspective. *Nature Neuroscience*, 8(11), 1458–1463.

Bechara, A., Berridge, K. C., Bickel, W. K., Morón, J. A., Williams, S. B., & Stein, J. S. (2019). A neurobehavioral approach to addiction: Implications for the Opioid Epidemic and the Psychology of Addiction. *Psychological Science in the Public Interest* 20(2), 96–127. doi:10.1177/1529100619860513

Bell, A. H., Meredith, M. A., Van Opstal, A. J., & Munoz, D. P. (2005). Crossmodal integration in the primate superior colliculus underlying the preparation and initiation of saccadic eye movements. *Journal of Neurophysiology*, 93(6), 3659–3673.

Bera, K., Shukla, A., & Bapi, R. S. (2021). Motor chunking in internally guided sequencing. *Brain Sciences*, 11(3). doi:10.3390/brainsci11030292

Bertalanffy, L. von. (1968). *General system theory*. New York: George Braziller.

Berridge, K. C., & Robinson, T. E. (1998). What is the role of dopamine in reward: Hedonic impact, reward learning, or incentive salience? *Brain Research Reviews*, 28(3), 309–369. doi:10.1016/S0165-0173(98)00019-8

Bickel, W. K., Athamneh, L. N., Basso, J. C., Mellis, A. M., DeHart, W. B., Craft, W. H., & Pope, D. (2019). Excessive discounting of delayed reinforcers as a trans-disease process: Update on the state of the science. *Current Opinion in Psychology*, 30, 59–64. doi:10.1016/j.copsyc.2019.01.005

Bickel, W. K., Johnson, M. W., Koffarnus, M. N., MacKillop, J., & Murphy, J. G. (2014). The behavioral economics of substance use disorders: Reinforcement pathologies and their repair. *Annual Review of Clinical Psychology*, 10, 641–677. doi:10.1146/annurev-clinpsy-032813-153724

Bigley, J., Griffiths, D., Prydderch, A., Romanowski, A. J., Miles, L., & Lidiard. H. (2010). Neurolinguistic programming used to reduce the need for anaesthesia in claustrophobic patients undergoing MRI. *The British Journal of Radiology*, 83, 113–117.

Blanke, O. (2012). Multisensory brain mechanisms of bodily self-consciousness. *Nature Reviews Neuroscience*, 13(8), 556–571. doi:10.1038/nrn3292

Bohns, V. K., & S. S. Wiltermuth (2012). It hurts when I do this (or you do that): Posture and pain tolerance. *Journal of Experimental Social Psychology*, 48(1), 341–345.

Bostic St Clair, C., & Grinder, J. (2002). *Whispering in the Wind*. Scotts Valley, CA: J & C Enterprises.

Bouton, M. E., & Moody, E. W. (2004). Memory processes in classical conditioning. *Neuroscience and Biobehavioral Reviews*, 28(7), 663–674. doi:10.1016/j.neubiorev.2004.09.001

Bradbury, A. (2011). 29: What is the FoNLP? FAQ 29 - What is the FoNLP? http://www.bradburyac.mistral.co.uk/nlpfax29.htm.

Braga, R. M., Fu, R. Z., Seemungal, B. M., Wise, R. J. S., & Leech, R. (2016). Eye movements during auditory attention predict individual differences in dorsal attention network activity. *Frontiers in Human Neuroscience*, 10, 164–164. doi:10.3389/fnhum.2016.00164

Braganza, D., & Piedmont, R. L. (2015). The impact of the Core Transformation process on spirituality, symptom experience, and psychological maturity in a mixed age sample in India: A pilot study. *Journal of Religion and Health*, 54(3), 888–902. doi:10.1007/s10943-0150049y

Braganza, D. J., Piedmont, R. L., Fox, J., Fialkowski, G. M., & Gray, R. M. (2019). Examining the clinical efficacy of core transformation: A randomized clinical trial. *Journal of Counseling & Development*, 97(3), 293–305. doi:10.1002/jcad.12269

Brown, N. (2019). Editor's note on correction to Crawley *et al. (2018). Archives of Disease in Childhood*, 104(10), e3–e3. doi:10.1136/archdischild-2017-313375ednote

Brown, R., Lau, H., & LeDoux, J. E. (2019). Understanding the higher-order approach to consciousness. *Trends in Cognitive Science*, 23, 754–768. doi:10.1016/j.tics.2019.

Buckner, R. L. (2010). The role of the hippocampus in prediction and imagination. *Annual Review of Psychology* 61(27–48), C21–C28. doi:10.1146/annurev.psych.60.110707.163508

Buzsáki, G. (2010). Neural syntax: Cell assemblies, synapsembles, and readers. *Neuron*, 68(3), 362–385. doi:10.1016/j.neuron.2010.09.023

Capra, F., & Luisi, P. L. (2017). *A Systems View of Life*. Cambridge, UK: Cambridge Univ. Press.

Carcea, I., & Froemke, R. C. (2019). Biological mechanisms for observational learning. *Current opinion in neurobiology*, 54, 178–185.

Carlei, C., & Kerzel, D. (2020). Looking up improves performance in verbal tasks. Laterality: asymmetries of body. *Brain and Cognition*, 25(2), 198–214. doi:10.1080/1357650X.2019.1646755

Carney, D. R., Cuddy, A. J. C., & Yap, A. J. (2010). Power posing: Brief nonverbal displays affect neuroendocrine levels and risk tolerance. *Psychological Science*, 21(10), 1363–1368.

Chartrand, T. L., & Bargh, J. A. (1999). The chameleon effect: The perception-behavior link and social interaction. *Journal of Personality and Social Psychology*, 76, 893–910.

Chomsky, N. A. (1965). *Aspects of the theory of syntax*. Cambridge: The MIT Press.

Chomsky, Noam (1957). *Syntactic Structures*. The Hague/Paris: Mouton, ISBN 978-3-11-021832-9

Clark, D. M. (1999). Anxiety disorders: Why they persist and how to treat them. *Behaviour Research and Therapy*, 37 (Suppl 1), S5–S27. 10.1016/s0005-7967(99)00048-0

Clark, D. A., & Taylor, S. (2009). The transdiagnostic perspective on cognitive-behavioral therapy for anxiety and depression: New wine for old wineskins? *Journal of Cognitive Psychotherapy: An International Quarterly*, 23, 60–66.

Cressey, D. R. (1960). The theory of differential association: An Introduction. *Social Problems*, 8(1), 2–6. doi:10.2307/798624

Damasio, A. R. (1989). The brain binds entities and events by multiregional activation from convergence zones. *Neural Computation*, 1, 123–132.

Daw, N. D., Gershman, S. J., Seymour, B., Dayan, P., & Dolan, R. J. (2011). Model-based influences on humans' choices and striatal prediction errors. *Neuron*, 69(6), 1204–1215. doi:10.1016/j.neuron.2011.02.027

DeLozier, J., & Grinder, J. (1995). *Turtles all the way down: Prerequisites to personal genius*, Oregon: Metamorphous press

de Rijk, L., Derks, L. A. C., & Hollander, J. (2019). NLP conceptual framework, tools and techniques – A Delphi Poll. In *Powered by NLP 2*, London.

Derks, L. A. C. (2018). *Mental space psychology: Psychotherapeutic evidence for a new paradigm*. Nijmegen, Netherlands: Coppelear b.v.

Derks, L. (2011). Social Panoramas, How to change unconscious landscapes to improve relationships. In L. M. Hall, & S. R. Charvet (Eds.), *Innovations in NLP for Challenging Times* (pp. 45–59). Crown House.

Diamond, D., Campbell, A., Park, C., Halonen, J., & Zoladz, P. (2007). The temporal dynamics model of emotional memory processing: A synthesis on the neurobiological basis of stress-induced amnesia, flashbulb and traumatic memories, and the Yerkes Dodson Law. *Neural Plasticity*, 1–33. doi:10.1155/2007/60803

Dilts, R. (1998). *Modeling With NLP*. Cupertino, CA: Meta Publications.

Dilts, Robert. (1995). *Strategies of Genius (3 vols.)*. Cupertino, CA: Meta Publications.

Dilts, R., & DeLozier, J. (2000) *NLP Encyclopaedia*. NLP University Press.

Dilts, R., Grinder, J., Bandler, R., & DeLozier, J. (1980). *Neuro-Linguistic Programming: Volume I. The Structure of Subjective Experience*. Cupertino, CA: Meta Publications.

Dresp-Langley, B. (2020). Seven properties of self-organization in the human brain. *Big Data and Cognitive Computing*, 4(2), 10. doi:10.3390/bdcc4020010

Duncan, S., & L. F. Barrett (2007). *Affect is a form of cognition: A neurobiological analysis*. Cognitive Emotion.

Dutton, D. G., & Aron A. P. (1974). Some evidence for heightened sexual attraction under conditions of high anxiety. *Journal of Personal Social Psychology*, 30(4), 510–517.

Edelman, G. M. (2003). Naturalizing consciousness: A theoretical framework. *Proceedings of the National Academy of Sciences of the United States of America*, 100(9), 5520–5524. doi:10.1073/pnas.0931349100

Edelman, G. M. (2005). *Wider than the sky. The phenomenal gift of consciousness*. New Haven, CT: Yale University Press.

Ehrlichman, H., & Micic, D. (2012). Why do people move their eyes when they think? *Current Directions in Psychological Science*, 21(2), 96–100. doi:10.1177/0963721412436810

Ehrlichman, H., Micic, D., Sousa, A., & Zhu, J. (2007). Looking for answers: Eye movements in non-visual cognitive tasks. *Brain and Cognition*, 64(1), 7–20. doi:10.1016/j.bandc.2006.10.001

Einspruch, E. L., & Forman, B. D. (1988). Neurolinguistic programming in the treatment of phobias. *Psychotherapy in Private Practice*, 6(1), 91–100

Ellis, A. (2017, May 17). *The Essence of REBT*. Retrieved June 18, 2020, from https://www.rebt.ws/albert_ellis_the_essence_of_rebt.htm

Engel, A. K., & Singer, W. (2001). Temporal binding and the neural correlates of sensory awareness. *Trends in Cognitive Science* (Regul. Ed.) 5, 16–25. doi:10.1016/s1364-6613(00)01568-0.

Farchione, T. J., Fairholme, C. P., Ellard, K. K., Boisseau, C. L., Thompson-Hollands, J., Carl, J. R., Gallagher, M. W., & Barlow, D. H. (2012). Unified protocol for transdiagnostic treatment of emotional disorders: A randomized controlled trial. *Behaviour Therapy*, 43(3), 666–678. doi:10.1016/j.beth.2012.01.001

Farrelly, F. & Brandsma, J. (1981) *Provocative therapy*. Cupertino, CA: Meta Publications

Feczko, E., Miranda-Dominguez, O., Marr, M., Graham, A. M., Nigg, J. T., & Fair, D. A. (2019). The heterogeneity problem: Approaches to identify psychiatric subtypes. *Trends in Cognitive Science*, 23(7), 584–601. doi:10.1016/j.tics.2019.03.009

Feil, J., Sheppard, D., Fitzgerald, P. B., Yücelc M., Lubman, D. I., & Bradshaw, J. L. (2010). Addiction, compulsive drug seeking, and the role of frontostriatal mechanisms in regulating inhibitory control. *Neuroscience and Biobehavioral Reviews*, 35(2), 248–275.

Feinberg, T. E., & Mallatt, J. (2020). Phenomenal consciousness and emergence: Eliminating the explanatory gap. *Frontiers in Psychology*, 11. doi:10.3389/fpsyg.2020.01041

Ferguson, David M. (1987). The effect of two audiotaped Neurolinguistic Programming (NLP) phobia treatments on public speaking anxiety. *Dissertation Abstracts International*, 49(4), 765. University of Tennessee, 95 pp. Order = DA8810355

Fernandez, R. S., Boccia, M. M., & Pedreira, M. E. (2016). The fate of memory: Reconsolidation and the case of Prediction Error. *Neuroscience Biobehaviour Review*, 68, 423–441. doi:10.1016/j.neubiorev.2016.06.004

Ferreira, F., Apel, J., & Henderson, J. M. (2008). Taking a new look at looking at nothing. *Trends in Cognitive* Sciences, 12, 405–410.

Field, E. S. (1990). Neurolinguistic programming as an adjunct to other psychotherapeutic/hypnotherapeutic interventions. *The American journal of clinical hypnosis* v, 32(3), 174–182.

Fineberg, N. A., Baldwin, D. S., Drummond, L. M., Wyatt, S., Hanson, J., Gopi, S., Kaur, S., Reid, J., Marwah, V., Sachdev, R. A., Pampaloni, I., Shahper, S., Varlakova, Y., Mpavaenda, D., Manson, C., O'Leary, C., Irvine, K., Monji-Patel, D., Shodunke, A., Dyer, T., Dymond, A., Barton, G., & Wellsted, D., (2018) *Optimal treatment for obsessive compulsive disorder: a randomized controlled feasibility study of the clinical-effectiveness and cost-effectiveness of cognitive-behavioural therapy, selective serotonin reuptake inhibitors and their combination in the management of obsessive compulsive disorder. International Clinical Psychopharmacology* Nov;33(6), 334–348. doi:10.1097/YIC.0000000000000237. PMID: 30113928; PMCID: PMC6166704.

Fingelkurts, A. A., Fingelkurts, A. A., & Neves, C. F. (2010). Natural world physical, brain operational, and mind phenomenal space-time. *Physics of Life Reviews*, 7(2), 195–249. doi:10.1016/j.plrev.2010.04.001. Epub 2010 Apr 13

Fishman, D. B.; Rotgers, F., & Franks, C. (1988). *Paradigms in behavior therapy: Present and promise.* New York: Springer Publishing.

Fredriskson, B. L. (2001). The role of positive emotions in positive psychology. The broaden-and-build theory of positive emotions. *The American psychologist*, 56(3), 218–226. doi:10.1037//0003-066x.56.3.218

Fredriskson, B. L. & T. Joiner (2018). Reflections on positive emotions and upward spirals. *Perspectives in Psychological Science*, 13(2), 194–199. doi:10.1177/1745691617692106.

Gallese, V., Keysers, C., & Rizzolatti, G. (2004). A unifying view of the basis of social cognition. *Trends in Cognitive Science*, 8(9), 396–403. doi:10.1016/j.tics.2004.07.002

Gendolla, G. H. E., & K. Brinkmann (2005). The role of mood states in self-regulation: Effects on action preferences and resource mobilization. *European Psychologist*, 10(3), 187–198. doi:10.1027/1016-9040.10.3.187

Genser-Medlitsch, M., Schütz, P. (1997, 2004). *Does Neuro-Linguistic psychotherapy have effect? New Results shown in the extramural section.* Martina Genser-

Medlitsch; Peter Schütz, ÖTZ-NLP, Wiederhofergasse 4, A-1090, Wien, Austria/ Nowiny Psychologiczne Psychological News. issue 1

Gibson, J. J. (1977). The theory of affordances. In R. Shaw, & J. Bransford (Eds.), *Perceiving, acting, and knowing: Toward an ecological psychology* (pp. 67–82). Hillsdale, NJ: Erlbaum.

Gillihan, Kessler, & Farah (2007). Memories affect mood: evidence from covert experimental assignment to positive, neutral, and negative memory recall. *Acta Psychol (Amst)* 125(2), 144–154.

Glenberg, A. M. (1997). What memory is for. *Behavioral and Brain Sciences* 20(1), 1–55. doi:10.1017/S0140525X97000010

Gordon, David (1978). *Therapeutic metaphors: Helping others through the looking glass*. Cupertino, CA: Meta Publications.

Gordon, D., & Dawes, G. (2005). *Expanding your world.* Author.

Gray, R. (2001). Addictions and the self: A self-enhancement model for drug treatment in the criminal justice system. *The Journal of Social Work Practice in the Addictions*, 2(1).

Gray, R. (2002). The Brooklyn Program: Innovative approaches to substance abuse treatment. *Federal Probation Quarterly*, 66(3).

Gray, R. (2006). Thinking About Drugs and Addiction Boulder CO: *NLP Comprehensive.* September 2005. Retrieved April 1, 2006 from http://www.nlpcomprehensive.com/articles/AddictionsGray.html

Gray, R. (2008/2012). *Transforming Futures: The Brooklyn Program Facilitators Manual.* 2nd ed. Lulu.com. http://www.lulu.com/content/2267218.

Gray, R. (2014). About addictions: Notes from psychology, neuroscience and NLP, 2nd ed. Lulu.com. http://www.lulu.com/content/3497961.

Gray, W., Fidler, J., & Battista, J. (1982). *General systems theory and the psychological sciences.* Intersystems Pubns.

Gray, R., & Liotta, R. (2012). PTSD: Extinction, reconsolidation, and the visual-kinesthetic dissociation protocol. *Traumatology*, 18(2), 3–16. doi:10.1177/1534765611431835.

Gray, R., Wake, L., Andreas, S., & Bolstad R. (2013). Indirect research into the applications of NLP. In Lisa Wake, Richard Gray, & Frank Bourke (Eds.), *The clinical efficacy of NLP: A critical appraisal* (pp. 153–193). London: Routledge.

Graziano, M. S., & Kastner, S. (2011). Human consciousness and its relationship to social neuroscience: a novel hypothesis. *Cognitive Neuroscience*, 2(January1(2)), 98–113. doi:10.1080/17588928.2011.565121. 2011.\

Grinder, J., & Bandler, R. (1976). *The structure of magic II.* Cupertino, California: Science and Behavior Books.

Grinder, J., & Bandler, R. (1981). *Trance-formations: Neuro-linguistic programming and the structure of hypnosis.* Andreas, C. (Ed.). Boulder, CO: Real People Press.

Grinder, J., & Pucelik, F. (2013). *Origins of neuro linguistic programming*. Bancyfelin: Crown House Publishing.

Grohol, J. M. (2019, June 24). *15 Common Cognitive Distortions*. Retrieved June 18, 2020, from https://psychcentral.com/lib/15-common-cognitive-distortions/

Gros, D. F. (2014). Development and initial evaluation of Transdiagnostic Behavior Therapy (TBT) for veterans with affective disorders. *Psychiatry Research*, 220(1), 275–282. doi:10.1016/j.psychres.2014.08.018

Hale, Richard L. (1986). *The effects of Neurolinguistic Programming (NLP) on public speaking anxiety and incompetence.* Dissertation Abstracts International, 47(5), 2167. Drake University, 93 pp. Order =DA8617682, 1986

Hall, L. M. (1996). *Meta-States: A domain of logical levels.* Grand Junction, CO: Empowerment Technologies.

Hall, L. M. (2010). Meta reflections 2010: The history of NLP. Neurons--*The International egroup of Neuro-Semantics* (17 Articles). Retrieved from http://www.neurosemantics.com/topics/nlp/the-history-of-nlp

Heap, M. (1988) Neurolinguistic programming: An interim verdict. In M. Heap (Ed.), *Hypnosis: Current clinical, experimental and forensic practices* (pp. 268–280). London: Croom Helm.

Holland, A. C., & Kensinger, E. A. (2010). Emotion and autobiographical memory. *Physics of life reviews*, 7(1), 88–131. doi:10.1016/j.plrev.2010.01.006

Hossack, A., & Bentall, R. P. (1996). Elimination of posttraumatic symptomatology by relaxation and visual-kinesthetic dissociation. *Journal of Traumatic Stress*, 9(1), 99–110.

Hung, I. W., & Labroo, A. A. (2011). From firm muscles to firm willpower: Understanding the role of embodied cognition in self regulation. *Journal of Consumer Research* 37(6), 1046–1064.

IASH & DeLozier, J. (2006). An Interview with our Keynote Speaker [Interview Transcript]. Retrieved from IASH 2006 Conference Web site: http://www.nlpiash.org/conference2006/Site/Presentations/DeLozierJudith.htm

Itti, L., Koch, C., & Niebur, E., (1998). A model of saliency-based visual attention for rapid scene analysis. *IEEE Transactions on Pattern Analysis and Machine Intelligence*, 20(11), 1254–1259, doi:10.1109/34.730558.

James, W., (1890). *The principles of psychology*. New York: Dover Publications, Inc.

James, W. (1950). *The principles of psychology. Authorized ed., unabridged.* (Dover ed.). Dover Publications.

Jerath, R., & Beveridge, C. (2019). Multimodal integration and phenomenal spatiotemporal binding: A perspective from the default space theory. *Frontiers in Integrative Neuroscience*, 13, 2. doi:10.3389/fnint.2019.00002

Jerath, R., Beveridge, C., & Jensen, M. (2019). On the hierarchical organization of oscillatory assemblies: Layered superimposition and a global bioelectric framework. *Frontiers in Human Neuroscience*, 13, 426. doi:10.3389/fnhum.2019.00426

Jerath, R., Crawford, M. W., & Barnes, V. A. (2015). A unified 3D default space consciousness model combining neurological and physiological processes that underlie conscious experience. *Frontiers in Psychology* Aug 27; 6, 1204. doi:10.3389/fpsyg.2015.01204.eCollection2015.

Kalinli, O., & Narayanan, S. S. (2007). *A top-down auditory attention model for learning task dependent influences on prominence detection in speech* In: Proceedings of the IEEE International Conference on Acoustics, Speech, and Signal Processing. ICASSP (Conference), pp. 3981–3984. doi:10.1109/ICASSP.2008.4518526.

Kammer, D., & Lanver, C. (1997) Schwochow, M.: *Controled treatment of simple phobias with NLP: evaluation of a pilot project.* University of Bielefeld, Department of Psychology, unpublished paper.

Kaplan, F., & Oudeyer, P. Y. (2007). In search of the neural circuits of intrinsic motivation. *Frontiers in Neuroscience*, 1(1), 225–236. doi:10.3389/neuro.01.1.1.017.2007

Kaya, E. M., & Elhilali, M. (2012). *A temporal saliency map for modeling auditory attention*, 2012 46th Annual Conference on Information Sciences and Systems (CISS), Princeton, NJ, 2012, pp. 1–6. doi:10.1109/CISS.2012.6310945.

Kemp, N. (2015, August 19). *Provocative therapy*. http://www.nickkemptraining.com/provocative-therapy-training/.

Kiefer, M., & Barsalou, L. W. (2013). Grounding the Human Conceptual System in Perception, Action, and Internal States. In W. Prinz, M. Beisert, & A. Herwig (Eds.), *Action Science: Foundations of an Emerging Discipline* (pp. 381–407). The MIT Press. https://mitpress.universitypressscholarship.com/view/10.7551/mitpress/9780262018555.001.0001/upso-9780262018555

Kilner, J. M., Friston, K. J., & Frith, C. D. (2007). Predictive coding: An account of the mirror neuron system. *Cognitive Processing*, 8(3), 159–166. doi:10.1007/s10339-007-0170-2

Kindt, M., & van Emmerik, A. (2016). New avenues for treating emotional memory disorders: towards a reconsolidation intervention for posttraumatic stress disorder. *Therapeutic Advances in Psychopharmacology*; May 1, 2016. doi:10.1177/2045125316644541

Kindt, M., Soeter, M., & Vervliet, B. (2009). Beyond extinction: erasing human fear responses and preventing the return of fear. *Nature Neuroscience*, 12(3), 256–258. doi:10.1038/nn.2271

Kirenskaya, A. V., Novototsky-Vlasov, V. Y., Chistyakov, A. N., & Zvonikov, V. M. (2011) The relationship between hypnotizability, internal imagery, and efficiency of neurolinguistic programming. *International Journal of Clinical and Experimental Hypnosis*. Apr; 59(2), 225–241.

Knudsen, E. I. (2018). Neural circuits that mediate selective attention: A comparative perspective. *Trends in Neuroscience*, 41(11), 789–805. doi:10.1016/j.tins.2018.06.006

Kolodny, O., Edelman, S., & Lotem, A. (2015). Evolved to adapt: A computational approach to animal innovation and creativity. *Current Zoology*, 61(2), 350–368. doi:10.1093/czoolo/61.2.350

Konefal, J., & Duncan, R. (1998). Social anxiety and training in neurolinguistic programming. *Psychological Reports*, 83, 1115–1122.

Konefal, J., Duncan, R., & Reese, M. (1992). Effect of neurolinguistic programming training on trait anxiety and internal locus of control. *Psychological Reports*, 70(819–832), 1992.

Kopp, B. (2012). A simple hypothesis of executive function. *Frontiers in Human Neuroscience*, *6*, 159. https://doi.org/10

Korzybski, A. (1994). *Science & sanity (5th ed.)*. European Society for General Semantics. Retrieved from http://esgs.free.fr/uk/art/sands.htm

Koziey, P. W., & McLeod, G., (1987) Visual-Kinesthetic dissociation in treatment of victims of rape (research and practice). *Professional Psychology: Research and Practice*. American Psychological Association.

Koul, A., Cavallo, A., Cauda, F., Costa, T., Diano, M., Pontil, M., & Becchio, C. (2018). Action observation areas represent intentions from subtle kinematic features. *Cerebral Cortex*, 28(7), 2647–2654. doi:10.1093/cercor/bhy098

Kragel, P. A., Reddan, M. C., Labar, K. S., & Wager, T. D. (2019). Emotion schemas are embedded in the human visual system. *Science Advances*, 5(7), eaaw4358. doi:10.1126/sciadv.aaw4358

Kringelbach, M. L. (2005). The human orbitofrontal cortex: Linking reward to hedonic experience. *Nature Reviews Neuroscience*, 6(9), 691–702. Retrieved from doi:10.1038/nrn1747

Kroes, M. C., & Fernández, G. (2012). Dynamic neural systems enable adaptive, flexible memories. *Neuroscience and Biobehavioral Reviews*, 36(7), 1646–1666. doi:10.1016/j.neubiorev.2012.02.014

Kuhnke, P., Kiefer, M., & Hartwigsen, G. (2021). Task-dependent functional and effective connectivity during conceptual processing. *Cerebral Cortex*. doi:10.1093/cercor/bhab026

Laeng, B., & Teodorescu, D. S. (2002). Eye scan paths during visual imagery re-enact those of perception of the same visual scene. *Cognitive Science: A Multidisciplinary Journal*, 26, 207–231.

Lamme, V. A. F. (2006). Towards a true neural stance on consciousness. *Trends in Cognitive Science*, 10, 494–501. doi:10.1016/j.tics.2006.09.001.

Lamme, V. A. F. (2010). How neuroscience will change our view on consciousness. *Cognitive Neuroscience*, 1(3), 204–220. doi:10.1080/17588921003731586

Lee, J. L. (2009). Reconsolidation: Maintaining memory relevance. *Trends in Neuroscience*, 32(8), 413–420. doi:10.1016/j.tins.2009.05.002

Leigh, R. J., & Kennard, C. (2004). Using saccades as a research tool in the clinical neurosciences. *Brain*, 127(3), 460–477. doi:10.1093/brain/awh035

Lewis, P. A., Critchley, H. D., Smith, A. P., & Dolan, R. J. (2005). Brain mechanisms for mood congruent memory facilitation. *Neuroimage*, 25(4), 1214–1223. doi:10.1016/j.neuroimage.2004.11.053

Lewis, B., & Pucelik, F. (1990). *Magic of NLP demystified. A pragmatic guide to communication and change*. Portland, Oregon: Metamorphous Press.

Liberman, M. B. (1984). *The treatment of simple phobias with Neurolinguistic Programming techniques*. Dissertation Abstracts International 45(6), St. Louis University.

Linden, A., & Perutz, K. (1998). *Mindworks: NLP tools for building a better life*. NY: Berkley Publishing Group.

Lyons, D. E., Santos, L. R., & Keil, F. C. (2006). Reflections of other minds: How primate social cognition can inform the function of mirror neurons. *Current Opinion in Neurobiology*, 16(2), 230–234. doi:10.1016/j.conb.2006.03.015

Malloy, T. E. (1995) Empirical evaluation of the effectiveness of a visual spelling strategy. In K. H. Schick (Ed.), Paderborn, Germany: Rechtschreibterapie, Paderborn, Junfermann Verlag.

Mannheim, K. (1998). *Ideology and Utopia*. NY: Routledge.

Mashour, G. A., Roelfsema, P., Changeux, J.-P., & Dehaene, S. (2020). Conscious processing and the global neuronal workspace hypothesis. *Neuron*, 105(5), 776–798. doi:10.1016/j.neuron.2020.01.026

Maslow, A. (1971). *The Farther Reaches of Human Nature*. Penguin / Esalen.

Mazurek, K. A., & Schieber, M. H. (2019). Mirror neurons precede non-mirror neurons during action execution. *Journal of Neurophysiology*, 122(6), 2630–2635. doi:10.1152/jn.00653.2019

McClure, S. M., Daw, N. D., & Montague, P. R. (2003). A computational substrate for incentive salience. *Trends in Neuroscience*, 26(8), 423–428. doi:10.1016/s0166-2236(03)00177-2

Merton, R. K. (1938). Social structure and anomie. *American Sociological Review*, 3, 672–682.

Micic, D., Ehrlichman, H., & Chen, R. (2010). Why do we move our eyes while trying to remember? The relationship between non-visual gaze patterns and memory. *Brain and Cognition*, 74(3), 210–224. doi:10.1016/j.bandc.2010.07.014

Miller, G. A. (1956). The magical number seven, plus or minus two: some limits on our capacity for processing information. *Psychological Review*, 63(2), 81–97. doi:10.1037/h0043158

Miller, G. A., Galanter, E., & Pribram, K. H. (1960). *Plans and the structure of behavior* [doi:10.1037/10039-000]. Henry Holt and Co. 10.1037/10039-000

Moore, B., Mischel, W., & Zeiss, A. (1976). Comparative effects of the reward stimulus and its cognitive representation in voluntary delay. *Journal of Personality and Social Psychology*, 34(3), 419–424. doi:10.1037/0022-3514.34.3.419

Mullally, S. L., & Maguire, E. A. (2014). Memory, imagination, and predicting the future: A common brain mechanism? *Neuroscientist*, 20(3), 220–234. doi:10.1177/1073858413495091

Muss, D. (1991). A new technique for treating post-traumatic stress disorder. *British Journal of Clinical Psychology*, 30(1), 91–92.

Muss, D. C. (2002). The rewind technique in the treatment of post-traumatic stress disorder: Methods and applications. In C. R. Figley (Ed.), *Brief treatments for the traumatized: A project of the Green Cross Foundation*. (pp. 306–314). Westport, CT US: Greenwood Press/Greenwood Publishing Group.

Naccache, L. (2018). Why and how access consciousness can account for phenomenal consciousness. *Philosophical Transactions of the Royal Society B: Biological Sciences*, 373(1755).

Nadel, L., Hupbach, A., Gomez, R., & Newman-Smith, K. (2012). Memory formation, consolidation and transformation. *Neuroscience & Biobehavioral Reviews*, 36(7), 1640–1645. doi:10.1016/j.neubiorev.2012.03.001

Nader, K. (2003). Memory traces unbound. *Trends in Neuroscience*, 26(2), 65–72. doi:10.1016/s0166-2236(02)00042-5

Nader, K., Schafe, G., & Le Doux, J. (2000). Fear memories require protein synthesis in the amygdala for reconsolidation after retrieval. *Nature*, 406(6797), 722–726. doi:10.1038/35021052

Nahari, A. A., and Hind, A. A. (2016). From memorising to visualising: The effect of using visualisation strategies to improve students' spelling skills. *English Language Teaching*, 9(6), 2016 ISSN 1916-4742 E-ISSN 1916-4750. doi: 10.5539/elt.v9n6p1 URL: 10.5539/elt.v9n6p1

Newby, J. M., McKinnon, A., Kuyken, W., Gilbody, S., & Dalgleish, T. (2015). Systematic review and meta-analysis of transdiagnostic psychological treatments for anxiety and depressive disorders in adulthood. *Clinical Psychology Review*, 40, 91–110. doi:10.1016/j.cpr.2015.06.002

NLPWIKI. (2014, December 7). NLP Journal Support (1) 12-7-14---v3000.doc. NLPWIKI.ORG. http://www.nlpwiki.org/nlp-research-information-document.pdf

Niedenthal, P. M., Barsalou, L. W., Winkielman, P., Krauth-Gruber, S., & Ric, F. (2005). Embodiment in attitudes, social perception, and emotion. *Personal Social Psychology Review*, 9(3), 184–211. doi:10.1207/s15327957pspr0903_1

Niedenthal, P. M., Winkielman, P. Mondillon, L., & Vermeulen, N. (2009). Embodiment of emotion concepts. *Journal of Personality and Social Psychology*, 96(6), 1120–1136.

Northoff, G., & Lamme, V. (2020). Neural signs and mechanisms of consciousness: Is there a potential convergence of theories of consciousness in sight? *Neuroscience and biobehavioral reviews*, 118, 568–587. Advance online publication. 10.1016/j.neubiorev.2020.07.019

Northoff, G., & Huang, Z. (2017). How do the brain's time and space mediate consciousness and its different dimensions? Temporo-spatial theory of consciousness (TTC). *Neuroscience & Biobehavioral Reviews*, 80, 630–645 10.1016/j.neubiorev.2017.07.013.Epub 2017 Jul 28.

O'Connor, J., & Seymour, J. (1990). *Introducing NLP*. London: Element.

O'Connor, J., & McDermott, I. (1997). *The art of systems thinking: Essential skills for creativity and problem solving*. London: Thorsons Publishing.

Ost, L. G. (2008). Efficacy of the third wave of behavioral therapies: A systematic review and meta-analysis. *Behaviour Research and Therapy*, 46(3), 296–321. doi: 10.1016/j.brat.2007.12.005

Ottaviani, R., & Beck, A. T. (1987). Cognitive aspects of panic disorders. *Journal of Anxiety Disorders*, 1(1), 15–28. doi:10.1016/0887-6185(87)90019-3

Park, S. A., Miller, D. S., Nili, H., Ranganath, C., & Boorman, E. D. (2020). *Map making: Constructing, combining, and inferring on abstract cognitive maps*. bioRxiv 810051; doi:https://doi.org/10.1101/810051

Park, H. D., & Tallon-Baudry, C., (2014). The neural subjective frame: from bodily signals to perceptual consciousness. *Philosophical Transactions of the Royal Society B*. 10.1098/rstb.2013.0208.

Pavlov, I. P. (1927) *Conditioned Reflexes*. London: Routledge.

Pedreira, M. E., Perez-Cuesta, L. M., & Maldonado, H. (2004). Mismatch between what is expected and what actually occurs triggers memory reconsolidation or extinction. *Learning & Memory*, 11(5), 579–585. doi:10.1101/lm.76904

Peelen, M. V., & Downing, P. E. (2007). The neural basis of visual body perception. *Nature Reviews Neuroscience*, 8(8), 636–648. doi:10.1038/nrn2195

Perrault, T., Stein, B., & Rowland, B. (2011). Non-stationarity in multisensory neurons in the superior colliculus. *Frontiers in Psychology*, 2(144). doi:10.3389/fpsyg.2011.00144

Perry, A., Stiso, J., Chang, E. F., Lin, J. J., Parvizi, J., & Knight, R. T. (2018). Mirroring in the human brain: Deciphering the spatial-temporal patterns of the human mirror neuron system. *Cerebral Cortex*, 28(3), 1039–1048. doi:10.1093/cercor/bhx013

Pessoa, L. (2017). A network model of the emotional brain. *Trends in Cognitive Science*, 21(5), 357–371. doi:10.1016/j.tics.2017.03.002

Polák, M., & Marvan, T. (2018). Neural correlates of consciousness meet the theory of identity. *Frontiers in Psychology*, 9(1269). doi:10.3389/fpsyg.2018.01269

Pomper, U., & Chait, M. (2017). The impact of visual gaze direction on auditory object tracking. *Scientific Reports*, 7(1), 4640. doi:10.1038/s41598-017-04475-1

Prigogine, I., & Stengers, E. (2017). *Order out of chaos: Man's new dialogue with nature*. London: Penguin/Random House.

Prochaska, J. O. (1994). Strong and weak principles for progressing from precontemplation to action on the basis of twelve problem behaviors. *Health Psychology*, 13(1), 47–51. doi:10.1037//0278-6133.13.1.47

Ramel, W., Goldin, P. R., Eyler, L. T., Brown, G. G., Gotlib, I. H., & McQuaid, J. R. (2007). Amygdala reactivity and mood-congruent memory in individuals at risk for depressive relapse. *Biol Psychiatry*, 61(2), 231–239. doi:10.1016/j.biopsych.2006.05.004

Ramsey, R., Kaplan, D. M., & Cross, E. S. (2021). Watch and learn: The cognitive neuroscience of learning from others' actions. *Trends in Neuroscience*. doi:10.1016/j.tins.2021.01.007

Redies C., Grebenkina, M., Mohseni, M., Kaduhm, A., & Dobel, C. (2020). Global image properties predict ratings of affective pictures. *Frontiers in Psychology*, 11, 953. doi:10.3389/fpsyg.2020.00953

Rescorla, R. A. (1988). Pavlovian conditioning. It's not what you think it is. *American Psychologist*, 43(3), 151–160. doi:10.1037//0003-066x.43.3.151

Richardson, D. C., Dale, R., & Spivey, M. J. (2007). *Eye movements in language and cognition: A brief introduction.* In M. Gonzalez-Marquez, I. Mittelberg, S Coulson, M. J..Empirical Methods in Cognitive Linguistics, 323–344.

Riskind, J. H., & Gotay, C. C. (1982). Physical posture: Could it have regulatory or feedback effects on motivation and emotion? *Motivation and Emotion*, 6(3), 273–298.

Rizzolatti, G., Cattaneo, L., Fabbri-Destro, M., & Rozzi, S. (2014). Cortical mechanisms underlying the organization of goal-directed actions and mirror neuron-based action understanding. *Physiology Review*, 94(2), 655–706. doi:10.1152/physrev.00009.2013

Rizzolatti, G., & Fogassi, L. (2014). The mirror mechanism: Recent findings and perspectives. *Philosophical Transactions of the Royal Society B: Biological Sciences*, 369(1644), 20130420. doi:10.1098/rstb.2013.0420

Rizzolatti, G., & Sinigaglia, C. (2010). The functional role of the parieto-frontal mirror circuit: Interpretations and misinterpretations. *Nature Reviews Neuroscience*, 11(4), 264–274. doi:10.1038/nrn2805

Sharpley, C. (1987). Research findings on neurolinguistic programming: Nonsupportive data or an untestable theory? *Journal of Counseling Psychology*, 34(1), 103–107.

Sharpley, C. (1984). Predicate matching in NLP: A review of research on the preferred representational system. *Journal of Counseling Psychology*, 31(2), 238–248.

Salo, V. C., Ferrari, P. F., & Fox, N. A. (2019). The role of the motor system in action understanding and communication: Evidence from human infants and non-human primates. *Developmental Psychobiology*, 61(3), 390–401. doi:10.1002/dev.21779

Schmidhuber, J. (2010). Formal theory of creativity, fun, and intrinsic motivation (1990–2010). *IEEE Transactions on Autonomous Mental Development*, 2, 230–247. doi:10.1109/TAMD.2010.2056368

Schutz, Alfred (1967). *The Phenomenology of the Social World.* (George Walsh and Frederick Lehnert, Trans.). Evanston, IL: Northwestern University Press.

Selcuk, E., Zayas, V., Günaydin, G., Hazan, C., & Kross, E. (2012). Mental representations of attachment figures facilitate recovery following upsetting autobiographical memory recall. J *Personal Social Psychology*, 103(2), 362–378. doi: 10.1037/a0028125

Sevenster, D., Beckers, T., & Kindt, M. (2012). Retrieval per se is not sufficient to trigger reconsolidation of human fear memory. *Neurobiology of Learning and Memory*, 97(3), 338–345. doi:10.1016/j.nlm.2012.01.009

Skinner, B. F. (1957). *Science and human behavior*. Garden City, NY, Free Press.

Sparks, D. L. (1999). Conceptual issues related to the role of the superior colliculus in the control of gaze. *Current Opinion in Neurobiology*, 9(6), 698–707. doi:10.1016/s0959-4388(99)00039-2

Stipancic, M., Reiner, W., Schütz, P., & Dond R. (2010). Effects of neuro-linguistic psychotherapy on psychological difficulties and perceived quality of life. *Counselling and Psychotherapy Research* 10(1) - Routledge: 39–49.

Sukenik, N., Vinogradov, O., Weinreb, E., Segal, M., Levina, A., & Moses, E. (2021). Neuronal circuits overcome imbalance in excitation and inhibition by adjusting connection numbers. *Proceedings of the National Academy of Sciences*, 118(12), e2018459118. doi:10.1073/pnas.2018459118

Sun, Y., Huang, Z., Yang, K., Liu, W., Xie, Y., Yuan, B., ... Jiang, X. (2011). Self-organizing circuit assembly through spatiotemporally coordinated neuronal migration within geometric constraints. *PLoS One*, 6(11), e28156. doi:10.1371/journal.pone.0028156

Tononi, G., Boly, M., Massimini, M., Koch, C. (2016). Integrated information theory: From consciousness to its physical substrate. *Nature Reviews Neuroscience*, 17, 450–461. doi:10.1038/nrn.2016.44.

Tosey, P., & Mathison, J. (2009). *Neuro-linguistic programming: A critical appreciation for managers and developers*. Palgrave-Macmillan.

Utuza, A. J., Joseph, S., & Muss, D. C. (2011). Treating traumatic memories in Rwanda with the rewind technique: Two-week follow-up after a single group session. *Traumatology*, 18(1), 75–78. doi: 10.1177/1534765611412795.

VA National Center for PTSD. (2014). *Using the PTSD Checklist for DSM-IV (PCL)* [Internet]. 2014 Jan. Washington, DC: US. Department of Veterans Affairs. http://www.ptsd.va.gov/professional/pages/assessments/assessment-pdf/PCL-handout.pdf Published January. 2014. Updated March 2016. Accessed July 4, 2016.

van Wingen, G. A., van Eijndhoven, P., Cremers, H. R., Tendolkar, I., Verkes, R. J., Buitelaar, J. K., & Fernández, G. (2010). Neural state and trait bases of mood-incongruent memory formation and retrieval in first-episode major depression. *Journal of Psychiatric Research*, 44(8), 527–534. doi:10.1016/j.jpsychires.2009.11.009

Varela, F., Thompson, E., & Rosch, E. (1991). *The embodied mind: Cognitive science and human experience*. Cambridge: MIT Press.

Veale, R., Hafed, Z. M., & Yoshida, M. (2017). How is visual salience computed in the brain? Insights from behaviour, neurobiology and modelling. *Philosophical Transactions of the Royal Society B: Biological Sciences*, 372(1714). doi:10.1098/rstb.2016.0113

Vetter, P., Smith, F. W., & Muckli, L. (2014). Decoding sound and imagery content in early visual cortex. *Current Biology*, 24(11), 1256–1262. doi:10.1016/j.cub.2014.04.020

Visser, R. M., Lau-Zhu, A., Henson, R. N., & Holmes, E. A. (2018). Multiple memory systems, multiple time points: how science can inform treatment to control the expression of unwanted emotional memories. *Philosophical Transactions of the Royal Society B: Biological Sciences*, 373(1742). doi:10.1098/rstb.2017.0209

Wake, L. (2008). *Neurolinguistic psychotherapy: A postmodern perspective*. Routledge

Wake, L. (2010). *NLP principles in practice*. St. Albans, Hertfordshire, UK: Ecademy Press.

Wake, L., Gray, R. M., & Bourke, F. S. (Eds.). (2013). *The clinical effectiveness of neurolinguistic programming: A critical appraisal.* Routledge.

Walsh, N. D., & Phillips, M. L. (2010). Interacting outcome retrieval, anticipation, and feedback processes in the human brain. *Cereb Cortex*, *20*(2), 271–281. doi:10.1093/cercor/bhp098

Watson, J. B., & Raynor, R. (1920). Conditioned emotional reactions. *Journal of Experimental Psychology* 3(1), 1–14.

Wells, A., & Hackmann, A. (1993). Imagery and core beliefs in health anxiety: Contents and origins. *Behavioural and Cognitive Psychotherapy*, 21(3), 265–273. doi:10.1017/S1352465800010511

White, B. J., Berg, D. J., Kan, J. Y., Marino, R. A., Itti, L., & Munoz, D. P. (2017). Superior colliculus neurons encode a visual saliency map during free viewing of natural dynamic video. *Nature Communications*, 8, 14263. doi:10.1038/ncomms14263

Williams, L., & Bargh, J. (2008). Experiencing physical warmth promotes interpersonal warmth. *Science*, 322, 606–607.

Witkowski, T. (2010) Thirty-five years of research on Neuro-Linguistic Programming. NLP research data base. State of the art or pseudoscientific decoration? *Polish Psychological Bulletin*, 41(2), 58–66.

Yamaguchi, M., Randle, J. M., Wilson, T. L., & Logan, G. D. (2017). Pushing typists back on the learning curve: Memory chunking improves retrieval of prior typing episodes. *Journal of Experimental Psychology: Learning, Memory, and Cognition*, 43(9), 1432–1447. doi:10.1037/xlm0000385

Yates, F. A. (1966). *The Art of Memory*. Chicago: The University of Chicago Press.

Yin, H. H., & Knowlton, B. J. (2006). The role of the basal ganglia in habit formation. *Nature Reviews Neuroscience*, 7(6), 464–476.

Zhou, H., & Desimone, R. (2011). Feature-Based Attention in the Frontal Eye Field and Area V4 during Visual Search. *Neuron*, 70(6), 1205–1217. doi:10.1016/j.neuron.2011.04.032

Zoja, L. (1990). *Drugs, addiction & initiation: The modern search for ritual.* Gloucester, MA: Sigo.

Part III

Furthering the field of NLP clinical treatments

11 Standards of training

Will Murray and Dr Lisa de Rijk

Introduction

This chapter summarises and updates the first edition's (Wake, Gray, & Bourke, 2013) debate about the status of NLP training. This chapter continues with the development of a clear training design for the public roll-out of the Reconsolidation of Traumatic Memories protocol (RTM) for treating Post Traumatic Stress Disorder (PTSD). The training development has been trialed, tested, adapted, and refined for both online and face-to-face training delivery. The training has also been coupled with clear monitoring of the clinical application of the protocol to ensure protocol fidelity. Recent research shows the efficacy of the training in a clinical setting (Gray, Davis, & Bourke, 2021).

The Reconsolidation of Traumatic Memories protocol (RTM) has promised to alleviate the suffering of millions of people with Post Traumatic Stress Disorder (PTSD). Many thousands of qualified mental health professionals will be needed to address these millions of PTSD clients. This chapter describes the design and delivery of certification training for licensed clinicians and describes the program to train and certify RTM trainers.

Summary of the status of NLP training

In the first edition of this book Wake, Bourke, Schutz, and Gray, (2013) highlighted the diversity of training standards in the field of NLP. These standards varied from distance learning, to full, year-long programmes, and finally to the rigorous standards over a four-year pathway required of NLP psychotherapists. More recently, the MA in applied coaching previously reported on, has been redesigned and approved by another UK University as an MA in Neurocoaching (The MA Neuro Coaching – The Neurocoaching Academy). This MA has NLP as its core modality.

The continued endeavours of the Research and Recognition Project (RandR; www.nlprandr.org) have now gained further recognition as a serious and credible player in the field of trauma treatment, as reported earlier

DOI: 10.4324/9781003198864-11

in this book. It is on this basis that the authors of this chapter present the training model for a robust clinical training.

Designing and delivering protocol training

The need

The Reconsolidation of Traumatic Memories protocol (RTM) has built into its very design the ability to be researched and tested. It is a manualized protocol that is standardized and replicable. The design of the training to certify qualified mental health professionals as RTM administrators, therefore, benefits from RTM's standardization, and the training itself is standardized and replicable. If the goal of the RandR project to certify 10,000 RTM administrators by 2025 is to be reached, then standardized and measurable training protocols are necessary. A large cadre of RTM trainers will carry out the RTM certification training to qualified mental health professionals. Additionally, if the success of the clinical trials is to be replicated in everyday clinical practice, a robust and clinically effective model of training is required.

RTM certification trainings have evolved since the first training sessions, with incremental improvements in delivery and materials, and then, in 2020, complete migration from live, in-person sessions to fully internet-based trainings. The training design, regardless of delivery channels, has remained the same, using the 4Mat approach.

Training design

The 4Mat approach to learning (McCarthy & McCarthy, 2005) underpins the RTM certification training. The 4Mat approach aims to address the learning styles of all training participants by formatting the training to answer four questions: *Why*?, *What*?, *How*? and *As If*. The *As If* section places the clinician into the future, as if they had acquired the skill, and what they could do with it.

The training sections each begin with the trainer's explanation of *Why* this topic is important and relevant, and then *What* the specific topic is. To address *How*, the trainer demonstrates the topic and gives the clinicians an exercise to practice the skill. The trainer then leads a discussion and question-and-answer session to explore *As If* – the consequences and future applications of using the presented skill, the benefits to the clinician and the client, and what the clinician will be able to do with the new skill. The clinician can mentally "try on" what it would be like to have the skill to employ in working with clients.

Demonstrations sometimes involve the entire group of clinician-trainees. The trainer leads the whole group at once to allow each clinician to experience the topic, such as in submodality shifts (e.g., moving internal images to different locations in the clinician's internal field of view). Other demonstrations use individuals, with the trainer using a volunteer demonstration subject at the front of the room for the rest of the clinicians to observe. Trainers strive to make demonstrations clearly exhibit the topic at hand (without mixing-in other elements) and accurate enough so that clinicians can easily understand the lesson. When the demonstration is about changes in the client's facial affect, the trainer's demonstration should focus wholly on that effect and not highlight other things such as new language patterns or movement of the client's feet. Trainers strive to select volunteer demonstration subjects who can clearly demonstrate the topic. A volunteer with a very light complexion might be a good subject for an initial demonstration of changes in skin tone, for example. In both the online and in-person training, some of the demonstrations appear as pre-recorded videos, and others as live demonstrations featuring one of the participating clinicians or a demonstration subject brought in specifically for that demonstration. It has happened that the demonstration subject has failed to appear at the training, in such cases the trainer would have previously selected a stand-in demonstration subject or a suitable video to show.

Exercises are a key part of the training. They are used to help clinicians gain facility with the clinical skills and gain competency in the complete RTM protocol. The trainer uses the 4Mat approach for exercises: explain *Why* this exercise is important, describe *What* the exercise is, demonstrate *How* to do the exercise, have clinicians complete the exercise, then conclude the exercise with a *What If* conversation.

Training Schedule

The training schedule has a daily format that spans the four days of the entire course.

The daily schedule appears in 90-minute blocks to facilitate optimum learning, with 75 minutes of training followed by a 15-minute break. These 90-minute blocks provide enough time for substantive work, yet enough breaks to keep the clinicians fresh and interested. The noon break is 90 minutes long to give the clinicians time to have a meal, to attend to pressing communications (phone calls, texts and emails), and to visit with one another. The training design allows trainers to complete the topic elements during those 75-minute time blocks, so that the work at hand fits the time blocks and trainers are not hurried to compress the task into the 75-minute period.

Opening metaphor

The daily schedule begins with an opening metaphor relevant to the day's topics. The purpose of the metaphor is to facilitate pre-teaching of the learning objectives of each day and facilitate unconscious receptivity towards learning. For example, the trainer might use a metaphor of a baking recipe as a way to get a tasty pastry, emphasizing how bakers who follow the recipe faithfully can expect a good bake time after time. Later in the day, when the trainer emphasizes the need for clinicians to faithfully follow the script of the RTM protocol, the trainer can refer again to the script being "like a baking recipe", connecting the metaphor with the topic at hand.

Closing metaphor

The trainer ends the training day with a closing metaphor that links the day's work with the following day's agenda. For example, the trainer might refer again to the baker's recipe and mention the similarity to a pilot's pre-flight checklist, which also intends to generate reproduceable results when followed. At the beginning of the next day, the trainer might refer to the closing metaphor to set up the clinicians' expectations.

RTM protocol elements

The training breaks down the elements of the RTM protocol into discrete units to be treated in the 4Mat approach. The trainers use 4Mat for each of the clinical skills and the discrete steps in the RTM protocol. That way, every clinician receives an explanation of their importance and a description of the element. They also watch a demonstration, practice the skill or step, and then discuss having the skill in the future (*as-if*). This ensures all learning styles are met.

In the latter part of the training, the trainer leads the clinicians in three separate experiences of the entire RTM protocol. Each clinician participating in the training gains experience in a range of perceptual positions: as clinician administering the protocol, as client, and as observer.

When serving as *administrator*, the clinician gains three complete experiences of administering the RTM protocol with one of their peers from the group, as if it were in a clinical setting.

When in the role of *client*, the clinician gains experience on the receiving end of the protocol. They are then better able to empathize with the client and can then authentically tell the client "I have experienced the protocol from another clinician. I know how this goes. I've been in your chair". This can help the clinician gain rapport and credibility with the client.

When in the role of *observer,* the clinician is able to see and hear the entire RTM protocol at close distance, watching and listening to both the administrator and the client, noticing the performance and effectiveness of the administrator and the responses of the client. The observer holds a copy of the RTM protocol script so that they can follow along with the protocol and may even assist the administrator in keeping to the script when necessary.

Every clinician participates in all three roles for three separate RTM sessions, giving each clinician nine experiences of the entire protocol.

Trainers and their assistants also observe the practice trios to gain evidence that each clinician can successfully administer the RTM protocol in its entirety.

Giving and Receiving Feedback

An important part of the RTM practice sessions is evaluation and feedback. The trainer instructs the trios (administrator, client, and observer) to provide feedback to each other at the close of the RTM session (not during). The trainer presents the following rules for feedback:

- Let the administrator provide self-evaluation first.
- Let the client provide feedback next.
- Let the observer provide feedback third.
- Focus on specific, observable behaviours.
- Begin with what went well.
- Follow up with what could have gone better.
- For the client and the observer, state suggestions for improvement in the form of a question, for example, "Would you consider giving the client more time to respond?" or "When you saw the client begin to stammer, what else could you have done to help the client to return to a calmer state?"

This form of giving and receiving feedback is supportive and gives the receiver more control over the feedback session. This positive form helps the receiver incorporate the learning into subsequent RTM sessions.

On-line training

Before March 2020, the RTM training consisted of four days of in-person training. When the COVID-19 pandemic made in-person gatherings impossible, the trainings shifted to an all-internet format. One format involved four days of live sessions over internet video (Zoom). This format replicated the in-person training as closely as possible. A second format was a combination of self-paced courses over an internet platform called Teachable (www.teachable.com) and live video conferencing. Participating clinicians in this format read about the elements of the training, view pre-recorded videos, and complete an on-line assessment of theoretical knowledge at their own pace. They must complete this part of the training and pass a test about the information at least two days before the live conferencing sessions begin.

The clinicians then participate in two and a half days of live conferencing during which they practice the clinical skills and elements of the RTM protocol, and then practice the entire protocol in trios as described above.

The internet conferencing format requires a large number of training assistants to monitor the practice trios as they do their work in separate (virtual) break-out rooms. Given the progression of the COVID-19 pandemic, it is unclear whether the trainings will revert to an in-person format, a hybrid of self-paced coursework in Teachable, or another asynchronous/synchronous format.

Safety and security during trainings

The RTM protocol itself is a non-traumatizing intervention. At no time does the client have to face the full force of the traumatic memory. The RTM certification training follows the same principle. Trainers instruct the participants to keep the practice sessions safe by interrupting at any time when in their judgment a client or trainee-partner exhibits evidence of negative sympathetic arousal, or expresses their discomfort.

Trainers also avoid using examples that may elicit negative sympathetic arousal in the training group. Trainers, as experienced RTM administrators, likely have had dozens or hundreds of gruesome stories related to them during client sessions that they may be tempted to use as examples. Trainers resist using these most traumatizing stories during the training so as to avoid installing negative internal representations or awakening unexpected trauma memories during the training. They also encourage the training participants to refrain from telling their colleagues similar stories.

At the beginning of the training session, trainers remind participants to treat the information conveyed by their colleagues during the practice sessions as confidential, just as they would in a clinical session.

Certification

To obtain certification, all trainees, having completed the on-line or in-person training, must submit videos of two successful treatments of PTSD using the RTM protocol. Pre- and post-treatment PSSI-5 documentation of treatment success must accompany the videos. These videos will be reviewed by a trainer or developer for adherence to the protocol, and for the provision of useful guidance for use with future clients. If the videos are unsatisfactory, the client will be asked to complete one or two more submissions with specific guidance on how to improve their efforts. After completion of the required review, trainees will be certified to use the RTM protocol in private client sessions. Certification at this level does not confer any right to teach the protocol or to employ it in other than individual sessions.

Training trainers

Certified RTM administrators who wish to become certified as RTM trainers must meet a set of qualifying prerequisites before being considered as a coach on the training for other therapists, complete a trainer course, then participate in four RTM certification training events as coach.

Prospective trainers must then meet the following prerequisites before being considered for leading trainings: RTM administrator certification, 15 successful RTM client administrations, and an *in vivo* demonstration of an RTM treatment session as a taught demonstration, consistent scores above-eight on a ten-point student feedback scale, with consistent success (>80%) by their students at certification.

The trainer course uses the same 4Mat approach as does the RTM certification training to rationalize, describe, demonstrate, and practice the key elements of the design and structure of the RTM certification training. Prospective trainers experience the *Why* for each element of the training and *What* each element does through explanation and discussion. They then experience and practice *How* to train each element and conclude with a discussion on *As If* they had that training skill.

Prospective trainers gain practical experience in four RTM certification trainings. In the first two trainings, they observe the trainer and serve as coaches to observe and assist the training participants as they conduct practice rounds. In the third training, the prospective trainer leads substantial portions of the training under observation and supervision of the lead trainer. In the fourth training, the prospective trainer serves as lead trainer under observation of the supervising trainer.

The supervising trainer evaluates prospective trainers on their ability to engage the training participants, faithfully follow the training structure, produce accurate explanations of the material, deliver precise demonstrations, and provide useful feedback.

Supporting materials

By design, RTM trainings are standardized and replicable on a large scale. Standardized training materials are key elements in reaching the numbers of certified administrators necessary to address PTSD at increasingly large scales. Training participants receive a comprehensive training manual (Research and Recognition Project, 2020) that explains the training format and provides everything that the participant will need during the course. Two copies of the RTM protocol script are included in the manual, one bound in as a permanent record and another separate copy that the participant can remove from the manual to use in practice sessions. The manual is provided in an everything-in-one-place bound or three-ring binder format, suitable for participants to use during and after the training.

The trainer also receives a trainer's manual (Research and Recognition Project, 2020). This manual contains everything the trainer will need to conduct an effective training including pre-event planning, logistics, room set up, equipment needs, and an explanation of the training format. The training protocol is scripted, ensuring consistency of training delivery.

A presentation file in PowerPoint (Research and Recognition Project, 2020) is provided to the trainees, in support of the training. This presentation file has key points and embedded videos to explain and demonstrate elements of the training and to help the trainer pace the sessions.

Internet-based trainings use Teachable as the training platform, which is compatible with the training manuals and supporting videos.

The participant manual, trainer manual, PowerPoint file, Teachable course, and supporting videos are copyrighted material.

Efficacy of the RTM training

Chapter 3 reports on the clinical effectiveness of the RTM protocol. One study (to date) presents evidence that the RTM training is effective in producing administrators who can successfully conduct the RTM protocol in a clinical setting. Gray et al. (2021) report that 18 clinicians from one site have successfully treated more than 95% of clients as measured by a standard PTSD symptom inventory (PSSI-5). Recent investigations of clinical certification calls, (the final step in the certification process, when RTM coaches interview prospective RTM administrators) have found no significant difference in the efficacy of clinicians trained by the different formats: in-person, four-day live internet conference and hybrid asynchronous self-paced and live internet conference.

Applications to other NLP training

While there are many different training formats, the 4Mat approach seems applicable to other NLP trainings that include skill acquisition. For NLP patterns such as Swish, Aligning Perceptual Positions, Core Transformation, the Wholeness Process, or Spinning Feelings, which rely on skill and practice, 4Mat would likely be a good approach.

The 90-minute-block format also seems useful in longer trainings, especially in internet-platform training. Training participants seem to benefit from planned 15-minute breaks at predictable intervals. The 75-minute learning periods work best when the task at hand is actually a 75-minute task. This enables the trainer to complete the material without hurrying.

The opening and closing metaphors seem a powerful way to gain the training participants' attention and to focus their subconscious attention on the most important information that the trainer wishes to impart. The trainer is unlikely to have the participants full attention at any time more than at the very beginning and end of each day. Therefore , the trainer may provide the participants with the most benefit at the start and end of a training day by using metaphors that embed specific and important learning points.

Actual practice of the skills seems paramount. Simple explanation and even demonstration without the learner gaining real experience by doing the skill will not result in the learner actually acquiring the skill. "The person that had took a bull by the tail once had learnt sixty or seventy times as much as a person that hadn't" (Twain, 1996, p. 74). Thorough practice, including effective feedback, is likely a key element in the efficacy of the RTM training, and something that trainers of other patterns may consider.

References

Gray, R., Davis, A., & Bourke, F. (2021). Reconsolidation of Traumatic Memories, The RTM Protocol: Albuquerque trainee results. Unpublished manuscript.

McCarthy, B., & McCarthy, D. (2005). *Teaching around the 4Mat Cycle: Designing instruction for learners with diverse learning styles.* Wauconda, IL: About Learning, Inc.

Reconsolidation of Traumatic Memories Participant Manual (2020). Research and Recognition Project. NLPRandR.org New York. Unpublished.

Twain, M. (1996). *Tom Sawyer abroad*, 6th edition. New York: Oxford University

Wake, L., Bourke, F., Schutz, P., & Gray, R. (2013). Certification and training. In Lisa Wake, Richard Gray, & Frank Bourke (Eds.), *The clinical efficacy of NLP: A critical appraisal* (pp. 219–233). London, Routledge.

Wake, L., Gray, R. M., & Bourke, F. S. (Eds.). (2013). *The clinical effectiveness of neurolinguistic programming: A critical appraisal.* Routledge.

12 The future of NLP research

Dr Lisa de Rijk and Dr Phil Parker

Introduction

We conclude this book with a reflection on the contents of this book and the progress made since the first edition. We bring to the fore gaps within the clinical evidence base and also present the reader with the controversies that remain within the field of clinical NLP. Practitioner led research has brought NLP to this point in time and we offer a perspective that encourages the continuation of practitioner led research alongside the current and future clinical trial agenda. This then enables us to offer recommendations for future research directions.

Research status

This book has presented a further 17 peer-reviewed clinical studies, providing evidence for NLP's application in PTSD, anxiety, occupational stress and general mental health, addiction patterns, post-surgical and birth pain management, strokes, chronic fatigue syndrome, ME and MS. Of these new studies, 5 are considered to be A level studies, randomised clinical trials, the perceived gold standard in clinical research. Of these studies, the PTSD RCTs have also resulted in Kitchiner, Lewis, Roberts, & Bisson (2019) recognising the RTM protocol as an emerging evidentiary medicine when mapped against ISTSS criteria, offering NLP as a serious contender in treating complex mental health presentations.

The Lightning Process is another significant addition to the field of A level studies bringing scientific rigour to the treatment of psychoneurological conditions with an NLP based therapy.

Two B level studies using the Lightning process, designed to treat psychoneurological conditions, have been added. Psychotherapy has also added to the list of B level studies with the first meta-analysis of NLP psychotherapy.

The remaining C and D level studies that have been added to the list since the first edition combine both qualitative and quantitative studies.

DOI: 10.4324/9781003198864-12

The qualitative case study series for the treatment of PTSD provide continued support of the more robust A level studies already published, as does the thematic analysis for the use of the Lightning Process.

Other studies of the use of NLP techniques in occupational stress and strokes utilise a quasi-experimental pre-post test design and both would have added greater value to the field had more research rigour been applied at research protocol design stage. The same lack of rigour in study protocol design can also be applied in a post cohort study measuring the effectiveness of NLP in post-combat veterans with PTSD, where researchers were invited to analyse data post-treatment.

A D level study measuring pain post-surgery has been classified as a D level study even though it was reported as an RCT, again lacking a robust study design protocol.

Gray continues to contribute significantly to this edition with his depth understanding of NLP and how ICD-11 and DSM-V diagnostics can be utilised from within an NLP frame to offer a treatment paradigm.

Notwithstanding the significant contribution that EANLPt colleagues have made in researching the clinical effectiveness of NLPt in a general psychotherapy population, de Rijk and Kamp have presented a case series utilising NLPt with clients with complex mental health conditions. They propose combining a general NLPt approach to the work of Heemskerk and Derks for treating eating disorder as a potential research avenue. This would offer a more protocol-based approach to treatment that could be measured through an RCT study design.

As this edition moves further into more specific conditions we see a further case series being offered as practitioner led research.

Derks and Gray present a further case study series through their discussion of the use of NLP techniques for the treatment of depression, anxiety, and phobias. This too could open up an avenue for a protocol-based study design to treat specific conditions that frequently present in general psychotherapy.

Turkowski offers a four-step theoretical model for the treatment of grief and bereavement. He brings this model to life through a case series and proposed that this model could be used in wider contexts of grief and loss, notably within the business world.

Gray concludes the research in this edition with a comprehensive review of supporting evidence for NLP in a clinical context.

Practitioner led research

Practitioner led research has brought NLP to this point in time, however, there are issues with this research approach and with research primarily designed and led by those with little working knowledge of the field. These issues and suggestions for potential solutions are discussed here.

Hierarchy of evidence

To identify the issues at play, it's important to understand how different types of studies are valued within research, as there are different levels of confidence in the quality of a studies results depending on the type of study methodology used. There is some variety in the way the hierarchy is presented and we've used the 6 divisions here that are generally used in psychosocial studies.

The least strong evidence is provided by editorials or experts opinions, which are simply reports of a particular expert's perspective and thoughts on an issue.

Next in strength are case reports and studies, which present information from one or a few selected cases which demonstrate new findings or approaches. This type of study is often favoured by practitioners as it fits their lived experience of seeing profound or interesting change in individual patients.

Case-controlled studies are next. These are non-experimental studies that rely on an approach based on epidemiology instead of collecting new data from a randomised population. So for example a group of patients with a specific disease, such as lung cancer, will be compared to a group of people who don't have that illness. This helps the researchers to identify any factors that may account for the increased chance of lung cancer in the 'case' group.

Next are Cohort studies where data is collected from a group (or cohort) of people with a shared characteristic (it could be a habit, illness or having attended an intervention) overtime to see what changes occur.

Randomised controlled trials (RCT) are often referred to as the gold standard of research as the evidence from them is considered to be of such high quality. They involve selecting a population of matched individuals randomising them one of a number of different treatment groups (called arms). One arm will deliver the intervention under research. The other arms (it is often only one but there can be more) will deliver a 'control' intervention which will be used as a comparison. It could be a passive control, where nothing is done, a placebo control, where a placebo or sham intervention is delivered or an active control where a standard treatment that has already been well researched is used as the comparison. This type of design allows researchers to evaluate if this new intervention is better than doing nothing, better than giving a placebo, or better than the current treatments available.

Even more highly valued than RCTs are meta-analyses and systematic reviews. These types of studies collate and report on a range of previously published research. By evaluating the quality and results of existing research they provide a rigorous assessment and overview of the available research in the field.

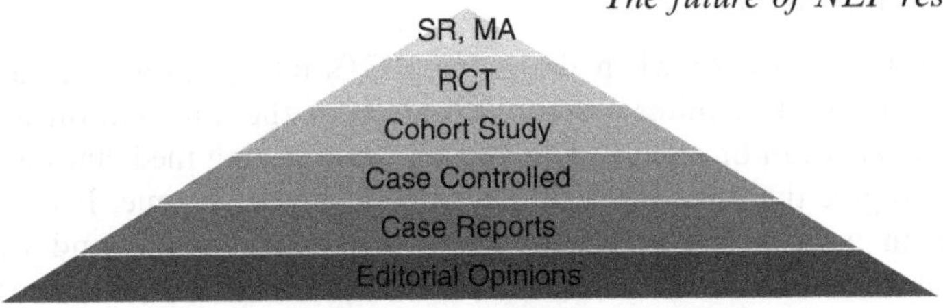

Issues

This identification of the hierarchy of evidence highlights some of the core issues within NLP research. It's been noted in other chapters that NLP has had a difficult relationship with early research endeavours, which prevented the development of an extensive evidence base until more recently. In recent years there has been an increase in RCTs, systematic reviews and meta-analyses, but, as noted above, these are still in the minority with most studies being of lower methodological quality.

The causes of this imbalance may be the result of several factors. First, a practitioner who is less well versed in the methodology of more complex research designs may favour simpler evidence collection from sources such as case histories. This is compounded by the absence of any research methodology education within the pragmatic and practical tools-based approach of NLP trainings. Second, there is a lack of understanding or familiarity with NLP concepts and its evidence base within academic institutions, as can be seen in the references by reputable academics NLP as a 'pseudoscience' (Norcross, Koocher, & Garofalo, 2006). This has resulted in a reluctance for many academics to become involved with a subject that appears to being disapproved of by their peers or which may cause a potential stumbling block for funding applications, ethics approval and publication of completed studies (Gordin, 2017; Arroll & Henwood, 2017). For these reasons the development of a strong high-quality evidence base for NLP is vital for the future of the field, as it is the only way to slowly redress the bias held in some academic quarters against NLP.

Models of research

One argument often raised by practitioners of non-pharmaceutical treatments such as therapy, NLP and coaching is that the standard research model, which is well suited to drug trials, is not fit for purpose in this context. They note that it is not possible to boil down the complexities of an individual interaction between a practitioner and their client to anything that can be standardised i.e., one session between the same practitioner and client will differ from week to week depending on that client needs. This perspective is fundamental to the person-centred approach (Rogers, 2004) which instead of prescribing a treatment that generally 'fits all', tailors the intervention for what this specific person needs in this moment.

This issue is of concern when designing RCTs into person-centred approaches, as an RCT requires a standardisation of the intervention under examination. This can be effectively achieved when testing medicines where it is simple to give the same drug of the same dosage each time. It is more challenging in approaches that vary from session to session and raises questions as to whether the research is measuring the same intervention across time and across different practitioners. This issue has received some useful suggestions for ways forward, using more appropriate methodologies, such as 'real-time monitoring of patient change in routine practice and in real-world eco-systems of clients that provide a reliable database for understanding and modelling therapeutic change' as outlined in the paper by The European Association of Psychotherapy (2021)

Evidence-based practice/practice-based evidence

These suggestions link to the debate within the research field between the merits of evidence-based practise (EBP), where the clinical work is guided by both research and practise-based evidence (PBE), where the evidence is derived from the clinical experience. EBP benefits from being methodologically well designed removing the factors that might bias the evidence using clear and transparent management of recruitment, randomisation and data collection processes. It suffers from being abstracted and distanced from direct clinical experience where clinicians will observe responses to interventions and develop new approaches based on 'what works'. It can be affected by researcher and publication biases and the increase in EBP research has not resulted in 'improvements in mental health prevalence or outcomes within the general population' and others note that well-designed trial does not represent the more variable experience of working with clients in the real world (Goh, 2021; Dubois, 2020). This final point is worth noting, if the way the intervention has been evaluated in the EBP study is not matched by the way it delivered in practice, then the research results cannot be applied to predict outcomes of such different versions of the intervention.

PBE has been defined as 'the systematic collection of patient-reported measures associated with a particular treatment goal or desired outcome' (Dubois, 2020). By evaluating clinical work in this way it can identify where outcomes diverge positively or negatively for the EBP findings. This approach raises the value of evaluation from a clinical perspective and helps bridge the gap between the sometimes-rarefied EBP and the real world and may provide some avenues for future NLP research.

There is also a history of well-respected interventions being created in this way, Motivational Interviewing (Miller, 1983) was developed from clinical experience of 'what worked' first and the formal research and theoretical underpinnings of the approach were developed later. Mindfulness with its 2,500-year-old history was created without a 'research base'. The evidence base that was developed particularly by Kabat-Zin millennia after its inception has resulted in its wide adoption by mainstream medicine.

These debates suggest there is a need for combining well-run and methodologically sound EBP and PBE to evaluate NLP in both clinical and in more formalised settings. This would give an opportunity to evaluate how much the flexibility of the process in real world clinical environments can be mapped to more standardised deliveries of the interventions. It could also help to identify which components, such as rapport, therapeutic alliance, practitioner experience, the balance of cognitive or somatic approaches, 1st generation (broadly resulting from therapeutic modelling), 2nd generation (focused on the interaction between self and other), 3rd generation (a generative, whole system perspective), etc., might be contributing factors to achieving positive outcomes and for whom (Vanson, 2014).

Recommendations for future research directions

NLP has now come to a crossroad. We have begun publishing randomized controlled trials and systematic reviews. There has been broad, if unacknowledged, acceptance of NLP patterns like rapport skills and calibration, and the large-scale, if unacknowledged use of submodalities and anchoring in advertising. NLPers have begun collaborations with main-line research institutions such as the Uniformed Services University's Center for Neurological and Restorative Medicine at Walter Reed Military Medical Center, the ongoing randomised control trial of the RTM Protocol with King's College, London/Belfast, as well as investigations of the Lightning Process with national and international institutions. Nevertheless, NLP remains an officially despised stepchild of the psychological enterprise (BPS, 2016; Wikipedia, 2021). Where then do we go from here?

We might begin by echoing an important point made by the early developers in NLP Vol1. (Dilts, Grinder, Bandler, & DeLozier, 1980, p. 9): "It is ... the shifting of environmental variables into decision variables by sorting and punctuating the way the variables fit into context, that is the goal of neurolinguistic programming." The early developers make no allowance for victimhood as an identity status. Every external barrier is transformed by NLP into opportunities for choice. What are the choices that we can make that will change our circumstances?

To this point we, the NLP community, have complained about our victimization by the scientific community. On some level this is true, but what are we to do about it? Do we remain victims, or do we take the environmental variables presented by the academic community and turn them to our own benefit? It is time that NLP applied some NLP to itself.

As ever, our first recommendation is pacing and leading. We encounter the scientific community as if we were their victims, and maintain the myopic perspective that if our results, our anecdotal results, are good enough, the world will beat a path to our door. On some level this is true, but the world has come to NLP, taken what it has found useful, rebranded it and used it on their own terms and NLP has gained nothing in the process.

What is the criterion of scientific respectability that we need to observe? What are the standards that would help to move NLP from a supposed pseudoscience, to a well-respected collaborator in the world of Psychology, Psychoneuroimmunology, and other fields? Here are a few suggestions.

NLP must begin to define itself and its theoretical structure in a standardized form. That is, as one of our authors has outlined in Chapter 10, we need to shake off our fear of theory and our fundamentalistic adherence to a creed that says these are ONLY patterns that are not subject to scientific and statistical evaluation. Theories are not allegations about TRUTH, they are frameworks for the creation of testable hypotheses. Observed patterns, as we have seen (Bateson, 1975; Shrout & Rodgers, 2018; Tosey & Mathison, 2009), are the roots of good theory and NLP's structural elements have been standard elements of the field for over 40 years. This is the kind of stable, observational material that good theory is made of. Every pattern developed from NLP's basic principles is a testable hypothesis. The Theory of Evolution is a set of predictions about the nature of biological (and psychological) change that is so well supported that most mainstream biologists accept it in some form as fact. Nevertheless, it is still referred to as the THEORY of Evolution because it is still subject to further evaluation. NLP, while certainly not comparable to evolution at this point, has a set of structural observations from which it makes certain predictions about behaviour. It is a theory and may be tested as a theory.

NLP is the scion of a proud lineage in the Maslowian and Rogerian traditions (Hall, 2010). As such, it places high value on the client's involvement in the process of change, respect for their personal maps, and a reticence to overly structure its approach to change work. This same tradition, which makes NLP so client friendly, has rendered many of us unintentionally paralysed with regard to the creation and testing of replicable patterns. Witness the difficulty detailed by Henwood (Arroll & Henwood, 2017) as she struggled with creating a standardized, replicable version of the Visual Kinesthetic Dissociation (V/K-D) Protocol, for scientific evaluation. Nevertheless, our fight for recognition on the battlefield of science requires that we do just that: create patterns and definitions that detail the structure of the behaviour in a manner that allows us to ask of each participant the same kinds of questions and provide them with the same kinds of instructions, with the understanding that their response will be idiosyncratic within the defined parameters. This kind of scientific structuring has led to the dissemination of Scientific tests of several NLP Patterns including the V/K-D Protocol (Arroll et al., 2017), the RTM Protocol (see Chapter 3), and the Lightning Process (See Chapter 8).

We are tempted to ask people to accept NLP in totality, without realizing that there are pathways to acceptance that we have not acknowledged. The scientific establishments will never accept us based upon patient satisfaction or our own claims of efficacy. To be accepted, we must meet science in its model of the world. It is only after we have successfully paced and modelled that perspective that we can join and perhaps even lead the scientific enterprise. Scientific recognition often follows in a stream of well structured, peer-reviewed studies. The alliances made by Parker, de Rijk, Schutz and his colleagues within EANLPt, and the Research and Recognition Project have developed out of successful publication and the cultivation of relationships with serious researchers from outside of the field. They respect us because we have earned their respect, not because we have demanded it.

There is an unfortunate shadow side to NLP, that we must also acknowledge and grow beyond. For as many who are altruistic in outlook, who honour the humanistic origins of NLP, and others who seek scientific respectability for the field, there are yet others for whom the multiplication of superficial trainings, a never-ending stream of egocentric blather, and the promotion of manipulative exercises have contributed to the field's bad name. If we talk about human potentials from a truly evolutionary and person-centred perspective, then NLP should also begin to look inward to find the farther reaches of our own human nature.

References

Arroll, B., & Henwood, S. M. (2017). NLP research, equipoise and reviewer prejudice. *Rapport*, 54, 24–26.

Arroll, B., Henwood, S. M., Sundram, F. I., Kingsford, D. W., Mount, V., Humm, S. P., Wallace, H. B., & Pillai, A. (2017). A brief treatment for fear of heights: A randomized controlled trial of a novel imaginal intervention. *The International Journal of Psychiatry in Medicine*, 52(1), 21–33. doi:10.1177/0091217417703285

Bateson, G. (1975). Introduction. In: R. Bandler & J. Grinder (Eds.), (1975). *The Structure of Magic* (pp. ix–xi). Real People Press.

British Psychological Society (BPS) (2016). 10 of the most widely led beliefs in psychology. https://digest.bps.org.uk/2016/07/29/10-of-the-most-widely-believed-myths-in-psychology/.

Dilts, R., Grinder, J., Bandler, R., & DeLozier, J. (1980). *Neuro-linguistic programming: Volume I. The structure of subjective experience*. Cupertino, CA: Meta Publications.

Dubois R. From evidence-based practice to practice-based evidence [Internet]. *Psychology Today*. 22/20 [cited 2021 Jun 21]. Available from: https://www.psychologytoday.com/gb/blog/the-digital-doctor/202009/evidence-based-practice-practice-based-evidence

Goh, S. (2021). The problem with evidence based medicine is really the clinicians, *BMJ*. 362, k2799.

Gordin M. D. (2017). The problem with pseudoscience. *EMBO Rep*. Sep 1;18(9), 1482–1485.

Hall, L. M. (2010). Meta reflections 2010: The history of NLP. *Neurons--The International egroup of Neuro-Semantics* (17 Articles). Retrieved from http://www.neurosemantics.com/topics/nlp/the-history-of-nlp

Kitchiner, N. J., Lewis, C., Roberts, N. P., & Bisson, J. I. (2019). Active duty and ex-serving military personnel with post-traumatic stress disorder treated with psychological therapies: systematic review and meta-analysis. *European Journal of Psychotraumatology*, 10(1). doi:10.1080/20008198.2019.1684226

Miller W. (1983). Motivational interviewing with problem drinkers. *Behavioural Psychotherapy*, 11, 147–172.

Neuro-linguistic programming. (2021, January 15). In Wikipedia. https://en.wikipedia.org/wiki/Neuro-linguistic_programming.

Norcross J. C., Koocher G. P., Garofalo A. (2006). Discredited psychological treatments and tests: A Delphi poll. *Professional Psychology: Research and Practice*, 37(5), 515–522.

Rogers, C. R. (2004). *On becoming a person a therapist's view of psychotherapy*. Edinburgh: Constable.

Shrout, P. E., & Rodgers, J. L. (2018). Psychology, science, and knowledge construction: Broadening perspectives from the replication crisis. *Annual Review of Psychology*, 69, 487–510. doi:10.1146/annurev-psych-122216-011845

The European Association of Psychotherapy. (2021). P*osition Paper on the Proper Nature and Policy Applications of Psychotherapy Research*. https://www.europsyche.org/app/uploads/2021/04/EAP-Research-Statement-March-13-2021-adopted.pdf

Tosey, P., & Mathison, J. (2009). *Neuro-linguistic programming: A critical appreciation for managers and developers*. Palgrave-Macmillan.

Vanson, S. (2014). *What is third generation NLP*. https://theperformancesolution.com/third-generation-nlp/ Accessed 23 June 2021.

Index

Note: **Bold** page numbers refer to tables and *italic* page numbers refer to figures.